D1555882

A RESTATEMENT OF THE ENGLISH
LAW OF CONTRACT

A RESTATEMENT OF
THE ENGLISH LAW
OF CONTRACT

ANDREW BURROWS

ASSISTED BY AN ADVISORY
GROUP OF ACADEMICS, JUDGES,
AND PRACTITIONERS

OXFORD
UNIVERSITY PRESS

OXFORD
UNIVERSITY PRESS

Great Clarendon Street, Oxford, OX2 6DP,
United Kingdom

Oxford University Press is a department of the University of Oxford.
It furthers the University's objective of excellence in research, scholarship,
and education by publishing worldwide. Oxford is a registered trade mark of
Oxford University Press in the UK and in certain other countries

First Edition published in 2016

Impression: 2

Published in the United States of America by Oxford University Press
198 Madison Avenue, New York, NY 10016, United States of America

British Library Cataloguing in Publication Data
Data available

Library of Congress Control Number: 2015952458

ISBN 978–0–19–875554–8 (hbk)
978–0–19–875555–5 (pbk)

Printed and bound by
CPI Group (UK) Ltd, Croydon, CR0 4YY

CONTENTS

ADVISORY GROUP

Lord Toulson, Supreme Court of the United Kingdom

Lord Justice Longmore, Court of Appeal of England and Wales

Lord Justice Gross, Court of Appeal of England and Wales

Lord Justice Lewison, Court of Appeal of England and Wales

Lord Justice Beatson, Court of Appeal of England and Wales

Mr Justice Hamblen, High Court of England and Wales

Stephen Moriarty QC, Fountain Court Chambers, London

Laurence Rabinowitz QC, One Essex Court, London

Marcus Smith QC, Fountain Court Chambers, London

Richard Calnan, Norton Rose Fulbright LLP

Professor Hugh Beale, University of Warwick

Professor Mindy Chen-Wishart, University of Oxford

Richard Hooley, University of Cambridge

Professor Ewan McKendrick, University of Oxford

Professor Gerard McMeel, University of Manchester

Dr Janet O'Sullivan, University of Cambridge

Professor Robert Stevens, University of Oxford

Professor Andrew Tettenborn, University of Swansea

Professor Simon Whittaker, University of Oxford

Dr Frederick Wilmot-Smith, University of Oxford

INTRODUCTION

This is the second Restatement of English law that I have undertaken. The first, *A Restatement of the English Law of Unjust Enrichment* ('*RELUE*'), was published by OUP in 2012. I was greatly encouraged by the welcome given to that book, both in the courts and by commentators,[1] and have thereby been inspired to believe that this type of work fills a gap in relation to English law. While knowing what the law of contract is in England and Wales does not involve the multi-jurisdictional problems that might be encountered in some other countries (for example, the USA), there nevertheless appears to be considerable benefit from setting out this law in as clear and accessible a form as possible.

The present Restatement largely follows the format, working methods, and approach of *RELUE*. I have again had the assistance of an advisory group. While I alone accept responsibility for the Restatement and commentary, and not all members of the Advisory Group agree with this version—indeed it may be that each member would express matters somewhat differently throughout—I wish to put on record the immense assistance I have derived from the Advisory Group for which I am extremely grateful. Further tremendous help on drafting has been given by Philip Davies, former Parliamentary Counsel.

It is hoped that, not least because so many lawyers here and abroad need to understand the English law of contract—it is one of the most respected systems of contract law in the world and by the device of a 'choice of law' clause is often chosen by foreign commercial parties as the applicable law to govern their contract—this work may attract an even wider readership than *RELUE*. This includes lawyers in civil law systems. One of the aims is for the reader to see quickly and easily how the different elements of this area of English law fit together. Civil lawyers, who are used to a statutory code, often find English law difficult for that reason.

The hope, therefore, is that all lawyers dealing with the English law of contract, whether as practitioners, judges, academics, or law students, will benefit from this Restatement. Non-lawyers too may find it of interest and help but the complexities are such that a degree of legal knowledge is likely to be necessary in order to understand all the provisions and commentary.

---

[1] See eg Rose (2013) 129 LQR 639, Lee [2013] RLR 228, and the review article by Barker, 'Centripetal Force: The Law of Unjust Enrichment Restated in England and Wales' (2014) 34 Oxford Journal of Legal Studies 155–79; and *RELUE* has been cited in many of the leading English cases on unjust enrichment since it was published (including in the Supreme Court in *Benedetti v Sawiris* [2013] UKSC 50, [2014] AC 938 and *Crown Prosecution Service v Eastenders Group* [2014] UKSC 26, [2015] AC 1 and in the Court of Appeal in *Relfo Ltd v Varsani* [2014] EWCA Civ 360 in which, at [74], Arden LJ described it as 'this valuable work').

Introduction

I have drawn inspiration from the American Law Institute's *Restatement (Second) of Contracts*,[2] from the *Unidroit Principles of International Commercial Contracts*,[3] and from the various European codification or restatement projects,[4] in particular the *Principles of European Contract Law*,[5] the *Draft Common Frame of Reference*,[6] and the earlier *Contract Code* drawn up by Harvey McGregor.[7] The work on the European harmonisation of contract law inevitably raises the question as to the value of a Restatement of *English law*. As with *RELUE*, it is my view that, whether one believes in European legal harmonisation or not, it is essential that the subtleties of English law are properly understood and appreciated before there is a consideration of whether they should be abandoned. Many English lawyers would also argue that English contract law has a particularly prominent and distinctive global role that should not be lightly given up.

The aim of this Restatement is to provide the best interpretation of the present English law of contract. It is believed that the interpretation put forward is both faithful to precedent (without requiring any change by the Supreme Court) and accurately summarises the core elements of the relevant legislation.

One might have thought that, because the law of contract is better understood and more 'worked out' than the law of unjust enrichment, this project would have posed less of a challenge than the last. That has not been so. On the contrary, there have been difficult issues raised in the course of this project that were non-problematic in the last. In particular, English contract law is in many areas very detailed. Almost inevitably, therefore, one has to draw a distinction between the 'general law' of contract and the law on specific contracts with this work being concerned with the former and not the latter (see the commentary to s 1(b)). But the drawing of that division between the general law and the rest is not straightforward. Closely connected with that is that there is more legislation in the law of contract than in the law of unjust enrichment and plainly some of that legislation has to be regarded as part of the general law of contract. Deciding which legislation falls within the general law of contract—and how to present the essence of that

---

[2] (1981). The ALI Restatements are non-legislative, but powerfully persuasive, statements of the law applying across the USA.

[3] (3rd edn, 2010). Unidroit is the International Institute for the Unification of Private Law.

[4] A non-binding code and a Restatement are clearly very similar. But a code, unlike a Restatement, does not need to be tied to the existing law. With a code, unlike a Restatement, one can simply start with a blank sheet of paper, decide on what is the best legal rule, and then set that out in the code. One cannot do that with a Restatement.

[5] (Eds Olé Lando and Hugh Beale, 2000). This was the work of the Commission on European Contract Law.

[6] (2009). Prepared by the Study Group on a European Civil Code and the Research Group on EC Private Law (Acquis Group).

[7] This was drawn up for the English Law Commission and was intended to embrace English and Scottish law. The final 1972 draft was published in 1993 in Italy at the instigation of Giuseppe Gandolfi (Milan: Guiffrè Editore).

legislation alongside the common law without losing overall coherence and accuracy—has been daunting and, as far as I am aware, is not an exercise that has been undertaken before. As with *RELUE*, the principal intellectual challenge has been in trying to restate complex judge-made law in as succinct and consistent a way as possible. Even though the law of contract is long-established and relatively well-settled, at almost every turn there can be (and, within the advisory group, there was) disagreement and heated debate as to what is the best interpretation of the law.

Nevertheless, the long pedigree of the English law of contract, in contrast to the recently developed English law of unjust enrichment, has meant that the distinction, between what the law is and views as to what it ought to be, can be drawn more sharply in this project than in the last. Put another way, there has been less 'room for manoeuvre' in restating the English law of contract than in restating the English law of unjust enrichment. So, for example, despite criticisms sometimes made, the Restatement adopts the conventional interpretation that: the doctrine of consideration is a fundamental feature of the English law of contract; past consideration is not good consideration; part payment of a debt is not good consideration for the creditor's promise to forgo the balance; the subsequent conduct of the parties cannot be taken into account in interpreting a contract; the exceptions to the approach to the award of an agreed sum in *White and Carter (Councils) Ltd v McGregor*[8] are rare; specific performance is a secondary, not a primary, remedy; there is a constant supervision bar to specific performance; and there is no doctrine of mistake (not induced by misrepresentation) rendering a contract voidable rather than void. It would surely require a radical reanalysis by the Supreme Court if it were to depart from those conventional interpretations.

This is not to deny that the Restatement has adopted, as the best interpretation of the law, some positions that may be regarded as controversial. These include that: one cannot accept in ignorance of an offer but the acceptance need not have been induced, or influenced, by the offer; acceptance in a unilateral contract is generally constituted by the promisee starting to perform; the promise to perform, or the performance of, a pre-existing duty is good consideration for a counter-promise of more money; there are three possible explanations for 'Wrotham Park damages'; there is a doctrine of unilateral and common mistake that renders a contract void; and there is a judge-made doctrine covering exploitation of weakness.

On two major issues of topical dispute it has been decided, after considerable debate, that the Restatement should restate the law in a neutral way (ie the text 'sits on the fence') while fully discussing the different approaches in the commentary. Those two issues are, first, whether Lord Hoffmann was correct in obiter dicta in

---

[8] [1962] AC 413.

Chartbrook Ltd v Persimmon Homes Ltd[9] to regard the continuing common intention needed for rectification as objective rather than subjective; and, secondly, what the correct approach should be to the defence of illegality which has been considered in no fewer than three recent cases in the Supreme Court.

It should be stressed that it is *not* intended that the Restatement should be enacted as legislation. On the contrary, the intention is for the Restatement to be a persuasive authority but non-binding; and it is envisaged that there may be periodic revisions of the Restatement to reflect new developments and thinking. It would be wholly contrary to the desires and aspirations of those who have been responsible for this project for the Restatement to be seen as working against the common law tradition. The essential idea is for the Restatement to supplement and enhance our understanding of the common law, and to make it more accessible, not to replace it.

It will be seen that the commentary attempts to state matters as succinctly as possible. Hypothetical or real examples have often been used in the belief that this is commonly the best way of understanding the law. The leading cases, but not all conceivable relevant cases, have been cited and the citation of academic literature has been kept to a minimum. The aim is to explain the Restatement, not to reproduce the (many excellent) textbooks in this area.

Where it has been thought helpful to refer to textbooks, I have steered towards books favoured by practitioners, in particular the superb detailed accounts of the English law of contract in *Chitty on Contracts*[10] and Peel, *Treitel on the Law of Contract*,[11] rather than to one of the many fine books principally intended for students.

Work started on this project in October 2013. Four five-hour meetings of the advisory group were held. In advance of those meetings, drafts of parts of the Restatement and the commentary were prepared and circulated electronically. Comments were then sent back and revised versions of the Restatement and commentary were again sent out in advance of each meeting. Those drafts were then discussed at the meetings. They were further revised in the light of the discussions. The Restatement and the commentary seek to reflect the insights gained from the written comments and the discussions in the meetings and the advice of former Parliamentary Counsel. It has been a rich and rewarding collaborative exercise.

---

[9] [2009] UKHL 38, [2009] 1 AC 1101.
[10] (32nd edn, 2015). The general editor is Hugh Beale.
[11] (14th edn, 2015).

Introduction

Thanks are owed to Norton Rose Fulbright LLP, who provided funding for this project, and to those involved at Oxford University Press, especially Alex Flach, Natasha Flemming, and Emily Brand, for their enthusiasm for publishing this work and for their efficiency and skill in doing so.

This Restatement has eight Parts and 50 sections.

This work is based on the law as at 1 October 2015,[12] subject to a few amendments at proof stage to deal with the Supreme Court's decisions, on penalties, in the conjoined appeals in *Cavendish Square Holdings BV v Talal El Makdessi* and *ParkingEye Ltd v Beavis.*[13]

---

[12] The major provisions of the Consumer Rights Act 2015 affecting contract law came into force on 1 October 2015 and apply to contracts made on or after that date: Consumer Rights Act 2015 (Commencement No 3, Transitional Provisions, Savings and Consequential Amendments) Order 2015 (SI 2015/1630).

[13] [2015] UKSC 67. The decision of the Supreme Court in *Marks and Spencer plc v BNP Paribas Securities Services Trust Co (Jersey) Ltd* [2015] UKSC 72, on terms implied by fact, came too late for inclusion. Section 15(3)–(4) of the Restatement, and the accompanying commentary, must be read in the light of that case (which appears to downplay the significance of Lord Hoffmann's recasting of the law in *Attorney General of Belize v Belize Telecom Ltd* [2009] UKPC 10, [2009] 1 WLR 1988).

A RESTATEMENT OF THE ENGLISH LAW OF CONTRACT

A RESTATEMENT OF THE ENGLISH LAW OF CONTRACT

A RESTATEMENT OF THE ENGLISH LAW OF CONTRACT

PART 1
GENERAL

1　**Scope**
This Restatement is concerned only with—
  (a) the law of England and Wales;
  (b) the general law applicable to contract (so that there are rules, especially in legislation, dealing with specific types of contract that are not mentioned in this Restatement).

2　**Definition of 'contract'**
A contract is an agreement that is legally binding because—
  (a) it is supported by consideration or made by deed (see section 8);
  (b) it is certain and complete (see section 9);
  (c) it is made with the intention to create legal relations (see section 10); and
  (d) it complies with any formal requirement needed for the agreement to be legally binding (see section 11(2)(a)).

3　**Non-contractual liability**
 (1) This Restatement does not cover in detail areas of law outside the law of contract (for example, the law of tort or unjust enrichment) even though liability under those areas of law may arise in the context of, for example, pre-contractual negotiations or a contract being defective or terminated.
 (2) A claim for breach of contract may be made concurrently with another claim (for example, for a tort or unjust enrichment).

4　**Parties**
 (1) A contract must have at least two parties but it may have more than two parties (a 'multiparty contract').
 (2) Although some issues arise in relation to multiparty contracts that do not arise in relation to two–party contracts (for example, whether the liability of a party is joint or several), the law as set out in this Restatement applies with appropriate modifications to multiparty contracts as it does to two-party contracts.
 (3) The parties to a contract are those who have entered into the legally binding agreement.

(4) In this Restatement, a person who is not a party to a contract is referred to as a 'third party'.

(5) In this Restatement, in relation to a contract—

    (a) references to A and B are references to the parties to the contract; and

    (b) a reference to C is to a third party.

5 Freedom of contract

(1) Subject to exceptions (especially provisions under the Equality Act 2010) one is free to make, or to refuse to make, a contract with whomever one chooses.

(2) Provided that the consent of a party is not impaired by, for example, misrepresentation, duress, undue influence or incapacity (sections 36 to 38 and 43), the parties to a contract are, in general, free to determine the terms of a contract.

(3) But the freedom in subsection (2) is qualified by the law on, for example—

    (a) the implication of some terms which do not rest on the parties' intentions (see section 15(1),(5), and (6));

    (b) the legislative control of exemption clauses and unfair terms (see sections 16 and 17);

    (c) penalties and forfeiture (see section 23);

    (d) illegality and public policy (see section 44);

    (e) legislation which provides that parties to a contract may not derogate from rules laid down in the legislation whether at all or to the detriment of one of the parties.

6 Meaning of words and phrases in this Restatement

(1) Unless the context otherwise requires, in this Restatement the phrase 'intentions of the parties' refers to what a reasonable person would understand those intentions to be (commonly referred to as 'objective intentions').

(2) In this Restatement—

'average consumer' means a consumer who is reasonably well-informed, observant and circumspect;

'consumer' means an individual acting for purposes that are wholly or mainly outside that individual's trade, business, craft or profession;

'consumer contract' means a contract between a consumer and a trader;

'excluding or limiting' in relation to a liability includes excluding or limiting a remedy in respect of that liability;

'exemption clause' means a term of a contract (in whatever form) excluding or limiting a liability for a breach of contract (or other cause of action);

'trader' means a person acting for purposes relating to that person's trade, business, craft or profession.

PART 2

FORMATION AND VARIATION OF CONTRACT

7 Agreement

(1) In general, the agreement in a contract is made by the acceptance of an offer or by the parties signing an agreement containing the agreed terms.

(2) But there are other ways in which the agreement may be made (as, for example, where participants in a competition or sporting event agree with each other to comply with the organiser's rules).

(3) An offer is an expression, by words or conduct, of a willingness to be bound by specified terms as soon as there is acceptance by the person to whom the offer is made ('the offeree').

(4) An offer is different from an invitation to treat which is an expression, by words or conduct, of a willingness to negotiate.

(5) The following are usually invitations to treat and not offers—
    (a) the display of goods for sale;
    (b) an advertisement of goods for sale;
    (c) an invitation to tender.

(6) An acceptance is the expression, by words or conduct, of assent to the terms offered.

(7) An acceptance must usually be communicated to (that is, received by) the person by whom the offer is made ('the offeror') although the offeror can waive the need for communication.

(8) The general rule in subsection (7) applies to an acceptance by e-mail.

(9) The general rule in subsection (7) is displaced where it would be inappropriate to allocate to the offeree the risk of the acceptance not being received as may be the case, for example, where the offeror has been at fault in not receiving the acceptance.

(10) An exception to the general rule in subsection (7) is that an acceptance by post usually takes effect when the letter is posted (the 'postal rule') although the offeror can displace this by stipulating, in the offer, that an acceptance will not be valid until it is received.

(11) The postal rule is displaced where it would be inappropriate to allocate to the offeror the risk of the letter not being received as may be the case, for example, where the offeree has been at fault in relation to a letter being lost or delayed in the post.

(12) The offeror may prescribe the mode of acceptance but, unless the offeror makes use of that mode of acceptance compulsory, any other mode of acceptance will suffice provided that it is no less advantageous to the offeror.

(13) There can be no acceptance in ignorance of an offer but the acceptance need not have been induced or influenced by the offer.

(14) Where an offeror makes a promise in return for performance by the offeree but the offeree does not promise to perform so that only the offeror is bound under the contract (a 'unilateral contract'), in general there is acceptance by the offeree (so that withdrawal by the offeror would constitute a breach) once the offeree starts to perform even if the offeror is not bound to perform until performance by the offeree is complete.

(15) An offer is terminated, so that it is no longer open for acceptance, by, for example—

    (a) the offeror's revocation;

    (b) the offeree's rejection (which may take the form of a counter-offer);

    (c) lapse of time (which may be either the expiry of the period specified in the offer or, where there is no period specified in the offer, the expiry of a reasonable time).

(16) The revocation of an offer, even one made by post, must generally be communicated to (that is, received by) the offeree; but the revocation may be communicated by a third party rather than by the offeror.

(17) The general rule in subsection (16) is displaced where it would be inappropriate to allocate to the offeror the risk of the revocation not being received as may be the case, for example, where the offeree has been at fault in not receiving the revocation.

8   Consideration

(1) To be legally binding, an agreement, unless made by deed, must be supported by consideration.

(2) 'Consideration' means that, in exchange for a promise by one party, a counter-promise or performance is given by the other party.

(3) The consideration need not be adequate and may be merely nominal.

(4) Past consideration (where A makes a promise to B in return for what B has already done) is not good consideration.

(5) If—

    (a) B owes a pre-existing duty to A under the general law or under a contract with C or under a contract with A, and

    (b) A makes a promise to B in exchange for B's promise to perform, or performance of, that pre-existing duty,

B's promise to perform, or performance of, that pre-existing duty is good consideration for A's promise although the contract may in certain circumstances be voidable for duress (see section 37) or unenforceable as being contrary to public policy (see section 44).

(6) B's promise to perform a part, or part performance, of a pre-existing duty (for example, part payment of a pre-existing debt) owed by B to A is not good consideration for A's promise to forgo the remaining part of the performance owing (for example, to forgo the balance of the pre-existing debt owed) although the law on promissory estoppel (see section 12) may operate to protect B.

9 **Certainty and completeness**
  (1) For an agreement to be legally binding, it must be certain and complete.
  (2) A conditional contract is legally binding, so that neither party can withdraw, even though neither party is bound to perform the principal obligations under the contract unless and until an agreed condition has been satisfied; but a party may be bound to perform, or abide by, subsidiary obligations that relate to the condition (for example, to use reasonable efforts to ensure that the condition is satisfied or not deliberately to prevent the condition being satisfied).

10 **Intention to create legal relations**
  (1) For an agreement to be legally binding, the parties must have an intention to create legal relations.
  (2) Unless the agreement is made by deed, there is a rebuttable presumption that there is no intention to create legal relations where the agreement is made in a social or domestic context.
  (3) There is a rebuttable presumption of an intention to create legal relations where an express agreement, that is certain and complete, is made in a commercial context.
  (4) An agreement expressed to be 'subject to contract' is not legally binding because, by using those words, the parties have made clear that they do not intend to create legal relations until a formal document has been drawn up.
  (5) It is commonplace in a written contract for there to be no intention to create legal relations until all the parties have signed the document.

11 **Formal requirements**
  (1) For most contracts there is no requirement as to form so that a contract may be made in writing, orally or by conduct (or by any combination of those methods).
  (2) There are legislative exceptions to the rule that there is no requirement as to form which include the following—
    (a) the rule that, subject to exceptions, a contract for the sale or other disposition of an interest in land is void unless it is made in writing and signed (see section 2 of the Law of Property (Miscellaneous Provisions) Act 1989);

(b) the rule that a contract of guarantee is unenforceable unless it is evidenced in writing and signed (see section 4 of the Statute of Frauds 1677).

12   Consensual variation or rescission and promissory estoppel

(1) A contract may be varied or rescinded by an agreement between the parties that is legally binding as satisfying the requirements in sections 8 to 11.

(2) A promise to forgo one's rights may to some extent be legally binding, even though it is not a contract or a term of a contract, under the doctrine of promissory estoppel.

(3) The doctrine of promissory estoppel applies where—

  (a) a clear and unequivocal promise is made by A to B to forgo A's existing rights against B;

  (b) that promise is relied on by B; and

  (c) that promise has not been induced by B's duress or other unfair conduct.

(4) Sometimes the reliance on the promise by B is required to be to B's detriment.

(5) Promissory estoppel may operate to extinguish, rather than just to suspend, A's existing rights against B.

(6) The remedies available for promissory estoppel may aim to put B into as good a position as if the promise had been kept and need not be limited to protecting B against loss incurred in reliance on the promise.

PART 3
TERMS OF A CONTRACT

13   Express terms

(1) The express terms of a contract may be oral or written or some may be oral and some written.

(2) There is a rebuttable presumption that, where there is a written contract, there are no terms other than the written terms.

(3) The terms of a contract must be distinguished from statements that are not incorporated as terms of the contract.

(4) The intentions of the parties determine whether or not a statement is incorporated as a contractual term; and there may be a term (commonly referred to as an 'entire agreement clause') that specifies which statements are the terms of the contract.

(5) Subsection (4) is subject to sections 11 to 12, 36 to 37, and 50 of the Consumer Rights Act 2015 whereby certain information provided by a trader to a consumer is to be treated as included as a term of the contract.

(6) Even where a contract has largely been concluded orally, A's written terms, including an exemption clause, may be incorporated into a contract with B by one of the following methods—
    (a) signature by B, provided that—
        (i) the document signed purports to have contractual effect; and
        (ii) the signature has not been induced by a misrepresentation;
    (b) reasonable notice given to B of those terms prior to the formation of the contract;
    (c) a consistent course of dealing on those terms between A and B;
    (d) a practice in a trade to which A and B belong that those terms are incorporated.
(7) Where a contract is concluded online between A and B, a standard method by which A's written terms are incorporated into the contract is by B clicking on a box agreeing to A's terms.

14   Interpretation

(1) The correct approach to interpreting a term of a contract is to ask what the term, viewed in the light of the whole contract, would mean to a reasonable person having all the relevant background knowledge reasonably available to the parties at the time the contract was made.
(2) In applying subsection (1), one must consider—
    (a) the natural and ordinary meaning of the words and syntax used;
    (b) the overall purpose of the term and the contract;
    (c) the facts and circumstances known or assumed by the parties at the time the contract was made;
    (d) commercial common sense as at the time the contract was made, if that can be ascertained;
but one must be careful to avoid placing too much emphasis on paragraph (b), (c), or (d) at the expense of paragraph (a).
(3) In interpreting a term of a contract the words or syntax must not be amended in order to protect one of the parties from having entered into a bad bargain; but exceptionally it may be decided that the parties must have used the wrong words or syntax.
(4) In interpreting a term of a contract the pre-contractual negotiations of the parties must not be taken into account except where one party seeks to establish that a fact relevant to the background was known to the parties; but they may be taken into account to establish that—
    (a) there is an estoppel by convention (which is a doctrine preventing a party from denying that, for example, certain words have a particular meaning where the parties have negotiated with each other on the common assumption that that meaning was correct); or

     (b) there should be rectification of a contract (see section 35(6)).

(5) In interpreting a term of a contract, the subsequent conduct of the parties must not be taken into account.

(6) Clear words will be needed if a term is to be interpreted as—

     (a) excluding a party from, or indemnifying a party against, liability for negligence; or

     (b) excluding a party from liability for a serious breach of contract.

(7) By reason of section 69 of the Consumer Rights Act 2015, if a term in a consumer contract could have different meanings, the meaning that is most favourable to the consumer is to prevail.

15   Implied terms

(1) Terms may be implied into a contract, or treated as included in a contract, by legislation (as, for example, the terms implied by sections 12 to 15 of the Sale of Goods Act 1979 and the terms treated as included in a consumer contract for the supply of goods, digital content or services by Part 1 of the Consumer Rights Act 2015).

(2) Apart from terms implied under subsection (1), terms may be implied into a contract—

     (a) by fact, or

     (b) by law,

but only if that is consistent with the express terms of the contract.

(3) A term implied by fact rests on the parties' intentions; and the underlying question to be asked in determining whether such a term should be implied is what the contract, viewed as a whole against the relevant background, would reasonably be understood to mean.

(4) In answering the question in subsection (3), it is helpful to apply one or both of the following tests—

     (a) whether, were an officious bystander to ask if the term was meant to be included, the parties would answer 'Of course' (commonly referred to as the 'officious bystander' test);

     (b) whether the term is necessary for the business efficacy of the contract (commonly referred to as the 'business efficacy' test).

(5) A term may be implied by law if the term is required by the type of contract or relationship in question (for example, there is an implied term not to destroy mutual trust and confidence in an employment contract).

(6) A term may be implied, whether by fact or law, requiring adherence to the custom or practice of the market, trade or locality relevant to the contract but such a term will only be implied if the custom or practice is certain, well-known, reasonable, regarded as intended to have legal consequences, and consistent with the express terms of the contract.

PART 4
LEGISLATIVE CONTROL OF EXEMPTION CLAUSES AND UNFAIR TERMS

16   Legislative control of exemption clauses in non-consumer contracts

(1) This section deals with legislation invalidating exemption clauses in a contract that is not a consumer contract, with subsections (3) to (5) and (7) referring to the Unfair Contract Terms Act 1977 and subsections (6) and (7) referring to section 3 of the Misrepresentation Act 1967.

(2) In this section, the party seeking to rely on the exemption clause is referred to as the defendant.

(3) If the liability of the defendant is business liability (for example, it arises while the defendant is acting in the course of a business)—

   (a) the defendant cannot by reference to a contract term exclude or limit liability for breach of a contractual obligation to use reasonable care, or breach of a duty of care in tort, causing death or personal injury;

   (b) the defendant cannot by reference to a contract term exclude or limit liability for breach of a contractual obligation to use reasonable care, or breach of a duty of care in tort, causing loss other than death or personal injury, unless the term satisfies the test of reasonableness;

   (c) if the claimant deals on the other's written standard terms of business, the defendant cannot by reference to a contract term exclude or limit liability for breach of contract (or claim to be entitled to render no performance or a substantially different performance than reasonably expected) unless the term satisfies the test of reasonableness;

   (d) in a contract for the sale of goods or hire-purchase, the defendant cannot by reference to a contract term exclude or limit liability for breach of the legislative implied term as to the title of the goods;

   (e) in a contract for the sale of goods or hire-purchase or hire or work and materials, the defendant cannot by reference to a contract term exclude or limit liability for breach of the legislative implied terms as to the goods' conformity with description or sample, satisfactory quality, or fitness for a particular purpose, unless the term satisfies the test of reasonableness.

(4) If the defendant is not acting in the course of a business so that the liability of the defendant is not business liability—

   (a) in a contract for the sale of goods or hire-purchase, the defendant cannot by reference to a contract term exclude or limit liability for breach of the legislative implied term as to the title of the goods;

13

(b) in a contract for the sale of goods or hire-purchase, the defendant cannot by reference to a contract term exclude or limit liability for breach of the legislative implied term as to the goods' conformity with description or sample, unless the term satisfies the test of reasonableness.

(5) Subsections (3) and (4) do not apply to certain types of contract (even though not a consumer contract), including—

(a) an international supply contract;

(b) a contract of insurance;

(c) a contract relating to the creation or transfer of an interest in land;

(d) a contract relating to the formation, dissolution, or constitution of a company;

(e) a contract relating to the creation or transfer of an intellectual property right;

(f) a contract relating to the creation or transfer of securities.

(6) A term in a contract that is not a consumer contract excluding or restricting liability for a misrepresentation by one party to the contract to the other before the contract was made is of no effect unless the term satisfies the test of reasonableness; but this subsection does not apply to an international supply contract.

(7) For the purposes of subsections (3), (4) and (6)—

(a) the test of reasonableness is whether the term is a fair and reasonable one to have been included having regard to the circumstances which were, or ought reasonably to have been, known to or in the contemplation of the parties when the contract was made;

(b) the burden of showing that the term is reasonable is on the defendant;

(c) factors that may be relevant in applying the test of reasonableness include—

(i) the bargaining power of the parties;

(ii) whether the claimant received an inducement to agree to the term or, in accepting it, had the opportunity to enter into a similar contract with someone else without that term (even if at a higher price);

(iii) whether the claimant knew or ought reasonably to have known of the term;

(iv) where the term excludes or limits liability if some condition is not complied with, whether it was reasonable at the time of the contract to expect that compliance with that condition would be practicable;

    (v) whether the goods or services were sold or supplied to the special order of the claimant;

    (vi) whether it is the practice in the trade for such a term to be enforced;

    (vii) the insurance that the parties have taken out or could have taken out;

    (viii) the nature of the breach, for example whether the breach is negligent;

    (ix) the financial impact of the term.

17   Legislative control of exemption clauses and unfair terms in consumer contracts

(1) This section deals with the provisions in the Consumer Rights Act 2015 (the '2015 Act') invalidating exemption clauses and unfair terms in a consumer contract.

(2) In a contract for the supply of goods or digital content by a trader to a consumer, a term is not binding on the consumer to the extent that it would exclude or limit the trader's liability for breach of a term (which the 2015 Act treats as being included in such a contract) that, for example—

    (a) the goods or digital content are of satisfactory quality, fit for a particular purpose made known to the trader by the consumer, and as described;

    (b) the trader has the right to supply the goods or digital content;

but, as regards paragraph (b), special provision applies in relation to a contract for the hire of goods.

(3) In a contract for the supply of services by a trader to a consumer, a term is not binding on the consumer to the extent that it would exclude or limit the trader's liability for breach of a term (which the 2015 Act treats as being included in such a contract) that, for example, the trader must perform the service with reasonable care and skill.

(4) A trader cannot exclude or limit liability in a consumer contract for breach of a contractual obligation to use reasonable care, or breach of a duty of care in tort, causing death or personal injury.

(5) A term of a consumer contract that is unfair is not binding on the consumer.

(6) A term is unfair for the purposes of subsection (5) if, contrary to the requirement of good faith, it causes a significant imbalance in the parties' rights and obligations under the contract to the detriment of the consumer.

(7) Factors that may be relevant in applying the test in subsection (6) include—

    (a) the bargaining power of the parties;

    (b) whether the consumer had an inducement to agree to the term;

    (c) whether the goods or services were sold or supplied to the special order of the consumer;

    (d) the extent to which the trader has dealt fairly and equitably with the consumer.

(8) But, provided that it is transparent and prominent (and not a term listed in Part 1 of Schedule 2 to the 2015 Act), a term cannot be assessed for fairness to the extent that—

    (a) it specifies the main subject matter of the contract; or

    (b) the assessment is of the appropriateness of the price payable under the contract by comparison with the goods, digital content or services supplied under it.

(9) A term is transparent if it is expressed in plain and intelligible language and (in the case of a written term) is legible; and a term is prominent if it is brought to the consumer's attention in such a way that an average consumer would be aware of the term.

(10) Where there are proceedings before a court which relate to a term of a consumer contract, the court must consider whether the term is fair even if not raised by the parties unless the court considers that it has insufficient legal and factual material to do so.

(11) Some of the above subsections do not apply to certain types of consumer contract so that, for example—

    (a) subsection (2) does not apply to a contract for a trader to supply coins or notes to a consumer for use as currency or to a contract for the supply of goods to a consumer that is intended to operate as a security;

    (b) subsections (3) and (5) do not apply to a contract of employment or apprenticeship;

    (c) subsection (4) does not apply to a contract of insurance or a contract relating to the creation or transfer of an interest in land.

PART 5
BREACH OF CONTRACT AND REMEDIES FOR BREACH

18   Breach of contract

(1) A party commits a breach of contract by failing to perform the contract in accordance with its terms.

(2) An anticipatory repudiation may also constitute a breach of contract (see sections 19(10) and (11)(b)).

(3) A party may commit a breach of contract without being at fault unless the terms of the contract impose merely an obligation to use reasonable care (or an equivalent standard requiring proof of fault).

(4) The rest of this Part deals with the remedies available to one party (the 'innocent party' or 'claimant') for a breach of contract by the other party (the 'other party' or 'defendant') (but, except in sections 19(13) and 26(4), it does not deal with the special remedies for a consumer in Part 1 of the Consumer Rights Act 2015).

19 Termination

(1) The innocent party has the right to terminate the contract for breach by the other party in the situations set out in subsection (8).

(2) Termination of a contract for breach depends on the election of the innocent party and does not occur automatically as a matter of law.

(3) Termination is effected by the innocent party making clear to the other party, by words or conduct, that it is treating the contract as at an end.

(4) Termination of the contract means that, subject to contrary agreement, the parties are discharged from their obligations under the contract which would arise after termination but not those which have arisen before.

(5) If a benefit has been obtained by one party from the other under a contract that has been terminated for breach, the right to restitution in respect of that benefit is governed by the law of unjust enrichment.

(6) An innocent party elects not to terminate, and thereby affirms, the contract, so that it cannot then change its mind and terminate the contract for the same breach, if, with knowledge of the facts constituting the breach and of the legal right to terminate, it unequivocally manifests an intention to continue with the contract.

(7) Under the Sale of Goods Act 1979, a buyer of goods (who is not a consumer buying from a trader) loses the right to terminate the contract of sale for breach of a condition by the seller if the buyer accepts the goods (as defined in section 35 of that Act) even though the acceptance does not constitute an affirmation.

(8) The situations referred to in subsection (1) are as follows—

    (a) there is the breach by the other party of a term that is a condition (rather than being a warranty or an innominate term);

    (b) there is the breach by the other party of an innominate term and the consequences of the breach are such as to deprive the innocent party of substantially the whole benefit of the contract; or

    (c) the other party repudiates the contract.

(9) For the purposes of subsection (8)(a) and (b)—

    (a) a term is a condition if it is such an important term of the contract that any breach of it would deprive the innocent party of substantially the whole benefit of the contract or if it is otherwise clear that the intention of the parties is that any breach of it should give the innocent party the right to terminate the contract;

    (b) a term is a warranty if it is such a minor term of the contract that no breach of it would deprive the innocent party of substantially the whole benefit of the contract;

    (c) an innominate term is a term that is neither a condition nor a warranty;

    (d) subject to legislation (for example, sections 12 to 15A of the Sale of Goods Act 1979), the intentions of the parties determine whether a term is a condition or a warranty or an innominate term but the fact that the contract refers to the term as a 'condition' is not conclusive.

(10) For the purposes of subsection (8)(c), the other party repudiates the contract if it makes clear to the innocent party, by words or conduct, that—

    (a) it is not going to perform the contract at all;

    (b) it is going to commit a breach of a condition; or

    (c) it is going to commit a breach of an innominate term and the consequences of the breach will be such as to deprive the innocent party of substantially the whole benefit of the contract.

(11) The repudiation may occur—

    (a) on or after the due date of performance; or

    (b) prior to the due date for performance (an 'anticipatory repudiation') in which case the innocent party, without waiting for the due date for performance, can elect to accept the repudiation thereby terminating the contract and becoming immediately entitled to damages for breach.

(12) The parties may include a term in the contract that provides for termination of the contract on an event other than a breach allowing termination under subsection (8).

(13) Subsection (8) is subject to provisions in Part 1 of the Consumer Rights Act 2015 (for example, sections 19, 20 and 42) which, in some circumstances, govern a consumer's right to terminate a contract for breach by a trader of a consumer contract for the supply of goods or digital content.

20   Compensatory damages

  (1) Where there has been a breach of contract, the claimant has a right to compensatory damages which—

    (a) have the purpose of providing a monetary equivalent to the claimant's loss caused by the breach;

    (b) are measured in accordance with the aim in subsection (2) (unless compensatory damages are being awarded as hypothetical release damages under section 22(4)(a)); and

    (c) are subject to the limits in section 21.

(2) The aim of compensatory damages for breach of contract is to put the claimant into as good a position as if the contract had been performed.

(3) In applying the aim in subsection (2), gains obtained by the claimant as a result of the breach will normally be deducted unless too far removed from the breach.

(4) In applying the aim in subsection (2), there is sometimes a choice between awarding—

    (a) the difference in value between the claimant's position after breach and the position the claimant would have been in had the contract been performed (the 'difference in value' measure); or

    (b) what it will, or has, cost the claimant to be put into as good a position as if the contract had been performed (the 'cost of cure' measure).

(5) If the cost of cure measure is higher than the difference in value measure, the former will not be awarded unless—

    (a) the claimant has incurred the cost of cure or intends to do so; and

    (b) it was, or will be, reasonable for the claimant to incur the cost of cure.

(6) The difference in value and cost of cure measures are usually assessed at the date of the breach of contract (the 'breach date' rule) but this is not an inflexible rule and may be departed from if, on the facts known at the date of assessment and taking into account section 21(1)(c), that rule would under-compensate or over-compensate the claimant.

(7) In applying the aim in subsection (2), the claimant can choose (as an alternative to a direct assessment of the position it would have been in if the contract had been performed) to be compensated for the wasted expenses, or other losses, incurred in reliance on, or in anticipation of, the contract; but by making this choice the claimant should not be put into a better position than if the contract had been performed (and the defendant has the burden of proving that the claimant would be put into that better position).

(8) In applying the aim in subsection (2), the claimant must prove the loss (applying the normal standard of proof on the balance of probabilities) subject to the following—

    (a) if the uncertainty relates not to a past fact but to a future or hypothetical event, other than the hypothetical conduct of the claimant, and the claimant has lost a substantial chance of making a gain or of avoiding a loss, damages can be awarded that are proportionate to the lost chance;

    (b) where the defendant had a choice under the contract as to the way in which the contract would be performed, damages will usually be assessed on the assumption that the defendant would have performed in the way most favourable to itself;

(c) in some rare situations, special rules apply to proving the causation of personal injury;

(d) in some rare situations, loss is presumed (for example, loss of credit is presumed where a bank in breach of contract fails to honour the claimant's cheque).

(9) In applying the aim in subsection (2), if the claimant is an individual who suffers a non-pecuniary loss as a result of the breach, damages may be awarded for that loss only—

(a) if it comprises loss of satisfaction (such as enjoyment or peace of mind) or distress and it was an important object of the contract that the claimant should have satisfaction or should not suffer distress;

(b) if it comprises physical inconvenience or discomfort or distress consequent on that inconvenience or discomfort; or

(c) if it comprises pain, suffering, or loss of amenity consequent on the claimant's personal injury.

21 Limits on compensatory damages

(1) The following rules limit compensatory damages for breach of contract—

(a) the loss must not be too remote from the breach (see subsections (2) and (3));

(b) an intervening action of the claimant or a third party or a natural event must not break the chain of causation between the breach and the loss;

(c) the claimant cannot recover for loss that it should reasonably have avoided;

(d) if there has been the breach of a contractual obligation to use reasonable care, and there is concurrent liability in the tort of negligence, damages may be proportionately reduced for any contributory negligence of the claimant.

(2) The general rule is that loss is too remote if that type of loss could not reasonably have been contemplated by the defendant as a serious possibility at the time the contract was made assuming that, at that time, the defendant had thought about the breach.

(3) Irrespective of the general rule in subsection (2)—

(a) loss is too remote if the defendant did not assume responsibility for that loss;

(b) loss is not too remote if the defendant assumed responsibility for that loss.

22 Hypothetical release damages or an account of profits

(1) As an alternative to compensatory damages assessed in accordance with the aim in section 20(2), a court may award—

   (a) hypothetical release damages (commonly referred to as '*Wrotham Park* damages'); or

   (b) an account of profits.

(2) Hypothetical release damages are assessed according to the price which the claimant could reasonably have charged the defendant for releasing the defendant from the obligation that has been broken had the defendant approached the claimant immediately before committing the breach.

(3) Hypothetical release damages will be advantageous to a claimant where, for example, damages assessed in accordance with the aim in section 20(2) would be nominal because no loss can be proved or the loss is otherwise irrecoverable.

(4) The purpose of hypothetical release damages may be—

   (a) to compensate the claimant for, for example, the loss of the claimant's opportunity to bargain with the defendant;

   (b) to reverse a benefit acquired by the defendant from the breach; or

   (c) to value the contractual right that has been infringed by the defendant.

(5) An account of profits is assessed according to the profits made by the defendant from the breach and the purpose of such an award is to remove those profits; but such an award will be made only in very exceptional circumstances where all other remedies for breach (including hypothetical release damages) are inadequate.

(6) Punitive or exemplary damages, which have the purpose of punishing the defendant, cannot be awarded for breach of contract.

23 Agreed damages, penalties and forfeiture

(1) The parties may include a term in the contract by which a stipulated sum is agreed to be the damages payable in the event of breach.

(2) But the agreed damages will be payable (as 'liquidated damages') instead of damages assessed by the court only if the stipulated sum is not a penalty (which is unenforceable).

(3) The stipulated sum is not a penalty if, judged at the time of the making of the contract, it is not out of all proportion to a legitimate interest of the claimant in the performance of the contract (so that, in particular, a genuine pre-estimate of the claimant's loss from the breach is not a penalty).

(4) A term which requires a sum to be paid on an event other than breach cannot be a penalty.

(5) Although not concerning agreed damages, subsection (3) is also applicable to determine whether a term is unenforceable for being a penalty if in the event of breach the term—

(a) requires the defendant to do something other than to make a stipulated payment (for example, to transfer shares); or

(b) allows the claimant not to pay the defendant a sum that would otherwise be owed.

(6) Where a term allows the claimant, in the event of the defendant's breach, to take away ('forfeit') from the defendant—

(a) a personal right to the repayment of money, or

(b) a proprietary or possessory right,

that term may be unenforceable or the defendant may otherwise be granted relief against forfeiture (for example, by being given further time for payment).

24   The award of an agreed sum

(1) Subject to section 23, the claimant is entitled to the award of an agreed sum, by which the defendant is required to pay the sum that it contracted to pay, provided that the agreed sum is due under the contract.

(2) Subject to legislation (in particular, section 49(1) of the Sale of Goods Act 1979) the terms of the contract determine whether the sum is due or not.

(3) Subject to subsection (2), the following rules apply—

(a) where the obligation or contract is interpreted as being 'entire', this means that substantial performance of it is required before payment is due;

(b) where the obligation or contract is interpreted as being 'severable', this means that payment is due once there has been substantial performance of a specified part of it.

(4) Where the contract has been repudiated by the defendant, the claimant is normally entitled to hold the contract open, to perform (where it is possible to do so without the defendant's co-operation), and to be awarded the agreed sum due for that performance; but, as a rare exception to that normal rule, a claimant is not so entitled where to hold the contract open, to perform, and to claim the agreed sum would be wholly unreasonable.

25   Interest

(1) Under section 17 of the Judgments Act 1838, simple interest of 8 per cent per annum is payable from the date of judgment on a judgment debt such as the award of an agreed sum or damages.

(2) A term of a contract may specify the interest that is payable on an agreed sum or damages.

(3) Under the Late Payment of Commercial Debts (Interest) Act 1998 (the '1998 Act'), there is an implied term in a commercial contract (other than an excepted contract) that simple interest is payable on an agreed sum—

(a) at base rate plus 8 per cent per annum,

(b) for the period from the day after the relevant day (as defined in the 1998 Act) and prior to there being a judgment debt,

but the interest may be remitted, wholly or in part, because of the creditor's conduct and, subject to exceptions, the implied term may be ousted or varied by the agreement of the parties.

(4) For the purposes of subsection (3), a commercial contract is a contract for the supply of goods and services where both parties are acting in the course of a business.

(5) Under section 35A of the Senior Courts Act 1981, the courts may award simple interest on an agreed sum or damages from the date of the breach of contract until the date of judgment or, if earlier, the date of payment; but no interest can be awarded under that section if the payment was made prior to the commencement of proceedings.

(6) Interest, including compound interest, may be awarded as damages for breach of contract (or in an account of profits) in accordance with the rules in sections 20 to 22.

26   Specific performance

(1) A court may make an order of specific performance which requires the defendant to perform a positive contractual obligation.

(2) A court will not order specific performance if, as will usually be the case, damages (or the award of an agreed sum) are adequate unless the contract is for the sale, or other disposition, of an interest in land.

(3) Even if (applying subsection (2)) specific performance would otherwise be ordered, it will not be ordered where any of the following applies—

(a) the contract is one of employment or for personal services and the order is sought against—

(i) the employee or person required to perform personal services; or

(ii) the employer or person entitled to receive personal services unless the employer or that person retains trust and confidence in the employee or person required to perform personal services;

(b) there would be a lack of mutuality in the sense that the defendant would have an inadequate remedy against the claimant if the claimant in turn failed to perform;

(c) the order would require constant supervision;

(d) performance would be physically or legally impossible;

(e) performance would entail severe hardship for the defendant;

(f) the order would be too uncertain;

(g) the contract was not supported by consideration or, if there was consideration, it was merely nominal;

(h) the defendant's consent to the contract was unfairly obtained;

(i) after the making of the contract, the conduct of the claimant has been such that the order should not be granted;

(j) the doctrine of laches applies (see section 30(7)).

(4) By reason of section 58 of the Consumer Rights Act 2015, some of the above bars (for example, the bar in subsection (2)) do not apply where an order of specific performance is sought enforcing a consumer's legislative right against a trader to the repair or replacement of goods or digital content or the repeat performance of a service.

(5) Specific performance may be ordered on terms.

(6) Specific performance is a final and not an interim order so that it can only be ordered at trial although a court can grant an interim mandatory injunction requiring performance of a positive contractual obligation.

27 Injunction

(1) A court may grant a prohibitory injunction which orders the defendant not to break a negative contractual obligation.

(2) A prohibitory injunction ordering the defendant not to break a negative contractual obligation will readily be granted so that, even if the adequacy of damages is a reason to refuse such an injunction, it will be a rare case in which, in this context, damages will be regarded as adequate.

(3) Equivalent bars to those set out for specific performance in section 26(3)(e) to (j) apply to bar a prohibitory injunction.

(4) A prohibitory injunction ordering the defendant not to break a negative contractual obligation will not be granted if its indirect practical effect would be to order the defendant to perform a positive contractual obligation in respect of which a court would not order specific performance (for example, because it would require performance of personal services).

(5) A court may grant a mandatory restorative injunction which orders the defendant to undo what it has done in breach of contract.

(6) An injunction may be a final or an interim order.

28 Damages in substitution for specific performance or an injunction

(1) Under section 50 of the Senior Courts Act 1981, a court may award damages in substitution for specific performance or an injunction.

(2) Subject to subsection (3), the purpose and assessment of such damages is governed by sections 20 to 22 above.

(3) Such damages can be awarded even though the claimant does not have a cause of action for breach of contract because, for example, a breach of contract is anticipated but has not yet occurred.

29 Declaration and nominal damages

(1) A court may make a declaration as to a party's contractual rights or remedies.

(2) Where there has been a breach of contract and no other monetary award is being made, the claimant has a right to nominal damages which have the purpose of recognising formally that there has been a breach of contract.

30 Limitation of actions

(1) The rules set out in subsections (2) to (6) are largely derived from the Limitation Act 1980.

(2) Subject to the exceptions in subsections (3) to (8), there is a limitation period of 6 years, or 12 years if the contract has been made by deed, to bring a claim for a monetary remedy for breach of contract which runs from when the cause of action accrues; and the cause of action for breach of contract accrues on the date of the breach.

(3) The limitation period does not run while the claimant is under 18 or lacks mental capacity; but once the period has started to run, it will not be suspended by reason of a supervening lack of mental capacity.

(4) If any fact relevant to the claim has been deliberately concealed from the claimant by the defendant, the limitation period does not start to run until the claimant has discovered, or could reasonably have discovered, the concealment.

(5) Where the defendant acknowledges a claim for the award of an agreed sum or liquidated damages, or makes any part payment in respect of such a claim, the limitation period (unless it has already expired) starts to run afresh from the date of the acknowledgement or part payment.

(6) There are legislative provisions (for example, where the damages are in respect of personal injury or the agreed sum is payable under certain types of loan) that displace the 6 or 12 year limitation period running from the date of the accrual of the cause of action.

(7) Under the doctrine of laches, an equitable remedy (for example, specific performance or an injunction) may be barred where there has been such unreasonable delay by the claimant in commencing the claim that to grant the remedy would be unjust to the defendant; but there can be no such unreasonable delay until the claimant has discovered, or could reasonably have discovered, that it has a claim against the defendant.

(8) In general (but subject, for example, to subsections (3) and (4)) the terms of a contract may govern—

    (a) the limitation period; and

    (b) when that period starts to run.

31 Combining remedies

(1) Subject to subsections (2) and (3), a remedy for breach of contract may be combined with any other remedy, whether for breach of contract or not (for example, damages for breach of contract may be combined with termination or with specific performance or with a monetary restitutionary award for unjust enrichment).

(2) Remedies cannot be combined if the combination is inconsistent (for example, termination for breach and specific performance, or rescission for misrepresentation and damages for breach).

(3) Satisfaction of more than one monetary remedy is not permitted to the extent that it would produce double recovery.

PART 6
FRUSTRATION OF CONTRACT

32 Change of circumstances constituting frustration

(1) Subject to the parties having expressly (see subsection (4)) or impliedly provided for the risk of this in the contract, a contract is frustrated where, after the making of the contract, there is such a change of circumstances that performance of the contract would be physically or legally impossible or would otherwise be rendered radically different from that which was promised.

(2) The mere fact that performance has been made more onerous or expensive does not constitute frustration.

(3) A contract is not frustrated where the party alleging a frustrating event is itself at fault for the occurrence of that event or chooses not to perform ('self-induced frustration').

(4) It is common for the parties to a written contract to deal with a change of circumstances outside their control, including what might otherwise be a frustrating event, by an express term (for example, what is commonly referred to as a 'force majeure' clause) which specifies the legal effects (such as termination, or suspension, of the contract and that money paid should be repaid) of there being a change of circumstances outside their control.

33 Effects of frustration

(1) Frustration terminates the contract automatically from the date of the frustration.

(2) Automatic termination means that the contract is terminated without any election by a party.

(3) Termination of the contract means that, subject to contrary agreement, the parties are discharged from their obligations under the contract which would arise after termination but not those which have arisen before.

(4) If a benefit has been obtained by one party from the other, under a contract that has been terminated for frustration, a right to restitution in respect of that benefit is governed by the law of unjust enrichment (which in this context is principally contained in the Law Reform (Frustrated Contracts) Act 1943).

PART 7
FACTORS RENDERING A CONTRACT DEFECTIVE

34 Void, voidable, unenforceable, rectifiable

(1) This Part makes provision about when a contract is—
    (a) void (as for mistake in limited circumstances);
    (b) voidable (as for, for example, misrepresentation or undue influence);
    (c) unenforceable (as for, for example, illegality);
    (d) rectifiable (as for mistake in limited circumstances).

(2) A void contract is invalid from the start and creates no contractual obligations but it may be that only one party can rely on the contract being void.

(3) A voidable contract is one that the party affected by the factor rendering the contract voidable (the 'claimant') can choose to rescind but is valid unless rescinded; and the effect of rescission is to invalidate the contract from the start.

(4) Rescission does not require an order of the court and is effected—
    (a) by the claimant informing the other contracting party that the contract is rescinded; or
    (b) where that is impossible, by the claimant making clear through any other act that the contract is rescinded.

(5) Rescission is barred where—
    (a) the claimant has affirmed the contract by unequivocally manifesting an intention to continue with it after knowing of the misrepresentation or non-disclosure or being free of the illegitimate threat, undue influence or weakness or incapacity;
    (b) a third party is a bona fide purchaser for value of property transferred under the contract without notice of the factor rendering the contract voidable;
    (c) restitution by the claimant to the other contracting party of benefits conferred on the claimant by the other contracting party is impossible; or
    (d) the claimant has delayed too long in seeking rescission so that, unless the rescission is at common law (as for, for example, fraudulent misrepresentation) rather than in equity (as for, for example, non-fraudulent misrepresentation or undue influence), the doctrine of laches applies (see section 30(7)).

(6) An unenforceable contract creates contractual obligations but cannot be enforced by one or, in some circumstances, either party.

(7) A rectifiable contract is a contract the written terms of which, because of a mistake by one or both parties, may in limited circumstances be amended by a court order for rectification (see section 35(6)).

(8) Rectification is barred where—

    (a) the party seeking rectification (the 'claimant') has affirmed the contract by continuing with it after knowing of the mistake;

    (b) a third party is a bona fide purchaser for value of property transferred under the contract without notice of the mistake; or

    (c) the claimant has delayed too long in seeking rectification so that the doctrine of laches applies (see section 30(7)).

(9) If a benefit has been obtained by one party from the other, under a contract that is defective in any of the ways set out in subsection (1), a right to restitution in respect of that benefit is governed by the law of unjust enrichment.

35   Mistake

(1) In this section, a mistake may include a mistake of law as well as a mistake of fact.

(2) Subject to the exceptions set out in subsections (3) to (6), a mistake made by both parties or by one party (whether or not known to the other) does not render the contract defective.

(3) A mistake in entering the contract renders the contract void if—

    (a) both parties make the same mistake so that, contrary to the parties' belief, performance of the contract is physically or legally impossible or the purpose of the contract cannot be achieved at the time the contract is made;

    (b) the parties have not expressly or impliedly provided in the contract for the risk of being so mistaken; and

    (c) the party who is alleging the mistake has not negligently induced the other party's mistake.

(4) A mistake in entering the contract renders the contract void (or, to put it another way, there is no acceptance of an offer and hence no contract) if—

    (a) the parties are at cross-purposes such that there is a central objective ambiguity as to what has been agreed; or

    (b) one party is mistaken and—

        (i) the other party knows, or ought reasonably to know, of that mistake;

(ii) the mistake is as to the terms of the contract or as to the identity of the other party; and

(iii) it is the mistaken party who is alleging that the contract is void.

(5) A signed contract is void under the doctrine of 'non est factum' if—

    (a) the document signed was mistakenly signed by the party who is alleging that it is void; and

    (b) that document is fundamentally different from what that party thought it to be; and

    (c) that party was not negligent in signing that document.

(6) The written terms of a contract may be rectified if—

    (a) those terms are inconsistent with the parties' outwardly manifested common intention that continued until the time the contract was made; or

    (b) one party was mistaken in entering into the contract and the other party knowing of that mistake unconscionably remained silent at the time the contract was made.

36   Misrepresentation

(1) A contract is voidable where a party to the contract ('the claimant') entered into it in reliance on a misrepresentation, whether fraudulent, negligent or innocent, by the other contracting party ('the defendant') or, in certain circumstances set out in section 39, by a third party.

(2) A misrepresentation is a false representation, by words or conduct, of present fact or law.

(3) A statement of intention contains a representation as to the present state of mind of the person making it.

(4) A statement of opinion contains a representation that the person making the statement holds that opinion; and in certain circumstances (as where the person making the statement may be expected to have special knowledge in relation to it) a statement of opinion contains a representation that the person making the statement has reasonable grounds for holding that opinion.

(5) To prove reliance it must be shown that the claimant would not have entered into the contract (whether at all or on the same terms) but for the misrepresentation unless—

    (a) the misrepresentation was fraudulent, in which case the misrepresentation need merely have been a reason for entering into the contract or present in the claimant's mind at the time the contract was entered into; or

    (b) the misrepresentation and another factor rendering the contract voidable (for example, duress) were each independently sufficient to induce the claimant to enter into the contract.

(6) A claimant who has relied on a misrepresentation in entering into a contract has a right to damages from the person by whom the misrepresentation was made (the 'misrepresentor')—

    (a) for the tort of deceit where the misrepresentation was fraudulent;

    (b) for the tort of negligence where the misrepresentation was negligent and there was a duty of care owed by the misrepresentor to the claimant;

    (c) under section 2(1) of the Misrepresentation Act 1967 (except where disapplied in relation to a misrepresentation to a consumer by section 2(4) of that Act) provided that—

        (i) the misrepresentor was a party to the contract, and

        (ii) the misrepresentor fails to prove that it had reasonable grounds to believe and did believe up to the time the contract was made that the representation was true.

(7) A claimant may both rescind a contract for misrepresentation and be awarded damages for the tort of deceit or negligence or under section 2(1) of the Misrepresentation Act 1967; but satisfaction of more than one monetary remedy is not permitted to the extent that it would produce double recovery.

(8) A claimant may be awarded damages instead of rescission for a non-fraudulent misrepresentation under section 2(2) of the Misrepresentation Act 1967 (except where disapplied in relation to a misrepresentation to a consumer by section 2(4) of that Act) but only where it is just to do so.

37   Duress

(1) A contract is voidable where a party to the contract ('the claimant') was induced to enter into it by an illegitimate threat ('duress') of the other contracting party or, in certain circumstances set out in section 39, of a third party.

(2) The illegitimate threat may be express or implied.

(3) For this purpose a threat—

    (a) is illegitimate if the conduct threatened is unlawful (as in the case of a threat to commit a crime or a tort or a breach of contract);

    (b) may in some circumstances be illegitimate even though the conduct threatened is lawful (as in the case of a threat to prosecute, or expose the truth about, the claimant or a member of the claimant's family).

(4) But if the illegitimate threat is a threat to break a contract (and possibly in respect of some other types of threat), the contract is voidable only if the claimant had no reasonable alternative to giving in to the threat.

(5) For the purposes of subsection (1)—

    (a) the standard test of causation is the 'but for' test by which it must be shown that the claimant would not have entered into the contract (whether at all or on the same terms) but for the illegitimate threat, but

    (b) there are exceptions to the 'but for' test where—

        (i) the threat was to the person in which case the threat need merely have been a reason for entering into the contract or present in the claimant's mind at the time the contract was entered into;

        (ii) duress and another factor rendering the contract voidable (for example, misrepresentation) were each independently sufficient to induce the claimant to enter into the contract.

38 Undue influence

(1) A contract is voidable if it was entered into while a party to the contract ('the claimant') was under the undue influence of the other contracting party ('the defendant') or, in certain circumstances set out in section 39, of a third party.

(2) A claimant is under the undue influence of another person if, because of the relationship between them, the claimant's judgement is not free and independent of that person.

(3) There is a rebuttable presumption of undue influence if—

    (a) the claimant was in a relationship of influence with the defendant or the third party at the time the contract was entered into; and

    (b) the contract was disadvantageous to the claimant in the sense that it was not readily explicable by reference to the motives on which people ordinarily act.

(4) A relationship of influence—

    (a) is to be treated as existing in certain relationships (for example, parent and young child, solicitor and client, doctor and patient, and spiritual adviser and follower), but

    (b) otherwise must be proved on the facts.

(5) It is for the defendant to rebut the presumption mentioned in subsection (3) by proving that the claimant exercised free and independent judgement; and an obvious way for the defendant to try to prove this is by showing that the claimant obtained the fully informed and competent independent advice of a qualified person, such as a solicitor or other legal adviser.

39   Misrepresentation, illegitimate threat or undue influence by a third party

(1) The misrepresentation or illegitimate threat or undue influence may be that of a third party but, if so, the contract is voidable by the party to the contract ('the claimant') only if—

    (a) the third party was acting as the agent of the other contracting party ('the defendant');

    (b) the defendant had actual notice of the misrepresentation or illegitimate threat or undue influence; or

    (c) the defendant is deemed to have had notice of the misrepresentation or illegitimate threat or undue influence under subsections (2) to (4).

(2) Unless subsection (3) applies, the defendant is deemed to have had notice of a misrepresentation, illegitimate threat or undue influence of a third party if—

    (a) the defendant is a financial institution with whom the claimant entered into a contract of suretyship guaranteeing the repayment of a loan made by the defendant other than a loan, including a joint loan, to the claimant; and

    (b) the claimant has a non-commercial relationship with the third party, known about by the defendant, and entered into the contract because the misrepresentation or illegitimate threat was made by the third party or while under the undue influence of the third party.

(3) The defendant is not deemed to have had notice of a misrepresentation or illegitimate threat or undue influence of a third party if, before the contract was entered into, it—

    (a) informed the claimant, by direct communication, that it required written confirmation from the claimant's adviser that the adviser had fully explained to the claimant the nature and practical implications of the contract;

    (b) forwarded to the claimant's adviser details of the financial circumstances regarding the loan application to it;

    (c) informed the claimant's adviser of any facts which had led the defendant to believe or suspect that there had been a misrepresentation, illegitimate threat, or undue influence by the third party; and

    (d) received confirmation from the claimant's adviser that the adviser had provided the claimant with fully informed and competent advice.

(4) In subsection (3) 'adviser' means a solicitor or other legal adviser.

40   Legislative consumer protection against misleading or aggressive commercial practices

(1) Under Part 4A of the Consumer Protection from Unfair Trading Regulations 2008, a consumer has a legislative right to redress in respect of

a contract with a trader for, for example, the sale or supply of a product by the trader, where—

    (a) there has been a commercial practice by the trader that is a misleading action or aggressive; and

    (b) that commercial practice was a significant factor in the consumer's decision to enter into the contract.

(2) A commercial practice is a misleading action if—

    (a) it contains false information or is likely to deceive the average consumer as to the existence or nature of the product or its main characteristics or the price or the rights of the parties; and

    (b) it is likely to cause the average consumer to take a transactional decision that would not otherwise have been taken.

(3) A commercial practice is aggressive if—

    (a) through the use of harassment, coercion, or undue influence, it is likely significantly to impair the average consumer's freedom of choice or conduct in relation to the product; and

    (b) it is likely to cause the average consumer to take a transactional decision that would not otherwise have been taken.

(4) The legislative right to redress includes the right to rescind the contract, the right to a discount, and the right to damages.

41   Exploitation of weakness

(1) A contract is voidable if one party to the contract ('the claimant') entered into it as the result of a weakness of the claimant having been exploited by the other contracting party ('the defendant').

(2) The weakness may be—

    (a) a mental weakness (such as inexperience, confusion because of old age, or emotional strain); or

    (b) in exceptional cases, a difficult position that the claimant is in.

(3) The claimant's weakness has been exploited by the defendant if—

    (a) the terms of the contract were clearly disadvantageous to the claimant, and

    (b) the defendant knew of the claimant's weakness and that the terms of the contract were clearly disadvantageous to the claimant,

unless the claimant obtained, and was able to act on, the fully informed and competent independent advice of a qualified person, such as a solicitor or other legal adviser.

42   Non-disclosure

(1) The general rule is that a contract is not voidable merely because one party to the contract ('the defendant') did not disclose to the other contracting party ('the claimant') an important matter of fact or law relevant to the contract.

(2) There are legislative provisions (for example, in respect of insurance contracts where the insured is not a consumer) which require the disclosure of information by one contracting party to the other.

(3) Other exceptions to the general rule in subsection (1) include—

    (a) that a contract is voidable for non-disclosure of a material circumstance if the defendant was in a fiduciary relationship with the claimant; and

    (b) that a contract of suretyship guaranteeing the payment of a debt to the defendant is voidable for non-disclosure of an unusual feature of that debt and, therefore, of the contract of suretyship.

(4) A contract is voidable under subsection (3) only if the defendant's non-disclosure induced the claimant to enter into the contract in the sense that the claimant would not have entered into the contract (whether at all or on the same terms) had it known about the matter of fact or law that was not disclosed.

43   Incapacity

(1) Subject to subsection (2), a contract with an individual who is under 18 (a 'minor') is unenforceable against the minor unless the minor ratifies the contract after becoming 18.

(2) A contract with a minor—

    (a) is voidable, and can be rescinded by the minor before, or within a reasonable time after, becoming 18 if the contract is—

        (i) a contract for the acquisition of an interest in land;

        (ii) a contract for the acquisition of shares in a company;

        (iii) a partnership agreement; or

        (iv) a marriage settlement;

    (b) is valid and enforceable by and against the minor if it is a contract for necessaries or a beneficial contract of service or an analogous contract.

(3) Subject to subsection (5), a contract is voidable where an individual enters into it while lacking mental capacity or while incapacitated by intoxication provided the other party to the contract knew of that lack of mental capacity or intoxication.

(4) For the purpose of subsection (3), an individual lacks mental capacity if at the time of entering into the contract he or she is unable to make the decision for himself or herself to enter into the contract because of an impairment of, or a disturbance in the functioning of, the mind or brain.

(5) There is a special rule applicable to a contract of compromise made by an individual while lacking mental capacity according to which the contract is voidable if, at the time of entering into it, he or she did not have a litigation friend (that is, an individual permitted to act in court proceedings on behalf of an individual who lacks capacity).

(6) By reason of section 39 of the Companies Act 2006, a contract with a non-charitable company is not void or otherwise defective on the ground that the company is acting outside the powers in its constitution.

(7) A contract made with a public authority acting outside its powers is void.

44 Illegality and public policy

(1) If the formation, purpose or performance of a contract involves conduct that is illegal (such as a crime) or contrary to public policy (such as a restraint of trade), the contract is unenforceable by one or either party if to deny enforcement is an appropriate response to that conduct.

(2) There are legislative provisions which—
    (a) prohibit a contract so that it is unenforceable by either party;
    (b) lay down that a contract or contract term is unenforceable by one or either party (or void).

(3) A contract that would otherwise be unenforceable as mentioned in subsection (1) or (2) may be severed so that the objectionable part of the contract is disregarded and the rest of the contract is enforceable; but severance is possible only if—
    (a) the objectionable part of the contract does not form the main consideration under the contract;
    (b) the objectionable part of the contract can be separated from the rest of the contract without rewriting; and
    (c) severance would not entirely alter the nature of the agreement.

(4) If a contract is unenforceable by one or either party as mentioned in subsections (1) and (2), a contract that is linked to such a contract may be unenforceable by one or either party for the same reasons.

(5) A term excluding liability for a person's own fraudulent misrepresentation is contrary to public policy and void.

(6) Where there are proceedings before a court relating to a contract involving conduct that appears to be illegal or contrary to public policy, the court must consider whether the contract or term is unenforceable or void even if not raised by the parties unless the court considers that it has insufficient legal and factual material to do so.

PART 8
PRIVITY OF CONTRACT AND THIRD PARTIES

45 Privity of contract

(1) A contract can be enforced only by, or against, a party to the contract (the 'privity of contract' rule).

(2) The rule in subsection (1) is subject to exceptions to, or circumventions of, that rule (see sections 47 to 50).

(3) For the purposes of this Part—

'the promisor' means the party to the contract against whom the contract is enforceable; and

'the promisee' means the party to the contract by whom the contract is enforceable.

46 Enforcement by the promisee

(1) A promisee's damages for breach of a contract made for the benefit of a third party are normally concerned to compensate the loss of the promisee, not the loss of the third party, so that those damages will often be nominal.

(2) A promisee may be granted specific performance requiring the promisor to perform for the benefit of the third party where a court is satisfied that the damages for the promisee, in particular nominal damages, would be inadequate to produce a just result.

(3) A prohibitory injunction may be granted to a promisee to enforce a negative contractual promise in favour of a third party.

(4) As an exception to subsection (1) a promisee can recover a third party's loss on a contract for the benefit of a third party relating to property (whether goods or land) where—

(a) the parties contemplated that the loss in respect of that property would be suffered by the third party; and

(b) the third party does not itself have a right against the promisor to recover the third party's loss.

47 Enforcement by a third party under the Contracts (Rights of Third Parties) Act 1999

(1) Under the Contracts (Rights of Third Parties) Act 1999 ('the 1999 Act') an expressly identified third party may enforce a term of the contract if—

(a) the contract expressly provides that the third party may; or

(b) the term purports to confer a benefit on the third party unless on a proper construction of the contract the parties did not intend the term to be enforceable by the third party.

(2) The requirement of express identification in subsection (1) means that the third party must be expressly identified in the contract by name, as a member of a class, or as answering a particular description but need not be in existence when the contract is entered into.

(3) A third party's right to enforce a term of a contract in subsection (1) means that, subject to the terms of the contract, there shall be available

to the third party any remedy that would have been available to the third party in an action for breach of contract had the third party been a party to the contract.

(4) Subject to an express term to the contrary, where a third party has a right under subsection (1), the parties may not extinguish or alter that right without the consent of the third party if—

    (a) the third party has communicated its assent to the term to the promisor, or

    (b) the third party has relied on that term and the promisor is aware of that reliance or could reasonably have foreseen it.

(5) Subject to an express term to the contrary, where a third party brings proceedings to enforce a right under subsection (1), the promisor may rely on any defence that would have been available to the promisor had the proceedings been brought by the promisee.

(6) Subject to the promisor not being made doubly liable for the same loss, the right of the third party under subsection (1) does not affect any right of the promisee to enforce the contract.

(7) A third party who has a right under subsection (1) to enforce a written arbitration agreement, or has a right under subsection (1) to enforce a term that, by reason of a written arbitration agreement, is conditional on resolving any dispute by arbitration, is to be treated as a party to the contract for the purposes of the Arbitration Act 1996.

(8) Some types of contract are excluded from the 1999 Act, including—

    (a) a contract on a bill of exchange, promissory note or other negotiable instrument;

    (b) in general, a contract for the carriage of goods.

48   Other exceptions to, or circumventions of, the privity of contract rule

In addition to section 47, the following rules exist by way of exceptions to, or circumventions of, the privity of contract rule—

    (a) an agent may make a contract on behalf of a principal, including an undisclosed principal (see section 49);

    (b) a right under a contract may be assigned to a third party (see section 50);

    (c) a promise to benefit a third party may be held by the promisee on trust for the third party;

    (d) a covenant concerning land, whether positive or negative, may in certain circumstances benefit or burden a third party;

    (e) a third party (C) may have a claim in the tort of negligence where A's breach of a contract with B also constitutes the breach of a duty of care owed by A to C, including where C's loss is the non-receipt of an economic benefit;

(f) a third party (C) may take the benefit of an exemption or exclusive jurisdiction clause in a contract between A and B where, in addition to that contract, C can establish that there is a unilateral contract by which A promises to be bound by the exemption or exclusive jurisdiction clause in exchange for a performance by C;

(g) a third party (C) may be burdened by an exemption or exclusive jurisdiction clause in a contract between A and B by which there has been a bailment or sub-bailment of C's goods provided C has consented to that bailment or sub-bailment;

(h) rules in legislation (for example, the Bills of Exchange Act 1882, section 11 of the Married Women's Property Act 1882, and the Carriage of Goods by Sea Act 1992) which, in respect of certain types of contract, allow enforcement of a contract by a third party.

49   Agency

(1) An agent makes a contract with a party ('the other party') on behalf of a principal where the agent has authority from the principal to do so.

(2) The agent's authority from the principal may be—

    (a) actual (whether express or implied);

    (b) apparent (where the principal represents to the other party that the agent has actual authority to make the contract on behalf of the principal even though the agent does not have that actual authority); or

    (c) retrospectively conferred by the principal's ratification.

(3) A principal may be—

    (a) disclosed (where the other party knows that the agent is acting on behalf of a principal); or

    (b) undisclosed (where the other party does not know that the agent is acting on behalf of a principal);

but a principal can only be undisclosed if the agent has actual authority.

(4) Where the principal is disclosed and the agent has actual authority or there has been ratification, the general position is that the parties to the contract are the principal and the other party so that the contract can be enforced by, and against, the principal.

(5) Where the principal is undisclosed, the general position is that both the agent and the principal are parties to the contract with the other party so that the contract may be enforced by, and against, each of them.

(6) Where the agent has apparent authority, and there has been no ratification, the contract can be enforced by the other party against the principal but cannot be enforced by the principal.

50   Assignment

(1) By an assignment, a party ('the assignor') may transfer to a third party ('the assignee'), without the consent of the other contracting party ('the debtor'), a right under a contract that the assignor has against the debtor.

(2) A right under a contract cannot be assigned if—

    (a) the contract involves a personal relationship between the assignor and the debtor such that it would be detrimental to the debtor to perform for the assignee rather than the assignor;

    (b) the contract prohibits the assignment;

    (c) the right under the contract is a right to (unliquidated) damages unless the assignee has a genuine commercial interest in taking the assignment; or

    (d) the assignment would be illegal or contrary to public policy.

(3) In a claim for breach of contract by the assignee against the debtor, the following general rules apply so as to avoid prejudice to the debtor—

    (a) the debtor can raise any defence that it could have raised against the assignor had the assignor been bringing the action against the debtor;

    (b) the assignee is not entitled to recover more from the debtor than what would have been the assignor's entitlement against the debtor had there been no assignment.

(4) If all the parties agree that a contract between two parties (A and B) is replaced by a new contract between one of the parties (A) and a third party (C) in which the same (or similar) duties are owed to, and by, C as were owed to, and by, B, this is known as a novation (which does not involve any assignment).

COMMENTARY

1 Scope

This Restatement is concerned only with—

    (a) the law of England and Wales;

    (b) the general law applicable to contract (so that there are rules, especially in legislation, dealing with specific types of contract that are not mentioned in this Restatement).

1(a)

This Restatement is concerned solely to restate English law (that is, the law as it applies in England and Wales). The English law on the law of contract differs in some significant respects from the Scottish law of contract. So, for example, the Scottish law of contract does not have a requirement of consideration and there is a judge-made doctrine of third party rights.

1(b)

It is widely recognised that a division can be usefully made between the general law of contract, both common law and legislation, and the law that applies to particular types of contract (for example, employment contracts, contracts for the sale of goods, contracts for the carriage of goods, construction contracts, insurance contracts, consumer credit agreements, arbitration agreements). That type of division is reflected, for example, in the division between Volumes 1 and 2 of *Chitty on Contracts* (32nd edn, 2015) the first being called *General Principles* and the second *Specific Contracts* (although it should be noted that, for the first time, the 32nd edition of *Chitty* pushes into Volume 2 in a new chapter on 'consumer contracts' the law on, for example, unfair terms in consumer contracts, which is treated in this Restatement as part of the general law). This Restatement is concerned only with the general law applicable to contract. This means that special rules applicable only to particular types of contract, whether at common law or, especially, by reason of legislation, will not be covered *unless* reference to the special rules assists in describing (or avoids a misleading description of) the general law, an obvious example being the terms implied by legislation into a contract for the sale of goods.

It is important to emphasise that the general law of contract comprises both common law (that is, judge-made law including equity) and legislation. So there are references to legislation at various points in the Restatement (for example, the Unfair Contract Terms Act 1977, the Consumer Rights Act 2015, the Limitation Act 1980, the Consumer Protection from Unfair Trading Regulations 2008, and the

Contracts (Rights of Third Parties) Act 1999). However, most of the general law of contract is common law so that most of this Restatement is concerned with the common law. Indeed if that were not the case and the general law of contract were mainly contained in legislation one might regard a Restatement as an inappropriate instrument. It further follows from this primary concern with the common law that *the law as set out in this Restatement is subject to any legislative provision, or provision of EU law, to the contrary.*

It is also usefully explained here that, although one might regard this as part of the general law of contract, the English private international law of contract has been excluded from this Restatement. This is for three main reasons. First, if there is to be a Restatement of that area of law, it is more coherently dealt with as part of a Restatement of English private international law generally. Secondly, the English private international law of contract is now largely governed by legislation, in particular the 'Rome I' EU Regulation (Regulation 593/2008) so that it is not clear that a Restatement is an appropriate instrument for that area. And, thirdly, it would be hard to improve on the treatment in Dicey, Morris, and Collins, *The Conflict of Laws* (15th edn, 2012).

2   Definition of 'contract'

A contract is an agreement that is legally binding because—

   (a) it is supported by consideration or made by deed (see section 8);
   (b) it is certain and complete (see section 9);
   (c) it is made with the intention to create legal relations (see section 10); and
   (d) it complies with any formal requirement needed for the agreement to be legally binding (see section 11(2)(a)).

2

Although rarely acknowledged, there has been a long-standing disagreement among commentators on the English law of contract as to whether, at root, a contract is best viewed as a legally binding *agreement* or a legally binding *promise*. It is submitted that, provided one takes a wide view of 'agreement' (so as to include, for example, unilateral contracts: see s 7(14)) the former is more accurate as an underpinning working definition. However, a problem, whether one focuses on agreements or promises, is that those terms are over-inclusive in the sense that there are legally binding agreements or promises that are not conventionally treated as contracts in English law: for example, an agreement or promise that is enforceable by the doctrines of promissory or proprietary estoppel (see s 12 and the accompanying commentary), a deed poll (which is explained in the commentary to s 8(1)), and the undertakings of a trustee or a gratuitous bailee (which are enforceable in actions for breach of trust or for the tort of negligence but not for breach of contract).

For that reason, it is necessary to narrow the definition so that, instead of just talking of a legally binding agreement, one adds in the further essential requirements of a contract in English law. These are listed in s 2(a) to (d) (and note as regards (d) that we are here concerned only with formal requirements that go to the existence of the contract, most importantly that contracts for the sale of land must be made in writing and signed). Their details are dealt with in ss 8–11. The notion of consideration is a particularly important feature of English contract law and is explained in s 8. Those further essential requirements are the positive requirements needed for an agreement to be binding as a contract. But a contract may still be defective for other reasons, which are dealt with in Part 7.

3   Non-contractual liability
(1) This Restatement does not cover in detail areas of law outside the law of contract (for example, the law of tort or unjust enrichment) even though liability under those areas of law may arise in the context of, for example, pre-contractual negotiations or a contract being defective or terminated.
(2) A claim for breach of contract may be made concurrently with another claim (for example, for a tort or unjust enrichment).

3(1)

This Restatement takes a conceptual, not a contextual, approach to what constitutes the law of contract. Applying that approach, tort and unjust enrichment are distinct areas of the law from contract and are seen as resting on different events/causes of action. This is not to deny that there may be claims in, for example, tort and unjust enrichment that arise in a contractual context. So, for example, a misrepresentation inducing a contract may be actionable as a tort. The details of that area of tort lie outside this Restatement. There may also be claims in the law of unjust enrichment (the 'unjust factor' usually being failure of consideration) for the restitution of the value of benefits conferred on the other party in anticipation of a contract that does not eventuate or is void or has been terminated for frustration. Even if a contract has been terminated for the other party's breach, the restitution of the value of benefits conferred on the contract-breaker for failure of consideration lies within the law of unjust enrichment not the law of contract. It is not a remedy to enforce the contract or for breach of contract but is instead reversing the unjust enrichment of the defendant at the claimant's expense. The details of the law of unjust enrichment fall outside this Restatement and within *A Restatement of the English Law of Unjust Enrichment* (2012) (see especially s 15).

3(2)

That there can be concurrent liability between breach of contract and tort was authoritatively accepted in *Henderson v Merrett Syndicates Ltd* [1995] 2 AC 145,

HL. The same principle of concurrence must be equally applicable as between other events/causes of action and breach of contract (for example, breach of fiduciary duty and breach of contract; or unjust enrichment and breach of contract). Acceptance of the principle of concurrence does not, of course, deny that the parties are free to include a term in their contract excluding another cause of action.

Combining remedies raises linked but separate issues to concurrent liability: see s 31.

4 Parties

(1) A contract must have at least two parties but it may have more than two parties (a 'multiparty contract').

(2) Although some issues arise in relation to multiparty contracts that do not arise in relation to two–party contracts (for example, whether the liability of a party is joint or several), the law as set out in this Restatement applies with appropriate modifications to multiparty contracts as it does to two-party contracts.

(3) The parties to a contract are those who have entered into the legally binding agreement.

(4) In this Restatement, a person who is not a party to a contract is referred to as a 'third party'.

(5) In this Restatement, in relation to a contract—

    (a) references to A and B are references to the parties to the contract; and

    (b) a reference to C is to a third party.

4

As a contract is a legally binding *agreement*, there must be at least two parties: one cannot have an agreement where there is only one party.

It also follows that, as s 4(3) makes clear, the parties to an agreement are those who have entered into the agreement. This includes a person who has accepted the offer in a unilateral contract: see s 7(14). Note that it is not necessary for a party to a contract to have provided consideration because a contract made by deed need not be supported by consideration and yet there are parties to that type of contract.

Contracts are sometimes divided into bilateral, unilateral, and multilateral contracts. However, that is a potentially confusing sequence because it mixes the number of parties with whether more than one party is bound.

So, for example, under a unilateral contract only one party is bound (because only one party makes a promise) but there can be a large number of parties in the sense that the offer of a unilateral contract can be made 'to the world at large' and many may accept the offer. Hence many of the classic examples of unilateral contracts which have arisen, or have been discussed, in past cases are ones where a promise of money is made at large in return for a requested act so that more than one person can accept: for example, the promise of a payment for walking from London to York; or the promise of a payment for using an anti-influenza smoke-ball in the correct way (and then catching flu) as in the famous case of *Carlill v Carbolic Smoke Ball Co* [1893] 1 QB 256, CA.

Moreover, it is not clear that there is any significant conceptual difference between a bilateral contract where there are two parties who are bound and a multilateral contract where many parties are bound: one can argue that a multilateral contract merely involves many bilateral obligations.

In the light of these difficulties, it seems preferable to avoid references to multilateral contracts as if different from bilateral contracts. Nevertheless, it is important to recognise, not least because they are very common in practice (even if this is not reflected in the law reports), that contracts can involve more than two parties. The terminology chosen to reflect this in s 4 is a 'multiparty contract'.

As s 4(2) makes clear, the general law of contract applies to multiparty contracts as it does to two-party contracts. However, there are some issues that arise in relation to multiparty contracts that do not arise at all or in the same way in two-party contracts: for example, whether a liability survives after the death of one of the parties, or whether a debt is discharged by payment by only one party, or whether the release of one party releases all, or whether separate consideration needs to be provided by each party, or whether one party alone can bring an action or must instead join all others. In determining those issues one may have to decide whether the liability under the contract is joint or several (or joint and several); or whether the entitlement under the contract is joint or several. That will turn on the interpretation of the contract and hence on the (objective) intention of the parties. Was it intended, on the liability side, that more than one party should be liable to perform the same promise or were separate promises being made? Was it intended, on the entitlement side, that more than one party should be entitled to sue for the same promise or were separate promises being made to separate parties? For a helpful examination of these issues, see Peel, *Treitel on the Law of Contract* (14th edn, 2015) ch 13; and for rescission in respect of multiparty contracts, see O'Sullivan, Elliott, and Zakrzewski, *The Law of Rescission* (2nd edn, 2004) paras 20.31–20.33.

Under the privity of contract doctrine, a contract can only be enforced by, and is only enforceable against, the parties to a contract (who in this Restatement will be referred to as A and B) and not a third party (C). This is explained in detail in Part 8.

5   Freedom of contract

(1) Subject to exceptions (especially provisions under the Equality Act 2010) one is free to make, or to refuse to make, a contract with whomever one chooses.

(2) Provided that the consent of a party is not impaired by, for example, misrepresentation, duress, undue influence or incapacity (sections 36 to 38 and 43),

the parties to a contract are, in general, free to determine the terms of a contract.

(3) But the freedom in subsection (2) is qualified by the law on, for example—

    (a) the implication of some terms which do not rest on the parties' intentions (see section 15(1),(5), and (6));

    (b) the legislative control of exemption clauses and unfair terms (see sections 16 and 17);

    (c) penalties and forfeiture (see section 23);

    (d) illegality and public policy (see section 44);

    (e) legislation which provides that parties to a contract may not derogate from rules laid down in the legislation whether at all or to the detriment of one of the parties.

5

The idea of freedom of contract (or party autonomy) is so fundamental to the English law of contract that it may be thought unnecessary to spell it out. Moreover, it may be regarded as a high level principle that does not in itself determine decisions of the courts. Nevertheless, it has been thought helpful to include this section not least because those looking across from a civilian background may find aspects of the English law of contract puzzling without there being a reference to this idea.

In trying to spell out in more concrete terms what freedom of contract means, it seems appropriate to focus on two aspects. Both are subject to significant exceptions.

The first (s 5(1)) is the freedom to contract, or to refuse to contract, with whomever one wishes. This freedom is subject to the major exception that one cannot refuse to contract with someone if that would contravene equality legislation: that is, the refusal to contract would constitute, for example, race, sex, disability, age, or religious discrimination.

Note that in *Norweb plc v Dixon* [1995] 1 WLR 636 a utility company's statutory obligation to supply electricity to those requesting that supply was held to be incompatible with there being a *contract* for the supply.

The second (s 5(2)) is the freedom of the parties to contract on whatever terms they choose. As Lord Toulson said in *Prime Sight Ltd v Lavarello* [2013] UKPC 22, [2013] 2 WLR 84, at [47], 'Parties are ordinarily free to contract on whatever terms they choose and the court's role is to enforce them.' This is on the assumption that the consent of a party is not impaired by factors such as mistake, misrepresentation, duress, undue influence, or incapacity. Those factors and others are dealt with in Part 7. This freedom is also subject to two types of exception. The first—set out in s 5(3)(a)—is that some terms are implied into contracts by legislation or by law irrespective of the parties' intentions. The second type of exception—set out in s 5 (3)(b)–(e)—is that some terms or contracts will be struck down for 'policy' reasons.

The last exception (s 5(3)(e)) needs explanation. This section has sought to avoid the terminology of 'mandatory provisions', which is not familiar to English lawyers (other than in the context of private international law, where it has a particular significance). Nevertheless, there are numerous legislative provisions which the parties cannot contract out of. So, for example, by s 7 of the Consumer Protection Act 1987, the relevant statutory liability laid down in the Act 'shall not be limited or excluded by any contract term'; by the Commercial Agents (Council Directive) Regulations 1993 (SI 1993/3053) reg 19, 'the parties may not derogate from regulations 17 and 18 to the detriment of the commercial agent before the agency contract expires'; by s 144(1) of the Equality Act 2010 (headed 'contracting out'), 'A term of a contract is unenforceable by a person in whose favour it would operate in so far as it purports to exclude or limit a provision of or made under this Act'; by the Timeshare, Holiday Products, Resale and Exchange Contracts Regulations 2010 (SI 2010/2960) reg 19, 'A term contained in a regulated contract is void to the extent that it purports to allow the consumer to waive the rights conferred on them by these Regulations'; and by s 10 of the Consumer Insurance (Disclosure and Representations) Act 2012 (headed 'contracting out') a contract term 'which would put the consumer in a worse position . . . than the consumer would be in by virtue of the provisions of this Act is to that extent of no effect'.

The default emphasis on the freedom to contract on whatever terms one wishes leads to another observation that civilian lawyers may find helpful in looking at the English law of contract. Comparative lawyers have stressed that English law has often traditionally favoured a term-based approach when civil law prefers rules. So, for example, in his seminal article 'Rules and Terms, Civil Law and Common Law' (1974) 48 Tulane Law Review 946, at 948–9, Nicholas wrote:

'In the field of contract, a fundamental difference between French law and the traditional Common law is that the Common law habitually attempts to derive all the consequences of a contract from the will of those who made it (or at least ostensibly to do so, for the French lawyer would say that the will from which those consequences are derived is a very artificial or objective one), whereas the French law (and the Civil law generally) will often have recourse to rules.'

Classic examples of this difference are the approaches to common mistake or frustration or a duty of good faith. It has often been argued (although this is not accepted in this Restatement) that English law has no doctrine of common mistake and that the relevant cases rest on an implied term in the contract. The so-called juristic basis of frustration has traditionally been said to rest on an implied term of the contract and/or its construction. English law does not recognise a duty to perform in good faith but instead relies on implied terms in particular situations to achieve similar results. Having said that, it can be strongly argued that the modern trend is for English law and doctrine to move closer to the civilian approach (so that, for example, apart from recognising a doctrine of common mistake, many would now accept that the doctrine of frustration is imposed for reasons of fairness in a situation where the parties' intentions have run out). However, as regards the duty to perform in good faith it remains clear that this is not yet seen as a free-standing rule in English law: see the commentary on s 15(3)–(4).

---

6   Meaning of words and phrases in this Restatement

(1) Unless the context otherwise requires, in this Restatement the phrase 'intentions of the parties' refers to what a reasonable person would understand those intentions to be (commonly referred to as 'objective intentions').

(2) In this Restatement—

'average consumer' means a consumer who is reasonably well-informed, observant and circumspect;

'consumer' means an individual acting for purposes that are wholly or mainly outside that individual's trade, business, craft or profession;

'consumer contract' means a contract between a consumer and a trader;

'excluding or limiting' in relation to a liability includes excluding or limiting a remedy in respect of that liability;

'exemption clause' means a term of a contract (in whatever form) excluding or limiting a liability for a breach of contract (or other cause of action);

'trader' means a person acting for purposes relating to that person's trade, business, craft or profession.

6(1)

There are references to the intentions of the parties in, for example, ss 10, 13(4), 15(3), and 19(9) of this Restatement. English law adheres to an objective, not a subjective, approach to ascertaining what the parties intended. The classic general authority for this is the judgment of Blackburn J in *Smith v Hughes* (1871) LR 6 QB 597, 607, although there have been many subsequent references to the same general idea: for example, *Ashington Piggeries Ltd v Christopher Hill Ltd* [1972] AC 441, 502, HL; *Paal Wilson & Co A/S v Partenreederei Hannah Blumenthal* [1983] 1 AC 854, 914, 915–16, 924, HL; *RTS Flexible Systems Ltd v Molkerei Alois Müller GmbH & Co KG (UK Production)* [2010] UKSC 14, [2010] 1 WLR 753, at [45] per Lord Clarke; *Spencer v Secretary of State for Defence* [2012] EWHC 120 at [62]–[63] per Vos J (upheld [2012] EWCA Civ 1368); *VTB Capital plc v Nutritek International Corp* [2013] UKSC 5, [2013] 2 AC 337, at [140] per Lord Neuberger.

What is less clear is what precisely the objective approach requires. A distinction is sometimes drawn between 'detached objectivity' (where one takes the stance of the reasonable observer) and 'promisee objectivity' (where one takes the intention of a party as the other party reasonably understood it) and it may be that the approach differs according to what the question relates to (for example, whether it relates to formation or interpretation). See generally Howarth, 'The Meaning of Objectivity in Contract' (1984) 100 LQR 265; Vorster, 'A Comment on the Meaning of Objectivity in Contract' (1987) 103 LQR 274.

The objective principle, with its emphasis on reasonableness, allows English contract law easily to feed into the law pragmatic considerations that are central to the thinking of commercial parties in practice. It is perhaps in this central sense that English contract law is widely regarded, and respected, as being closely allied to the expectations of those in business.

It must also be stressed that to say that there is an objective approach to the intention of the parties leaves open the extent to which the law recognises that the mistake of one or both parties will render a purported contract defective. What is here said, therefore, must be read alongside s 35 on mistake.

6(2)

There are references to 'average consumer', 'consumer', 'consumer contract', or 'trader' in, for example, ss 14(7), 16–17, 19(7), 26(4), and 40 of this Restatement. The meanings of those terms set out here derive from the Consumer Rights Act 2015, ss 2(2), 2(3), 61(3), and 64(5).

There are references to 'excluding or limiting liability' and to an 'exemption clause' in, for example, ss 16–17 of this Restatement. An exemption clause is an umbrella term that includes both an exclusion clause and a limitation clause. That an exemption clause may take various forms is made clear in, for example, the Unfair Contract Terms Act 1977, s 13.

This is the most appropriate place to mention that the term 'legislation' and the adjective 'legislative' have been used in the Restatement to refer to both primary legislation (that is, an Act of Parliament/a statute) and secondary legislation (that is, a statutory instrument). Sometimes in the commentary it has been found convenient to use the adjective 'statutory' somewhat loosely to refer to both primary and secondary legislation.

7 Agreement

(1) In general, the agreement in a contract is made by the acceptance of an offer or by the parties signing an agreement containing the agreed terms.

(2) But there are other ways in which the agreement may be made (as, for example, where participants in a competition or sporting event agree with each other to comply with the organiser's rules).

(3) An offer is an expression, by words or conduct, of a willingness to be bound by specified terms as soon as there is acceptance by the person to whom the offer is made ('the offeree').

(4) An offer is different from an invitation to treat which is an expression, by words or conduct, of a willingness to negotiate.

(5) The following are usually invitations to treat and not offers—
   (a) the display of goods for sale;
   (b) an advertisement of goods for sale;
   (c) an invitation to tender.

(6) An acceptance is the expression, by words or conduct, of assent to the terms offered.

(7) An acceptance must usually be communicated to (that is, received by) the person by whom the offer is made ('the offeror') although the offeror can waive the need for communication.

(8) The general rule in subsection (7) applies to an acceptance by e-mail.

(9) The general rule in subsection (7) is displaced where it would be inappropriate to allocate to the offeree the risk of the acceptance not being received as may be the case, for example, where the offeror has been at fault in not receiving the acceptance.

(10) An exception to the general rule in subsection (7) is that an acceptance by post usually takes effect when the letter is posted (the 'postal rule') although the offeror can displace this by stipulating, in the offer, that an acceptance will not be valid until it is received.

(11) The postal rule is displaced where it would be inappropriate to allocate to the offeror the risk of the letter not being received as may be the case, for example, where the offeree has been at fault in relation to a letter being lost or delayed in the post.

(12) The offeror may prescribe the mode of acceptance but, unless the offeror makes use of that mode of acceptance compulsory, any other mode of acceptance will suffice provided that it is no less advantageous to the offeror.

(13) There can be no acceptance in ignorance of an offer but the acceptance need not have been induced or influenced by the offer.

(14) Where an offeror makes a promise in return for performance by the offeree but the offeree does not promise to perform so that only the offeror is bound under the contract (a 'unilateral contract'), in general there is acceptance by the offeree (so that withdrawal by the offeror would constitute a breach) once the offeree starts to perform even if the offeror is not bound to perform until performance by the offeree is complete.

(15) An offer is terminated, so that it is no longer open for acceptance, by, for example—

    (a) the offeror's revocation;

    (b) the offeree's rejection (which may take the form of a counter-offer);

    (c) lapse of time (which may be either the expiry of the period specified in the offer or, where there is no period specified in the offer, the expiry of a reasonable time).

(16) The revocation of an offer, even one made by post, must generally be communicated to (that is, received by) the offeree; but the revocation may be communicated by a third party rather than by the offeror.

(17) The general rule in subsection (16) is displaced where it would be inappropriate to allocate to the offeror the risk of the revocation not being received as may be the case, for example, where the offeree has been at fault in not receiving the revocation.

7(1)

Offer and acceptance is the conventional legal description of the process by which the agreement in a contract is established. It therefore also (usually) tells us where and when the contract is made.

Although it can be criticised as sometimes being 'forced' to fit the facts (see, for example, Lord Wilberforce in *New Zealand Shipping Co Ltd v AM Satterthwaite & Co Ltd, The Eurymedon* [1975] AC 154, 167) the courts have continued to regard offer and acceptance as usually being the correct method of analysing the making of the agreement (even in respect of the 'battle of the forms': see the commentary to s 7(6)).

However, in many contracts where the parties sign the same document, there can be no dispute that the parties have made an agreement so that the need to use an offer and acceptance analysis does not arise (see, emphasising this point, Cartwright, *Formation and Variation of Contracts* (2014) para 3.47).

7(2)

Exceptions to s 7(1) are where an agreement (that is legally binding) is made but the agreement can neither be helpfully analysed in terms of offer and acceptance nor is there the signing of an agreement containing the agreed terms.

The classic exception in the reported cases is a contract between competitors in a yacht race: see *The Satanita* [1895] P 248, CA (affirmed, without discussing this point in any detail, by the House of Lords *sub nom Clarke v Dunraven* [1897] AC 59). Presumably on the facts the agreement was made at the place where, and at the moment when, the yachts began to sail: see [1895] P 248, 255. Although the competitors made an agreement with each other there was no offer and acceptance as such: see Peel, *Treitel on the Law of Contract* (14th edn, 2015) para 2-076. A similar example may be the contract that governs the legal relations between members of an unincorporated association, such as a social club.

7(3)–(4)

English law draws a distinction between an offer and a prior indication of a willingness to negotiate (an 'invitation to treat'). There is no contract if an invitation to treat is accepted.

Example 1

A e-mails B, 'Will you sell me your car? E-mail me lowest cash price.' B e-mails back, 'Lowest price for my car £900.' A replies by e-mail, 'I agree to buy your car for £900.' There is no contract because B's e-mail was an invitation to treat not an offer. (This example, substituting a car for land and e-mails for telegrams, is based on *Harvey v Facey* [1893] AC 552, PC.)

Example 2

In February, B, a city council, responds by letter to a request by A, a tenant of a council house, to buy that house. B's letter says that B 'may be prepared to sell the house to you at the purchase price of … £2,180 … ' The letter goes on to say, 'If you would like to make formal application to buy your council house please complete the enclosed application form and return it to [B] as soon as possible.' In March, A completes the application form and returns it to B. B then changes its policy and decides not to sell council houses. There is no contract of sale between A and B. B's February letter was an invitation to treat not an offer. (This example is based on *Gibson v Manchester City Council* [1979] 1 WLR 294, HL.)

7(5)

This subsection gives three of the classic illustrations from the case law of common situations where it has been held that there is an invitation to treat not an offer. For s 7(5)(a), see, for example, *Fisher v Bell* [1961] 1 QB 394; *Pharmaceutical Society of Great Britain v Boots Cash Chemist (Southern) Ltd* [1953] 1 QB 401, CA. For s 7(5) (b), see, for example, *Partridge v Crittenden* [1968] 1 WLR 1204 (but for a famous exception, where an advertisement was held to be an offer, see *Carlill v Carbolic Smoke Ball Co* [1893] 1 QB 256, CA). For s 7(5)(c), see, for example, *Spencer v Harding* (1870) LR 5 CP 561 (but for an exception, where the express words used made clear that the invitation to tender was an offer, see *Harvela Investments Ltd v Royal Trust Co of Canada (CI) Ltd* [1986] AC 207, HL).

In working out whether there is a willingness to be bound (an offer) or merely a willingness to negotiate (an invitation to treat), the judges consider what a reasonable person would understand the intentions to be, and this often involves reasoning back from the result of adopting one or other analysis. So, for example, goods on display for sale and adverts of goods for sale are normally invitations to treat because the person selling normally has only a limited stock and would not therefore be willing to be bound under multiple contracts which could not be fulfilled. There may also, for example, be problems about entering into contracts for the sale of certain goods (for example, medicines) without supervision (as in the *PSGB v Boots* case).

As between the buyer and seller of goods at an auction, the holding of the auction is an invitation to treat. The person making the bid is making an offer which may or may not be accepted by the auctioneer by bringing down the hammer. *Barry v Davies* [2000] 1 WLR 1962, CA, makes clear that, as between the buyer and the auctioneer, the holding of an auction sale without reserve is an offer by the auctioneer to sell to the highest bidder.

7(6)

That the acceptance can be by conduct is shown in, for example, *Brogden v Metropolitan Railway Co* (1877) 2 App Cas 666, HL.

The acceptance must match the terms offered (this is sometimes called 'the mirror-image rule').

Example 3

B offers to sell his farm to A for £100,000. A responds by saying that he will give £95,000 for it. This is not an acceptance but rather a counter-offer which B is free to accept or not. (This example is based on *Hyde v Wrench* (1840) 3 Beav 334: see also, on this case, s 7(15)(b).)

Commonly, parties exchange their standard terms and yet those standard terms do not precisely match. In this 'battle of the forms' situation, is there a contract and on whose terms? Although doubts have sometimes been expressed about this (see, for example, the judgment of Lord Denning MR in *Butler Machine Tool Co Ltd v Ex-Cell-O Corporation (England) Ltd* [1979] 1 WLR 401, CA) the answer in English law is that, except where there is a long-term clear course of dealing between the parties on particular terms, the normal rules of offer and acceptance must be applied; and, applying those rules, the standard result will be that the party who sends its terms last (the party who 'fires the last shot') will win because that will be the offer which is regarded as accepted by the other party's conduct. See the judgments of Lawton and Bridge LJJ in the *Butler Machine Tool* case; and, most importantly, *Tekdata Interconnections Ltd v Amphenol Ltd* [2009] EWCA Civ 1209, [2010] 1 Lloyd's Rep 357.

Example 4

A, the buyer of goods, sends a purchase order with its terms to the seller, B, who responds with an acknowledgement containing its standard terms, which include an exemption clause. The goods are sent and accepted by A. A then alleges that the goods are defective and that the exemption clause is not part of the contract. B 'wins' this battle of the forms, and the exemption clause is part of the contract, because B fired the last shot, which was accepted by the conduct of A. (This example is based on *Tekdata Interconnections Ltd v Amphenol Ltd.*)

7(7)

Classic illustrations of the general rule that, putting to one side postal acceptances, an acceptance must be received by the offeror are shown in cases in which the question at issue was the place where the contract was made: see, for example, *Entores Ltd v Miles Far East Corp* [1955] 2 QB 327, CA; *Brinkibon Ltd v Stahag Stahl and Stahlwarenhandelsgesellschaft mbH* [1983] 2 AC 34, HL.

Example 5

A in London makes an offer by fax to B in New York. B sends back from New York an acceptance by fax which is received by A on its fax machine in London. The contract is made in London. (This example, substituting fax for 'telex', is based on *Entores Ltd v Miles Far East Corp.*)

Example 6

A shouts an offer to B across a river. B shouts back her acceptance but A cannot hear it because of aircraft noise. There is no contract. The acceptance has not been received by A. (This was one of the examples given by Denning LJ in *Entores Ltd v Miles Far East Corp.*)

Example 7

A makes an offer to B on the telephone. B accepts the offer but A cannot hear his acceptance because of sudden interference on the telephone line. There is no contract. (This is based on one of the examples given by Denning LJ in *Entores Ltd v Miles Far East Corp.*)

The offeror can waive the need for communication by making clear by words or conduct that he or she need not receive the acceptance. In contrast, the offeror cannot insist, against an unwilling offeree, that silence shall constitute acceptance: *Felthouse v Bindley* (1862) 11 CB (NS) 869.

7(8)

Although there is no direct English authority on this, it is clear that an e-mail acceptance should be treated in the same way as an acceptance by telephone or fax or any other mode of 'instantaneous communication'. This general requirement of communication to (that is, receipt by) the offeror probably means that the acceptance takes place when the e-mail arrives on the offeror's e-mail server (or possibly when it appears in the offeror's inbox) even though it may not be opened and read by the offeror until later. See, generally, Nolan, 'Offer and Acceptance in the Electronic Age', in *Contract Formation and Parties* (eds Burrows and Peel, 2010) 61.

7(9)

An exception to the need for communication is where the reason that the acceptance is not received by the offeror is the offeror's fault or where, otherwise, the risk should lie with the offeror: *Brinkibon Ltd v Stahag Stahl and Stahlwarenhandelsgesellschaft mbH* [1983] 2 AC 34, 42, 50, HL.

Example 8

A makes an offer to B on the telephone. B replies that he will need a short time to think about it and ten minutes later accepts by leaving a message on A's answering machine. A cannot hear the message because her answering machine is not working properly. It would appear that there is a valid contract because it is A's fault that she cannot hear the acceptance.

7(10)

The classic exception to the general rule that acceptance takes effect when received is the 'postal rule' whereby a letter of acceptance usually takes effect when posted rather than when (and if) the letter arrives: see, for example, *Household Fire and Carriage Accident Insurance Co Ltd v Grant* (1879) 4 Ex D 216, CA; *Holwell Securities Ltd v Hughes* [1974] 1 WLR 155, CA. This rests on the policy that, as between the offeror and the offeree, the risk of loss or delay is more appropriately borne by the offeror.

This can be explained as follows. In contrast to 'instantaneous communications', there is an inevitable risk of delay or loss if the post is used; the law therefore has to allocate that risk to the offeror or the offeree; as the offeror has set the process of offer and acceptance going, in a way that makes postal communication acceptable, it is appropriate that that risk should in general be borne by the offeror. It follows from this risk-allocation that, in general, a letter of acceptance takes effect on posting (and, as we shall see, a letter of revocation takes effect when received).

However, as *Holwell Securities Ltd v Hughes* also shows, the postal rule will be displaced by the offeror making clear in the offer that the acceptance must be received (that is, the offeror has then cast the risk of loss or delay onto the offeree).

Example 9

B offers to buy 100 shares from A. A sends a letter of acceptance to B but that letter is lost in the post. There is a contract because the letter of acceptance takes effect when posted. (This example is based on *Household Fire and Carriage Accident Insurance Co Ltd v Grant*.)

Example 10

B offers to buy shares from A and states that any acceptance must be received by her. A sends a letter of acceptance to B but that letter is lost in the post. There is no valid contract because B has displaced the general rule by specifying that an acceptance must be received.

A long-debated question, on which there is no clear authority, is whether an offeree who has posted a letter of acceptance can retract the acceptance by a speedier means of communication. The answer is probably 'yes', applying the reasoning that the risk in relation to the post is on the offeror. As it was put by Hudson, 'Retraction of Letters of Acceptance' (1966) 82 LQR 169, 170: 'If the offeror can be said to take the risks of delay and accidents in the post it would not seem to strain matters to say that he also assumes the risk of a letter being overtaken by a speedier means of communication.'

7(11)

Although there is no clear authority on this, the best view (not least in ensuring consistency with s 7(9)) is that the postal rule will not apply where the reason for the delay or loss of the letter of acceptance is the fault of the offeree or where the risk of that delay or loss should otherwise be borne by the offeree.

Example 11

B offers by letter to sell shares to A. A sends a letter of acceptance to B but that letter is lost in the post. B sells the shares to someone else and informs A.

The reason for the loss of the letter is that the address written by A was illegible. There is no contract between A and B because the fault of A means that the risk of the loss should be borne by A.

7(12)

This rule was laid down in *Manchester Diocesan Council for Education v Commercial and General Investments Ltd* [1970] 1 WLR 241.

Example 12

B offers to buy land from A stating that A's acceptance should be sent to B's address. A sends an acceptance to B's surveyor. Even though that acceptance has not been sent to the address specified, it will suffice if receipt by B's surveyor is no less advantageous to B. (This example is based on *Manchester Diocesan Council for Education v Commercial and General Investments Ltd.*)

7(13)

Although there is no clear authority in English law, a rule that one cannot accept in ignorance of an offer is a good explanation of why identical cross-offers do not constitute a binding contract: *Tinn v Hoffman & Co* (1873) 29 LT 271, 279. It also follows from the root idea of a contract being a legally binding *agreement* (see s 2 above) that one cannot accept in ignorance of an offer.

Example 13

B offers £100 to any person who swims across the Mersey on New Year's Day. A, knowing nothing of the offer, fulfils that condition. A is then told of the offer and claims the £100. B is not contractually bound to pay A the £100.

In contrast, provided one knows of the offer, it would seem unnecessary for the acceptance to be in reliance on the offer (that is, it need not have been induced or influenced by the offer). That is the best interpretation of *Williams v Carwardine* (1833) 4 B & Ad 621, which stressed that the offeree's motive in accepting is irrelevant. It did not matter that the offeree gave the information, thereby accepting the offer of a reward, not in order to claim the reward but to ease her conscience. This is the approach put forward by Mitchell and Phillips, 'The Contractual Nexus: Is Reliance Essential?' (2002) 22 OJLS 115 (the authors argue that the contrary obiter dicta in *Lark v Outhwaite* [1991] 2 Lloyd's Rep 132, 140 is incorrect).

7(14)

A unilateral contract is an agreement binding one party only. So if A offers a reward of £500 for the finding of her lost laptop, and B accepts that offer, only A is bound because only A makes a promise. B is not promising to do anything. Similarly in the classic examples mentioned in the commentary under s 4 above, the offeree (or offerees) is (are) not bound to walk to York or to use the smoke-ball and cannot therefore be sued for breach of contract for failure to do so.

Although there has been some doubt about this, one principled interpretation of recent cases (and that adopted in s 7(14)) is that there is an acceptance of the offer of a unilateral contract, so that the offer cannot be revoked, once the offeree *starts* to perform the requested act: see *Errington v Errington* [1952] 1 KB 290, CA; *Daulia Ltd v Four Mill Bank Nominees Ltd* [1978] Ch 231, 239; *Soulsbury v Soulsbury* [2007] EWCA Civ 969, [2008] Fam 1, CA. Some may argue that that straightforward analysis strains the concept of consideration (see s 8) because it involves saying that the consideration for the promise is starting, rather than completing, performance. If one is troubled by that (but one can surely say that the offeror starts to be benefited when performance starts) there is an alternative more complicated two–contract analysis, which in practice leads to the same result. According to this alternative, there is a subsidiary unilateral contract whereby the offeror promises not to revoke the offer of the main unilateral contract once the offeree has started to perform.

It cannot be overstated that it is a distinct question, which turns on the terms of the unilateral contract, when it is that the offeror is bound to perform (for example, the offeror will often not be bound to pay until the requested act has been completed). Of course, as this is a unilateral contract, the offeree has made no promise and is never bound to perform.

Example 14

B, A's former husband, promises A £100,000 on his death if she does not seek any ancillary relief from him. A refrains from claiming any ancillary relief. B fails to give her the promised £100,000 in his will. There is a binding contract as soon as A refrains from seeking the ancillary relief albeit that, by the terms of B's promise, B—and hence his estate—is only bound to pay A on B's death. (This example is based on *Soulsbury v Soulsbury*.)

The rule as to when a unilateral contract is accepted can only be stated as a general rule because the offer may make clear that the offeror is free to revoke the offer at any time (that is, that there can be no acceptance) until the performance has been completed.

7(15)

As regards revocation, see s 7(16). Note that in English law even a 'firm offer' (that is, one which specifies that it will be held open until a particular date) can be revoked prior to acceptance. This is because the promise to hold open is not itself binding unless there is consideration for it (in which case it is described as an option contract).

One of the commonest forms of rejection (s 7(15)(b)) is a counter-offer. Subject conceivably to the counter-offeror making it clear that the counter-offer is not a rejection, a counter-offer 'kills' (that terminology was used in *Butler Machine Tool Co Ltd v Ex-Cell-O Corp England) Ltd* [1979] 1 WLR 401, CA) the original offer: see *Hyde v Wrench* (1840) 3 Beav 334.

Example 15

B offers to sell his farm to A for £100,000. A responds by offering £95,000. B refuses that counter-offer. A then writes to B to say that he accepts the original offer to sell at £100,000. There is no contract. The original offer was terminated by the counter-offer and was therefore no longer open to be accepted. (This example is based on *Hyde v Wrench*.)

However, one must be careful to distinguish between a counter-offer and a mere enquiry (that is, a request for further information). The latter does not terminate the original offer: *Stevenson, Jacques & Co v McLean* (1880) 5 QBD 346.

Example 16

B offers to sell a quantity of iron to A for £400 per tonne cash on delivery. A e-mails back asking if B would allow two months for payment. B sells the iron to a third party. A, not knowing of this, e-mails B accepting the original offer. There is a valid contract. A's first e-mail was not a counter-offer but a mere enquiry so that the original offer remained open. (This example is based on *Stevenson, Jacques & Co v McLean* with e-mails substituted for telegrams.)

Two other ways, not expressly mentioned in s 7(15), by which an offer is terminated are: first, the occurrence of an event which, as the offer expressly or impliedly provides, terminates the offer; or secondly, in some circumstances the death or supervening incapacity of the offeror or the offeree. On these, see *Chitty on Contracts* (32nd edn, 2015) paras 2-105–2-116 and Peel, *Treitel on the Law of Contract* (14th edn, 2015) 2-66–2-74.

7(16)

Consistently with the risk of loss or delay in the post generally being placed on the offeror (see the commentary to s 7(10)), the general rule for a revocation even by post is that the revocation must be received by the offeree: *Byrne & Co v Van Tienhoven & Co* (1880) 5 CPD 344.

Example 17

On 1 October, B, in Cardiff, posts a letter to A, in New York, offering to sell A 1,000 boxes of tinplate at a certain price. A receives this letter on 11 October and immediately e-mails its acceptance. The price of tinplate goes up during the first week of October. On 8 October, B therefore posts a letter to A withdrawing its offer. That letter is not received by A until 20 October. There is a valid contract. A validly accepted on 11 October and that was before B's revocation was received. (This example is based on *Byrne & Co v Van Tienhoven & Co* with e-mails substituted for telegrams.)

Although not free from controversy, it would appear that the revocation can be communicated by a third party rather than the offeror: *Dickinson v Dodds* (1876) 2 Ch D 463, CA.

Example 18

B makes a written offer to A to sell A a horse for £80,000. The next day A hears from a third party that B has sold the horse to X. Nevertheless, later that day, A hands a letter of acceptance to B. There is no valid contract. B's offer has been revoked by the third party's communication to A.

7(17)

As with the rules on acceptance, the rule in 17(16) is only a general rule. It would appear that that rule does not apply, for example, where the offeree's answering machine is not working properly (as the offeree should have known) so that the revocation is not received. Another different type of exception is that an offer made to the public at large (for example, the offer of a reward) can be revoked by the same means as were used to make the offer.

8   Consideration
(1) To be legally binding, an agreement, unless made by deed, must be supported by consideration.
(2) 'Consideration' means that, in exchange for a promise by one party, a counter-promise or performance is given by the other party.
(3) The consideration need not be adequate and may be merely nominal.
(4) Past consideration (where A makes a promise to B in return for what B has already done) is not good consideration.
(5) If —
    (a) B owes a pre-existing duty to A under the general law or under a contract with C or under a contract with A, and
    (b) A makes a promise to B in exchange for B's promise to perform, or performance of, that pre-existing duty,
B's promise to perform, or performance of, that pre-existing duty is good consideration for A's promise although the contract may in certain circumstances be voidable for duress (see section 37) or unenforceable as being contrary to public policy (see section 44).

(6) B's promise to perform a part, or part performance, of a pre-existing duty (for example, part payment of a pre-existing debt) owed by B to A is not good consideration for A's promise to forgo the remaining part of the performance owing (for example, to forgo the balance of the pre-existing debt owed) although the law on promissory estoppel (see section 12) may operate to protect B.

8(1)

Although sometimes criticised (see, for example, Atiyah, *Consideration in Contracts: A Fundamental Restatement* (1971)), the need for consideration, as defined in s 8(2), is a major distinguishing feature of English law in contrast to civil law systems.

An exception to the need for consideration is where the contract is made by deed. So what is a contract made by deed?

An agreement made by deed must satisfy the two requirements for a deed to be valid as set out in section 1 of the Law of Property (Miscellaneous Provisions) Act 1989. These are as follows. First, it must be made clear on the face of the instrument that the person or parties making it intend(s) it to be a deed (s 1(2)(a) of the 1989 Act). Secondly, the deed must be validly executed, which, in the case of a deed made by an individual, requires that: (i) signature and attestation requirements are satisfied (ss 1(2)(b) and 1(3)(a) of the 1989 Act); and (ii) the instrument is 'delivered as a deed' (s 1(3)(b) of the 1989 Act), which has the particular meaning, as established by the case law (see, for example, *Vincent v Premo Enterprises Ltd* [1969] 2 QB 609, 619; *Bibby Financial Services Ltd v Magson* [2011] EWHC 2495 (QB) at [335]), that the individual making the deed must make clear by word or act that the deed is regarded as binding. In the case of a company, the requirements for the valid execution of a deed are in the Companies Act 2006, s 44 (see *Chitty on Contracts* (32nd edn, 2015) para 1-128).

Those requirements encompass the need for there to be an intention to create legal relations (and any formal requirement) so that provided the agreement in the deed is complete and certain, it will be a contract.

In order to understand fully what is meant by a contract made by deed (and, in particular, to explain why deed polls are not normally treated as contracts: see also commentary to s 2 above) three examples may be helpfully distinguished.

Example 1

A agrees to purchase land from B for £100,000. Their agreement, supported by consideration, is made in the form of a deed. This is indisputably a contract, albeit made by deed.

Example 2

A agrees to pay £10,000 to B in a deed signed by both A and B, that is, it is a deed inter partes. Although this is a gratuitous agreement or promise (there being no consideration for A's promise) this is also regarded as a contract made by deed.

Example 3

A agrees to pay £1,000 to each of those in a class of which B is a member (for example, future adult children of A) made by deed poll (that is, it is not a deed inter partes). It is signed only by A; and B may know nothing of it. It appears that this is not regarded as a contract. This is because, although one might say that there is a legally binding promise, one cannot say that there is an agreement, even in a wide sense, because the deed is binding even though the promisee knows nothing about it. (For a rare judicial examination of a deed poll, see *Moody v Condor Insurance Ltd* [2006] EWHC 100 (Ch), [2006] 1 WLR 1847.)

Examples 1 and 2 (but not 3) are contracts and fall within this Restatement.

Apart from contracts made by deed—and although falling outside the general law of contract (and hence outside this Restatement) because they concern specific types of contract—two other apparent exceptions to the need for consideration are worth noting. First, by reason of the Consumer Rights Act 2015, s 30, a guarantee in relation to goods supplied to a consumer takes effect 'as a contractual obligation owed by the guarantor'. This means that it is unnecessary for the consumer to prove the normal requirements for a contract (such as consideration). Secondly, in so far as a banker's irrevocable letter of credit is treated as a contract (rather than as a *sui generis* payment obligation) it appears to be an exception to the need for consideration in the sense that the bank appears to be bound as soon as it notifies the beneficiary (for example, the seller of goods) that it has opened the letter of credit (that is, prior to the provision of any consideration by the beneficiary).

8(2)

Consideration is the legal description of the necessary element of exchange. Its practical effect is to ensure that gratuitous promises (unless made by deed) are not binding whereas bargains are.

Example 4

A promises B £1,000. B cannot enforce that promise because B has provided no consideration (nothing in exchange) for it.

Example 5

A promises B £10,000. B relies on that promise to buy a car. B cannot enforce that promise because B has provided no consideration (nothing in exchange) for it.

Example 6

A promises B £20,000 in return for B's promise to transfer his car to A. B makes that promise. B's promise is consideration for A's promise and B can therefore enforce A's promise.

8(3)

A contract is not invalid merely because there is a gross disparity of value between what each party is doing or promising to do for the other. Leading cases include *Thomas v Thomas* (1842) 2 QB 851 (a widow's promise to pay £1 a year and to keep a cottage in good repair was good consideration for the promise to allow her to live there for the rest of her life); and *Chappell & Co Ltd v Nestle Co Ltd* [1960] AC 87, HL (chocolate bar wrappers, although of trivial or no value, were held to be part of the consideration for the purchase of a record). The latter case also indicates that a counter-promise or counter-performance of no clear economic value counts: see also, for example, *Ward v Byham* [1956] 1 WLR 496, CA, where Morris LJ regarded the wife's promise, that the child would be well looked after and happy, as consideration for the husband's promise to pay her £1 a week. (Cf *White v Bluett* (1853) 23 LJ Ex 36, where a father's promise of money, in exchange for his son's ceasing to complain about his unequal treatment, was held not to be supported by valid consideration: but that is probably better explained on the ground that there was no intention to create legal relations (see s 10).)

Example 7

A promises B (his nephew) £5,000 to give up smoking and drinking alcohol for a year. B does so. A is contractually bound to pay the £5,000 assuming that there is the necessary intention to create legal relations. (This example is based on the famous US case of *Hamer v Sidway* 124 NY 538 (1891).)

8(4)

A promise to pay for what the promisee has already done is a gratuitous promise. The denial that past consideration is good consideration is therefore consistent with consideration marking the divide between enforceable bargains and unenforceable gratuitous promises. Although sometimes criticised (see, for example, Law Revision Committee, *Sixth Interim Report (Statute of Frauds and the Doctrine of Consideration)* (1937, Cmd 5449)), leading cases showing that past consideration is not good consideration include *Eastwood v Kenyon* (1840) 11 Ad & E 438, *Roscorla v Thomas* (1842) 3 QB 234, and *Re McArdle* [1951] Ch 669.

Example 8

A promises B £5,000 for work that B has already done to A's house. B cannot enforce that promise because the consideration for it is past. (This example is based on *Re McArdle*.)

However, one needs to be careful: what might at first sight look like past consideration may, on closer examination, turn out not to be. This will be so where, although the promise of payment is subsequent to an act, the promisor requested that act and there was an understanding throughout that the requested act was to be remunerated: *Lampleigh v Brathwait* (1615) Hob 105; *Pao On v Lau Yiu Long* [1980] AC 614, PC.

8(5)

The law on consideration and pre-existing duty has been much discussed especially in the light of the leading modern case of *Williams v Roffey Bros & Nicholls* [1991] 1 QB 1, CA. The trend appears to be towards finding consideration in these situations; and, while some may dispute how far one can generalise from what was said in *Williams v Roffey* (and might regard the Restatement as here departing from precedent) it is submitted that, applying a principled understanding of *Williams v Roffey* and other decisions, the best interpretation is that, whatever the source of the pre-existing duty, B's promise or performance of a pre-existing duty does give A 'a practical benefit' (to use the language of Glidewell LJ in that case). That benefit comprises either a direct right against B that A did not otherwise have or simply the increased likelihood of performance by B. There therefore appears to be no need to find that B is doing something more than required by its pre-existing duty; and cases apparently denying this are best interpreted as treating the contract as invalid for reasons other than there being no consideration (for example, duress or public policy).

Examples of support for the principle in s 8(5), where the source of the pre-existing duty is *the general law* (for example, legislation), include Denning LJ's judgments in *Ward v Byham* [1956] 1 WLR 496, CA, and *Williams v Williams* [1957] 1 WLR 148, CA. But sometimes there will be a public policy objection to upholding a contract where one party is being paid to do what it is bound to do by the general law (as in, for example, *Collins v Godefroy* (1831) 1 B & Ad 950, KB; and *Glasbrook Brothers Ltd v Glamorgan County Council* [1925] AC 270, HL).

Example 9

A, a football club, agrees to pay the local police force, led by B, to maintain law and order on public land (away from the football club's stadium) at a home match. B does so but A then refuses to pay. A is not contractually bound to pay. This is best explained, not by saying that there was no consideration for A's promise, but rather that there is a public policy objection to upholding a contract under which the police are paid to do what they are already under a public duty to do. The position would be different, and there would be no public policy objection, if the police were going beyond their public duty and providing special police services. (This fact-situation is exemplified by *Leeds United FC Ltd v Chief Constable of West Yorkshire Police* [2013] EWCA Civ 115, [2014] QB 168; and see also the Police Act 1996, s 25(1).)

Example 10

B is about to carry out major work to the foundations of her terraced house. A, her neighbour, is concerned about the impact on his house and agrees to pay B £5,000 to shore up A's house while the work is going on. Under the general law of support, B is required to shore up A's house for free. There is consideration for A's promise so that, prima facie, A would have a contractual entitlement to damages if B did not shore up the house and B could sue for the £5,000 if the shoring up work was done. Any objections to upholding the contract should turn not on the doctrine of consideration but on whether enforcement (for example, by B) is contrary to public policy.

The application of s 8(5), where the pre-existing duty is under *a contract between B and a third party C*, is illustrated by, for example: *Shadwell v Shadwell* (1860) 9 CB (NS) 159, Common Bench; *Scotson v Pegg* (1861) 6 H & N 295, Court of Exchequer; *New Zealand Shipping v Satterthwaite, The Eurymedon* [1975] AC 154, 168, PC; *Pao On v Lau Yiu Long* [1980] AC 614, PC.

Example 11

B is bound by a contract with C to deliver a cargo of coal to A. A promises to unload the coal at a stated rate in return for B delivering the coal to A. A fails to unload the coal at the stated rate. A is in breach of contract. A's promise was contractually binding even though the consideration for it was the delivery of coal that B was already under a duty to deliver to A under its contract with C. (This example is based on *Scotson v Pegg*.)

Williams v Roffey Bros & Nicholls was dealing with where A is promising B more for what B is already bound to do *under a contract with A*. The Court of Appeal held that B was giving good consideration by promising to do what it was already bound to do provided A obtained 'a practical benefit'. But it would seem that A would always obtain such a practical benefit because, in return for the promise to pay or payment of extra money, A has the increased likelihood that B will fully perform.

Assuming no duress, why else would A promise to pay the extra? (For a carefully reasoned and slightly different view—that the consideration is the completion of performance by B under a separate unilateral contract—see Chen-Wishart, 'A Bird in the Hand: Consideration and Contract Modifications' in *Contract Formation and Parties* (Burrows and Peel, 2010) 89–113.) The old case of *Stilk v Myrick* (1809) 2 Camp 317, where, following two desertions, the rest of the crew was promised extra wages to get the ship home to England, is probably better explained as being based on the fear of permitting duress by a ship's crew rather than lack of consideration.

Example 12

B is under a contractual duty to A to provide the carpentry work on a block of flats. After the work has been partly completed, B runs into financial difficulties. A promises to pay B more for the job to be completed on time. B completes the job on time but then A refuses to pay the extra money. Assuming no duress, A is contractually bound to pay the extra money promised (that is, B is providing valid consideration for A's promise to pay the extra) even though B was initially contractually bound to complete the work at the original price. (This example is based on *Williams v Roffey Bros & Nicholls*.)

8(6)

One can powerfully argue that, in principle, the same reasoning that has been applied in relation to s 8(5) should be applied to the part performance of a pre-existing duty, most obviously, part payment of a debt: that is, that B's part payment of a pre-existing debt owed to A can be good consideration for A's promise to forgo the balance of the debt. A obtains a practical benefit in return for its promise because of the increased likelihood that B will pay off some part of the debt. However, it would appear that one can only accept that reasoning if one departs from the House of Lords' decision in *Foakes v Beer* (1884) 9 App Cas 605. Certainly in *Re Selectmove Ltd* [1995] 1 WLR 474, CA, the Court of Appeal was of the view that such a move could only be made judicially by the House of Lords (now the Supreme Court) or, perhaps even more appropriately, by the Legislature. The view taken here is that the law in *Foakes v Beer* is so well entrenched that it would require a very bold Supreme Court to use the 1966 Practice Statement to depart from that previous decision in order to assimilate promises to pay more with promises to accept less (and note that in any event, it can be strongly argued that promissory estoppel provides a better route round *Foakes v Beer* than the doctrine of consideration: see *Collier v P & MJ Wright (Holdings) Ltd* [2007] EWCA Civ 1329, [2008] 1 WLR 643). For these reasons, the Restatement adheres to the traditional rule in *Foakes v Beer*.

9   Certainty and completeness

(1) For an agreement to be legally binding, it must be certain and complete.

(2) A conditional contract is legally binding, so that neither party can withdraw, even though neither party is bound to perform the principal obligations under the contract unless and until an agreed condition has been satisfied; but a party may be bound to perform, or abide by, subsidiary obligations that relate to the condition (for example, to use reasonable efforts to ensure that the condition is satisfied or not deliberately to prevent the condition being satisfied).

9(1)

Although absolute certainty and total completeness are not required, an agreement that is too vague or too incomplete is not binding. Normally the courts will strive to cure vagueness: see, for example, *Hillas & Co Ltd v Arcos Ltd* (1932) 147 LT 503, HL (cf *Scammell and Nephew Ltd v Ouston* [1941] 1 AC 251, HL). And, if no price has been fixed, a reasonable price will normally be payable: *Foley v Classique Coaches* [1934] 2 KB 1, CA, *Sudbrook Trading Estate Ltd v Eggleton* [1983] 1 AC 444, CA, s 8 Sale of Goods Act 1979 (cf *May and Butcher Ltd v R* [1934] 2 KB 17n, HL). See also *Pagnan SpA v Feed Products Ltd* [1987] 2 Lloyd's Rep 601, CA (contract held to be complete with subsidiary and legally inessential terms to be settled later). It may therefore be said that a degree of uncertainty or incompleteness is tolerated provided it is either insignificant or can be resolved by the courts.

In *Scammell v Dicker* [2005] EWCA Civ 405, [2006] 1 P & CR 4, at [30], Rix LJ helpfully stressed that a contract will rarely fail for uncertainty:

'[I]t is simply a non sequitur to argue from a disagreement about the meaning and effect of a contract to its legal uncertainty. Parties are always disagreeing about the contracts which they make. They take those arguments, if necessary, to the courts, or to arbitration, for their resolution: and sometimes the resolution is very difficult indeed to arrive at. That is equally true of disputes as to the meaning of contracts and of disputes as to the application of contracts to the facts and of disputes as to the proper understanding of the facts. None of that makes a contract uncertain. For that to occur—and it very rarely occurs—it has to be legally or practically impossible to give to the parties' agreement any sensible content.'

See similarly *Durham Tees Valley Airport Ltd v Bmibaby Ltd* [2010] EWCA Civ 485, [2011] 1 Lloyd's Rep 68, at [54]–[55] and [88]–[92].

However, a primary reason given for why agreements to negotiate in good faith (or agreements to agree, or agreements to use reasonable endeavours to agree) are not binding in English law is that they are too uncertain: *Walford v Miles* [1992] 2 AC 128, HL (dealing with a 'lock-in agreement' albeit accepting that a 'lock-out agreement' of fixed duration is sufficiently certain). This does not seem convincing and commentators have criticised the reasoning in *Walford v Miles*: for example Berg, 'Promises to Negotiate in Good Faith' (2003) 119 LQR 357. Moreover, *Walford v Miles* has been distinguished in some subsequent cases. For example, in *Emirates Trading Agency LLC v Prime Mineral Exports Pte Ltd* [2014] EWHC 2104 (Comm), [2015] 1 WLR 1145, it was held that an express dispute resolution clause in an otherwise binding contract, requiring the parties to seek to resolve a dispute in good faith and within a limited period of time prior to arbitration, was enforceable.

It should be noted that there is a very close link between the requirement of completeness (or finality) and the requirement of an intention to create legal relations. This explains why some of the material (for example, on an agreement 'subject to contract') considered under s 10 of this Restatement is sometimes examined in the books as an aspect of completeness.

9(2)

It is helpful at this point to distinguish a conditional contract from a contract that is invalid because it is uncertain or incomplete. An agreement may be contractually binding—so that the parties cannot withdraw—even though the parties' main obligations to perform are dependent on a condition being satisfied: see, for example, *Smith v Butler* [1900] 1 QB 694, CA; *Wishart v National Association of Citizens Advice Bureaux* [1990] ICR 794, CA (employment offered subject to satisfactory references). This is what is meant by a conditional contract. For a helpful discussion of conditional contracts, see *Chitty on Contracts* (32nd edn, 2015) paras 2-161–2-165.

Example 1

A contracts to take a lease of a pub from B on condition that a loan to B, secured by a mortgage in respect of the pub, is transferred to A. A is in breach of contract by seeking to withdraw before B can arrange the transfer. (This example is based on *Smith v Butler*.)

Sometimes in conditional contracts there are subsidiary obligations (usually implied rather than express: for implied terms, see s 15) relating to the condition. For example, a term may be implied that neither party will, without justification, deliberately prevent the fulfilment of the condition: and non-compliance with that obligation will constitute a breach of contract. There was an excellent judicial discussion of this by Scott J in *Thompson v ASDA-MFI Group plc* [1988] Ch 241 (rejecting as Scottish law, and not English law, that part of the reasoning in *Mackay v Dick* (1881) 6 App Cas 251, HL (SC), supporting the idea that a condition may be treated as fictionally fulfilled).

Example 2

A contracts with B to buy an excavating machine from B on condition that it can excavate at a specific rate on A's property. A refuses to provide facilities for a proper trial of the excavator and then seeks to withdraw from the contract. It is likely that there would be held to be an implied term that neither party deliberately prevents the fulfilment of the condition so that A would be in breach of contract. (This fact-situation is exemplified by *Mackay v Dick*.)

In other situations, there may be an obligation to make reasonable efforts to ensure that the condition is fulfilled.

Example 3

A contracts with B (a foreign buyer) to sell goods to B on condition that A obtains a licence necessary to export the goods. A seeks to withdraw from the contract before obtaining the licence. It is likely that there would be held to be an implied term that A should use reasonable effects to obtain the licence. If so, A would be in breach of contract if she did not use such efforts.

A conditional contract is to be distinguished from the agreements referred to in ss 10(4) and (5) where the parties are free to withdraw.

10   Intention to create legal relations
  (1) For an agreement to be legally binding, the parties must have an intention to create legal relations.
  (2) Unless the agreement is made by deed, there is a rebuttable presumption that there is no intention to create legal relations where the agreement is made in a social or domestic context.
  (3) There is a rebuttable presumption of an intention to create legal relations where an express agreement, that is certain and complete, is made in a commercial context.
  (4) An agreement expressed to be 'subject to contract' is not legally binding because, by using those words, the parties have made clear that they do not intend to create legal relations until a formal document has been drawn up.
  (5) It is commonplace in a written contract for there to be no intention to create legal relations until all the parties have signed the document.

10(1)

As has been made clear in s 6(1), the intentions of the parties refer to what a reasonable person would understand those intentions to be.

10(2)

Social and domestic agreements are not binding unless the claimant can prove that there was an intention to create legal relations. Agreements were held not to be binding, because of the lack of intention to create legal relations, in, for example, *Balfour v Balfour* [1919] 2 KB 571, CA, and *Jones v Padavatton* [1969] 1 WLR 328, CA. Cf *Radmacher v Granatino* [2010] UKSC 42, [2011] 1 AC 534 (pre-nuptial agreements).

As regards contracts made by deed, the requirements for the deed to be valid (see commentary to s 8(1)) inevitably mean that there is an intention to create legal relations; and even in respect of social and domestic agreements made by deed, there is certainly, therefore, no presumption against there being such an intention.

10(3)

Turning to commercial contracts, it has sometimes been indicated that there is a presumption of an intention to create legal relations in all commercial agreements, provided certain and complete, and that there is a heavy onus on the party seeking to rebut that presumption: see, for example, *Esso Petroleum Co Ltd v Commissioners of Customs and Excise* [1976] 1 WLR 1, HL. However, the better view is that that presumption applies only to *express* commercial agreements that are certain and complete (which also explains why the requirement of an intention to create legal relations is rarely raised in respect of such agreements); and that in respect of contracts that are wholly or partly implied from conduct, there is no such presumption, so that it is for the party alleging that there is a contract to prove that intention, without the benefit of any presumption: see, for example, *Blackpool and Fylde Aero Club v Blackpool BC* [1990] 1 WLR 1195, 1202; *Baird Textile Holdings Ltd v Marks & Spencer plc* [2001] EWCA Civ 274, [2002] 1 All ER (Comm) 737 at [62]; *Assuranceforeningen Gard Gjensidig v The International Oil Pollution Compensation Fund* [2014] EWHC 3369 (Comm) [89]–[103].

It should be noted that, provided sufficiently complete and certain, a 'letter of intent' or 'letter of comfort' or 'memorandum of understanding' or 'heads of agreement' (which are all terms to describe preliminary agreements between negotiating parties) are commonly held to be contracts unless there are words negating contractual intent: see, for example, *RTS Flexible Systems Ltd v Molkerei Alois Müller GMBH & Co KG (UK Production)* [2010] UKSC 14, [2010] 1 WLR 753 (cf *British Steel Corp v Cleveland Bridge and Engineering Co Ltd* [1984] 1 All ER 504 where Robert Goff J preferred a solution within the law of unjust enrichment rather than the law of contract).

10(4)

An agreement that is 'subject to contract' is not a contract because, by the use of that phrase, the parties have made clear that their agreement is not final. There is no intention to create legal relations until a formal contract is drawn up (that is, their agreement is subject to a condition that a formal contract is drawn up). The initial agreement for the sale or lease of land is almost invariably made 'subject to contract' so that, even though made in writing, it is not binding and either party can withdraw: see, for example, *Winn v Bull* (1877) 7 Ch D 29.

10(5)

This subsection has been inserted because it is often not appreciated that many commercial agreements are not binding unless and until there has been signature by all the parties. Although agreement has been reached, the best analysis of why the agreement is not binding is that the parties do not intend to create legal relations until there has been signature (that is, their agreement is subject to a condition, sometimes expressed but commonly implied, that all parties must sign). See generally *Von Hatzfeldt-Wildenburg v Alexander* [1912] 1 Ch 284; *Okura & Co Ltd v Navara Shipping Corp SA* [1982] 2 Lloyd's Rep 537, CA; cf *Ateni Maritime Corp v Great Marine Ltd, The Great Marine (No 2)* [1990] 2 Lloyd's Rep 250 (where it was held that the contract had already been concluded prior to signature of a memorandum of agreement).

11 Formal requirements
(1) For most contracts there is no requirement as to form so that a contract may be made in writing, orally or by conduct (or by any combination of those methods).
(2) There are legislative exceptions to the rule that there is no requirement as to form which include the following—
  (a) the rule that, subject to exceptions, a contract for the sale or other disposition of an interest in land is void unless it is made in writing and signed (see section 2 of the Law of Property (Miscellaneous Provisions) Act 1989);
  (b) the rule that a contract of guarantee is unenforceable unless it is evidenced in writing and signed (see section 4 of the Statute of Frauds 1677).

11(1)–(2)

Most contracts do not require any particular form. They are valid whether made orally or in writing or by conduct. Subsection (2) sets out the main general exceptions to that. The justification for these exceptions presumably rests on these being contracts in which one or more of the parties need an added degree of protection lest they commit themselves too easily.

11(2)(a)

Section 2(1) of the Law of Property (Miscellaneous Provisions) Act 1989 reads as follows: 'A contract for the sale or other disposition of an interest in land can only be made in writing and only by incorporating all the terms which the parties have expressly agreed in one document or, where contracts are exchanged, in each.' By s 2(3) there must be signature by or on behalf of each party.

Exceptions to the need for writing for a disposition of an interest of land are set out in s 2(5) of the 1989 Act and include a contract to grant a short lease and a contract made in the course of a public auction.

The precise effect on the contract of a failure to comply with the formality depends on the statute in question. It used to be the case that a failure to comply with the writing requirement for contracts for the sale of land merely made the contract unenforceable rather than void. However, under the 1989 Act it is clear that an oral contract for the sale of land is now void.

11(2)(b)

The Statute of Frauds 1677, s 4, reads:

'No action shall be brought ... whereby to charge the defendant upon any special promise to answer for the debt default or miscarriages of another person ... unless the agreement upon which such action shall be brought or some memorandum or note thereof shall be in writing and signed by the party to be charged therewith or some other person thereunto by him lawfully authorized.'

Here the words of the statute make clear that the contract is unenforceable ('no action shall be brought') rather than void.

It was established that e-mails may satisfy the requirements of writing and signature under the 1677 Act in *Golden Ocean Group Ltd v Salgaocar Mining Industries* [2012] EWCA Civ 265, [2012] 1 WLR 3674.

12 Consensual variation or rescission and promissory estoppel
(1) A contract may be varied or rescinded by an agreement between the parties that is legally binding as satisfying the requirements in sections 8 to 11.
(2) A promise to forgo one's rights may to some extent be legally binding, even though it is not a contract or a term of a contract, under the doctrine of promissory estoppel.
(3) The doctrine of promissory estoppel applies where—
    (a) a clear and unequivocal promise is made by A to B to forgo A's existing rights against B;
    (b) that promise is relied on by B; and
    (c) that promise has not been induced by B's duress or other unfair conduct.
(4) Sometimes the reliance on the promise by B is required to be to B's detriment.
(5) Promissory estoppel may operate to extinguish, rather than just to suspend, A's existing rights against B.
(6) The remedies available for promissory estoppel may aim to put B into as good a position as if the promise had been kept and need not be limited to protecting B against loss incurred in reliance on the promise.

12(1)

The parties may amend or rescind the contract but to do so their agreement must comply with the normal requirements for a valid contract. Very importantly, unless made by deed, the agreement to vary or rescind must be supported by consideration. In the old language, there must be both accord and satisfaction. Where neither party has performed (that is, the original contract is executory) this presents no difficulty, because each party is promising not to enforce the other's original promise and those mutual promises are consideration for each other. However, where one party has already performed (that is, the contract is executed), that party's promise not to enforce the other's original promise needs fresh consideration if it is to be binding.

Example 1

A and B enter into a contract for the sale of goods. It has been performed by neither party (that is, it is an executory contract). A and B make an agreement rescinding the contract. That rescission by agreement is a valid contract because each party is promising to release the other from its obligations under the original contract in return for its own release. That is, there is consideration for each party's promise.

Example 2

A and B enter into a contract for the sale of goods. A performs by delivering conforming goods to B. B has not yet paid for the goods but title has passed to B. A and B make an agreement 'rescinding' the contract. If by this B agrees to revest title to the goods in return for A's release of B, there is consideration and the rescission by agreement is a valid contract. But if only outstanding obligations are discharged, so that B is no longer obliged to pay but will retain the title to the goods although A has already fully performed, that rescission by agreement is not a valid contract because there is no consideration for A's promise to release B.

There is no requirement that a contract made by deed has to be rescinded or varied by a contract made by deed: *Berry v Berry* [1929] 2 KB 316. Moreover, the fact that formal requirements applied to the original contract does not mean that those requirements are also needed to rescind, rather than to vary, the contract: *Morris v Baron & Co* [1918] AC 1, HL (contract for the sale of goods that, at the time, was unenforceable unless evidenced in writing was rescinded orally albeit that the new oral replacement contract was itself unenforceable).

12(2)–(6)

Even though not supported by consideration, a promise to forgo one's existing rights (for example, under the original contract) may be legally binding, at least to some extent, under the doctrine of promissory estoppel.

Promissory estoppel (sometimes referred to as 'equitable estoppel') has been one of the most discussed doctrines in English law since it was relied on by Denning J in *Central London Property Trust Ltd v High Trees House Ltd* [1947] 1 KB 130. Promissory estoppel does not create a cause of action (*Combe v Combe* [1951] 2 KB 215, CA; *Baird Textiles Holdings Ltd v Marks and Spencer plc* [2001] EWCA Civ 274, [2002] 1 All ER (Comm) 737) but operates as a defence which means, in practice, that it applies to a promise to give up an existing right but not to a promise to confer a new right.

The promise must be clear and unequivocal (*Woodhouse AC Israel Cocoa SA v Nigerian Produce Marketing Co Ltd* [1972] AC 941, HL); and the promise must not have been induced by the promisee's inequitable conduct (*D & C Builders v Rees* [1966] 2 QB 617, CA, where the promisee exerted duress). The promise must have been relied on by the promisee although it is a controversial question whether reliance is sufficient or whether detrimental reliance must be shown. Certainly detrimental reliance is not always required: see *WJ Alan & Co Ltd v El Nasr Export and Import Co* [1972] 2 QB 189, CA; *Société Italo-Belge pour le Commerce et l'Industrie SA v Palm and Vegetable Oils (Malaysia) Sdn Bhd, The Post Chaser* [1981] 2 Lloyd's Rep 695. But in the latter case, Robert Goff J regarded the crucial question as being whether it was inequitable for the promisor to enforce its rights and considered that, on the facts—where the promisee had merely relied on the promise by presenting documents which were rejected by the promisor two days later—detrimental reliance was held to be required and was not present.

Although a promise only to suspend rights will obviously not, as a matter of straightforward interpretation, extinguish those rights, so that the original rights can be reverted to at least if reasonable notice is given, a promise that is not so limited will, it would seem, extinguish the original rights. This is the best interpretation of the difficult case of *Tool Metal Manufacturing Co Ltd v Tungsten Electric Co Ltd* [1955] 1 WLR 761, HL. See also *Collier v P & MJ Wright (Holdings) Ltd* [2007] EWCA Civ 1329, [2008] 1 WLR 643, at [42] (per Arden LJ) (cf at [48] per Longmore LJ).

Example

In 1940, a landlord, A, promises its tenant, B, who sub-lets flats, to forgo one-third of the rent owing during a period when B cannot sub-let the flats because of wartime conditions. In reliance on that promise, B pays the two-thirds rent but no more. In 1945, after the war has ended, A sues for the one-third of the rent for the period of the war 1940–5. A's claim will fail because of the doctrine of promissory estoppel. (This example is based on *High Trees* although in that case the landlord was not claiming arrears back to 1940.)

Although not a cause of action, in its role as a defence the doctrine can protect the promisee's expectations although it is sometimes erroneously thought that it is merely concerned to protect the promisee against reliance loss. The extinguishment of the landlord's original rights in the *High Trees* case (see the example just given) illustrates the protection of the promisee's expectations.

This is the most convenient point in the commentary to refer to several other concepts that are not mentioned in the Restatement but which may be regarded as related to promissory estoppel. These are: (i) waiver, (ii) proprietary estoppel, and (iii) contractual estoppel.

(i) Waiver

The Restatement does not refer anywhere to a 'waiver' of a party's rights. The term 'waiver' is best avoided because it can cover a range of different situations. These include variation of a contract and promissory estoppel. But waiver may also be used to describe, for example, where a party has chosen to affirm a contract rather than terminating it for breach (see s 19(6)) or rescinding it for, for example, misrepresentation (see s 34(5)).

Although in practice largely, if not entirely, subsumed by promissory estoppel, there is also a somewhat obscure common law doctrine of 'waiver' or 'forbearance' that suspends rights and does not require reliance by the promisee. See Peel, *Treitel on the Law of Contract* (14th edn, 2015) paras 3-069–3-075; Phipps, 'Resurrecting the Doctrine of Common Law Forbearance' (2007) 123 LQR 286.

(ii) Proprietary estoppel

Although not contractual, and not merely concerned with promises to forgo rights, it is also worth pointing out here that English law enforces certain types of agreement or promise through the doctrine of *proprietary* estoppel. Proprietary estoppel applies where a person makes a promise to confer rights over its own land (or goods), which is then detrimentally relied on by the promisee such that it would be unconscionable for the promisor to go back on its promise. In contrast to promissory estoppel, proprietary estoppel creates a cause of action. The remedy may protect the promisee's expectations. Leading cases include *Crabb v Arun DC* [1976] Ch 179, CA; *Cobbe v Yeoman's Row Management Ltd* [2008] UKHL 55, [2008] 1 WLR 1752; *Thorner v Major* [2009] UKHL 18, [2009] 1 WLR 776. Proprietary estoppel falls outside this Restatement because the agreement or promise enforced by proprietary estoppel is not viewed as a contract and the liability is not seen as contractual. Moreover, in contrast to promissory estoppel, which is restricted to provisions to forgo rights, proprietary estoppel does not naturally belong alongside variation as a method of consensually changing a contract.

(iii) Contractual estoppel

So-called 'contractual estoppel' is also conveniently contrasted with promissory estoppel. This type of estoppel has been developed in the specific context of the exclusion of liability for misrepresentation (see generally the commentary to s 16(6)). The explanation for the operation of a 'no reliance' or 'no representation' clause (excluding liability for misrepresentation)—the explanation for why such a clause can contradict the truth that the claimant *has relied on a representation*—has been said to turn on a 'contractual estoppel', which differs from other forms of estoppel by not requiring (detrimental) reliance: *Peekay Intermark Ltd v Australia and New Zealand Banking Group Ltd* [2006] EWCA Civ 386, [2006] 2 Lloyd's Rep 511, at [56]–[57] per Moore-Bick LJ; *Springwell Navigation Corp v JP Morgan Chase* [2010] EWCA Civ 1221 at [165]–[169], [177].

However, if that is correct it would appear that a 'contractual estoppel' can have importance beyond explaining how 'no reliance' or 'no representation' clauses work and can apply more generally to prevent parties denying the existence of a state of affairs which was the basis of their contract. This is most clearly understood if one cites what Moore-Bick LJ said in the *Peekay* case at [56]:

'There is no reason in principle why parties to a contract should not agree that a certain state of affairs should form the basis for the transaction, whether it be the case or not. For example, it may be desirable to settle a disagreement as to an existing state of affairs in order to establish a clear basis for the contract itself and its subsequent performance. Where parties express an agreement of that kind in a contractual document neither can subsequently deny the existence of the facts and matters upon which they have agreed, at least so far as concerns those aspects of their relationship to which the agreement was directed. The contract itself gives rise to an estoppel'.

This paragraph makes clear that the scope of contractual estoppel can extend beyond 'no reliance' and 'no representation' clauses and may apply to all situations in which a party has warranted that a certain state of affairs exists. For example, it may be a term of a contract to sell a business that equipment is of a certain age, or that there are no outstanding claims against the business, or that the order books are full. The party providing that warranty cannot then deny that the state of affairs is different than warranted. Indeed one might query whether there is any need to refer to a contractual estoppel at all given that a party denying the state of affairs that it has warranted to be true would be in breach of contract and the other party would be entitled to standard remedies for breach (see the analysis by Andrew Smith J in *Credit Suisse International v Stichting Vestia Groep* [2014] EWHC 3103 (Comm) esp at [309]); and that one is dealing with breach of a term might explain why, in relation to this type of estoppel, it is irrelevant to consider whether a party relied or detrimentally relied on what was agreed. However, if one were seeking to defend the language of estoppel here, one might say that its importance, going beyond the normal consequences of breach of a term, is that it explains there being a rule of evidence that the party cannot deny that the state of affairs is different than warranted. The ordinary rules as to breach perhaps cannot explain that rule of evidence (although a contrary view is that the language of estoppel here reflects nothing more than the idea that a party may be prevented by a court from being in breach of contract).

For a sharp denunciation of the notion of 'contractual estoppel', see McMeel, 'Documentary Fundamentalism in the Senior Courts: The Myth of Contractual Estoppel' [2011] LMCLQ 185; 'Banks, the Judiciary and "Documentary Fundamentalism"', *Counsel*, April 2015, 10–12.

Finally, it should be noted that separate from a 'contractual estoppel' is an 'estoppel by convention'. For this type of estoppel, see s 14(4).

13   Express terms

(1) The express terms of a contract may be oral or written or some may be oral and some written.

(2) There is a rebuttable presumption that, where there is a written contract, there are no terms other than the written terms.

(3) The terms of a contract must be distinguished from statements that are not incorporated as terms of the contract.

(4) The intentions of the parties determine whether or not a statement is incorporated as a contractual term; and there may be a term (commonly referred to as an 'entire agreement clause') that specifies which statements are the terms of the contract.

(5) Subsection (4) is subject to sections 11 to 12, 36 to 37, and 50 of the Consumer Rights Act 2015 whereby certain information provided by a trader to a consumer is to be treated as included as a term of the contract.

(6) Even where a contract has largely been concluded orally, A's written terms, including an exemption clause, may be incorporated into a contract with B by one of the following methods—

    (a) signature by B, provided that—

       (i) the document signed purports to have contractual effect; and

      (ii) the signature has not been induced by a misrepresentation;

    (b) reasonable notice given to B of those terms prior to the formation of the contract;

    (c) a consistent course of dealing on those terms between A and B;

    (d) a practice in a trade to which A and B belong that those terms are incorporated.

(7) Where a contract is concluded online between A and B, a standard method by which A's written terms are incorporated into the contract is by B clicking on a box agreeing to A's terms.

13(1)

We have seen in s 11(1) that a contract may be made in writing, orally, or by conduct. In whichever way the contract is made, the terms of the contract are express or implied (for the latter, see s 15). The express terms are written or oral or a combination of both.

13(2)

This subsection attempts to capture the essence of the so-called 'parol evidence rule'. On its face, that 'rule' lays down that, where there is a written agreement, neither party can adduce evidence extrinsic to that agreement to establish that there are other terms. But that formulation of the 'rule' is so riddled with exceptions that few believe in its existence in the modern law. For example, implied terms (s 15) and collateral warranties (see commentary to s 13(4) below) are obvious exceptions. Indeed, as that 'rule' can be departed from wherever a court is satisfied that to do so accords with the parties' intentions, the better view is that there is no such rule. See Law Commission, *Law of Contract: The Parol Evidence Rule* (1986), Report No 154. Nevertheless, this subsection seeks to make clear that the starting point is that the written agreement is all that one needs to look at, so that a court will require persuasion, by the party alleging it, that the parties have agreed that there are additional terms outside the written agreement.

13(3)

It is important to know which statements relied on in entering a contract have become incorporated as terms of the contract and which remain 'mere' representations outside the contract. The latter do not trigger liability for breach of contract although they may (as may representations incorporated as terms) trigger liability in tort (for the torts of deceit or negligence) or under s 2 of the Misrepresentation Act 1967.

13(4)

That the parties' intentions determine, at common law, whether a statement is incorporated as a term was laid down in *Heilbut Symons & Co Ltd v Buckleton* [1913] AC 30, HL. Sometimes the statement may be given contractual force by treating it as a separate collateral contract (often referred to as a collateral warranty): see *Chitty on Contracts* (32nd edn, 2015) paras 13-004–13-006; Peel, *Treitel on the Law of Contract* (14th edn, 2015) paras 9-056–9-058.

Where there is a written contract, the parties may seek to avoid disputes as to whether there are additional terms, whether within the main contract or as collateral warranties, by including an 'entire agreement clause'. Entire agreement clauses are often combined with clauses seeking to exclude liability for misrepresentation and the phrase 'entire agreement clause' is often loosely used to encompass all such clauses. However, strictly speaking, an entire agreement clause does not exclude liability for misrepresentation: its role is to help to identify the terms of the contract. See, for example, *Government of Zanzibar v British Aerospace (Lancaster House)*

Ltd [2000] 1 WLR 2333; *Axa Sun Life Services plc v Campbell Martin Ltd* [2011] EWCA Civ 133, [2011] 2 Lloyd's Rep 1. For the exclusion of liability for misrepresentation, see the commentary to s 16(6).

There is an interesting, but as yet unresolved, question as to the impact of an entire agreement clause on implied terms. This will ultimately turn on the wording and interpretation of the entire agreement clause although it may also be relevant to consider the reason why the term is being implied: see *Exxonmobil Sales and Supply Corp v Texaco Ltd* [2003] EWHC 1964 (Comm), [2003] 2 Lloyd's Rep 686, at [27].

13(5)

The Consumer Rights Act 2015 lays down that certain information provided by a trader to a consumer is to be treated as included as a term of the contract: see Consumer Rights Act 2015 ss 11–12 (goods contracts), ss 36–37 (digital content contracts), and s 50 (services contracts). These provisions provide that the information in question is that specified or mentioned in the Consumer Contracts (Information, Cancellation and Additional Charges) Regulations (SI 2013/3134).

13(6)

The typical situation in which the question arises as to whether one party's written terms have been incorporated into a contract is where the contract has largely been made orally but one party insists that its standard written terms (commonly including an exemption clause) have been incorporated. This subsection sets out the four methods by which the written terms may be incorporated. In principle the last three of these methods of incorporation could apply even to oral and not written terms although all the reported cases have been concerned with written (and indeed standard written) terms. It should be noted that, prior to the legislative control of exemption clauses (see Part 4), the non-incorporation of an exemption clause, along with *contra proferentem* interpretation (see s 14(6)), were the somewhat blunt 'techniques' at common law for controlling unfair exemption clauses. Although still relevant, they are less likely to be 'distorted' now that there is finely tuned legislative control.

13(6)(a)

The leading case of *L'Estrange v F Graucob Ltd* [1934] 2 KB 394 establishes that terms are incorporated by signature whether or not the person signing has read the terms. The first proviso is illustrated by, for example, *Grogan v Robin Meredith Plant Hire* [1996] CLC 1127, CA, where the signed document was a time sheet. The second proviso is illustrated by *Curtis v Chemical Cleaning and Dyeing Co* [1951] 1 KB 805, CA. (Of course the whole contract, and not merely the exemption clause, could be voidable for, for example, misrepresentation, duress, or undue influence or void for mistake (including the doctrine of *non est factum*).)

Example 1

A takes a white satin dress to B for cleaning. A is asked to sign a document which B tells A excludes B from liability just for damage to the beads and sequins on the dress. That is untrue because the exclusion clause exempts B from any damage to the dress. A signs. The dress is returned by B to A with an unexplained stain. The exclusion clause is not incorporated into the contract despite A's signature because that signature was induced by B's misrepresentation. (This example is based on *Curtis v Chemical Cleaning and Dyeing Co.*)

13(6)(b)

It was established in *Parker v The South Eastern Railway Co* (1877) 2 CPD 416, CA, that incorporation may be brought about by reasonable notice. What amounts to reasonable notice was discussed in, for example, *Thornton v Shoe Lane Parking Ltd* [1971] 2 QB 163, CA; *Interfoto Picture Library Ltd v Stiletto Visual Programmes Ltd* [1989] QB 433, CA; *AEG (UK) Ltd v Logic Resource Ltd* [1996] CLC 265, CA; and *O'Brien v MGN Ltd* [2001] EWCA Civ 1279, [2002] CLC 33. They show that greater notice is needed for a term that is particularly onerous or unusual.

The reasonable notice must be given prior to the formation of the contract, otherwise it is too late: *Chapelton v Barry UDC* [1940] 1 KB 532, CA; *Olley v Marlborough Court Ltd* [1949] 1 KB 532, CA.

Example 2

A is a long-term paying guest at B's hotel. Valuable items are stolen from A's room. There is an exclusion clause on a notice in the room excluding B from liability for theft from hotel rooms. That notice was not incorporated into the contract because the contract was made at the hotel reception when A first booked in. The notice was therefore too late. (This example is based on *Olley v Marlborough Court Ltd.*)

13(6)(c)

There was incorporation on this basis in *Henry Kendall & Sons v William Lillico & Sons Ltd* (sub nom *Hardwick Game Farm v Suffolk Agricultural Poultry Producers Assoc*) [1969] 2 AC 31, HL, where the course of dealing comprised three or four transactions a month for three years. In contrast, three or four transactions over five years were held insufficient to amount to a course of dealing in *Hollier v Rambler Motors (AMC) Ltd* [1972] 2 QB 71, CA.

13(6)(d)

The leading case is *British Crane Hire Corp Ltd v Ipswich Plant Hire Ltd* [1975] QB 303, CA.

Example 3

A and B are both in the business of plant hire. B urgently needs a crane and telephones A. Over the phone B agrees charges with A and the crane is promptly delivered. A's printed form is subsequently sent to B but B does not sign it. The crane sinks in marshland. A has to incur great expense to recover it. A claims an indemnity for its costs from B in accordance with the terms on the printed form. Those terms are incorporated because such terms are customarily included in the trade to which both parties belong. (This example is based on *British Crane Hire Corp Ltd v Ipswich Plant Hire Ltd.*)

13(7)

Given the prevalence of online contracting, it has been thought helpful to include this subsection which clarifies that the clicking of a box agreeing to the standard terms is analogous to a signature.

14 Interpretation

(1) The correct approach to interpreting a term of a contract is to ask what the term, viewed in the light of the whole contract, would mean to a reasonable person having all the relevant background knowledge reasonably available to the parties at the time the contract was made.

(2) In applying subsection (1), one must consider—

   (a) the natural and ordinary meaning of the words and syntax used;

   (b) the overall purpose of the term and the contract;

   (c) the facts and circumstances known or assumed by the parties at the time the contract was made;

   (d) commercial common sense as at the time the contract was made, if that can be ascertained;

   but one must be careful to avoid placing too much emphasis on paragraph (b), (c), or (d) at the expense of paragraph (a).

(3) In interpreting a term of a contract the words or syntax must not be amended in order to protect one of the parties from having entered into a bad bargain; but exceptionally it may be decided that the parties must have used the wrong words or syntax.

(4) In interpreting a term of a contract the pre-contractual negotiations of the parties must not be taken into account except where one party seeks to establish that a fact relevant to the background was known to the parties; but they may be taken into account to establish that—

   (a) there is an estoppel by convention (which is a doctrine preventing a party from denying that, for example, certain words have a particular meaning where the parties have negotiated with each other on the common assumption that that meaning was correct); or

    (b) there should be rectification of a contract (see section 35(6)).

(5) In interpreting a term of a contract, the subsequent conduct of the parties must not be taken into account.

(6) Clear words will be needed if a term is to be interpreted as—

    (a) excluding a party from, or indemnifying a party against, liability for negligence; or

    (b) excluding a party from liability for a serious breach of contract.

(7) By reason of section 69 of the Consumer Rights Act 2015, if a term in a consumer contract could have different meanings, the meaning that is most favourable to the consumer is to prevail.

14

The law on the interpretation of contracts is of huge importance in practice because most contractual disputes turn on it. What this section seeks to do is to outline the relevant modern principles of interpretation. For a similar and useful attempt to set out the key principles, see Calnan, *Principles of Contractual Interpretation* (2013). More detailed principles are set out in the leading work for practitioners, Lewison, *The Interpretation of Contracts* (6th edn, 2015). See also McMeel, *The Construction of Contracts* (2nd edn, 2011). Although all the leading reported cases have concerned written contracts, it would appear that the same principles apply to interpreting an oral contract.

14(1)

The modern approach to interpreting a contract was laid down by Lord Hoffmann in *Investors Compensation Scheme Ltd v West Bromwich Building Society* [1998] 1 WLR 896, HL. He stressed that one is seeking to ascertain 'the meaning which the [contract] would convey to a reasonable person having all the background knowledge which would reasonably have been available to the parties in the situation they were in at the time of the contract' (at 912). This is therefore an objective, not a subjective, approach; and it is focusing on the context (often referred to as the 'matrix of fact') rather than the literal or dictionary meaning of the words. In *Bank of Credit & Commerce International SA v Ali* [2002] 1 AC 25 at [39] Lord Hoffmann marginally adjusted what he had said by clarifying that the background knowledge must be relevant: 'I meant anything which a reasonable man would have regarded as *relevant*.'

    In *Cherry Tree Investments Ltd v Landmain Ltd* [2012] EWCA Civ 736, [2013] Ch 305, the majority (Longmore and Lewison LJJ, Arden LJ dissenting) suggested that the courts should be more cautious about using background material when interpreting a contract in a public document (in the case itself, a registered legal charge) rather than an ordinary contract. This may be thought controversial not least because almost all contracts are assignable so that the contextual approach to interpretation may commonly potentially prejudice third parties who do not know the background between the parties. However, it is probably true to say that there is a workable distinction between, on the one hand, interpreting registers and the like, where the intended audience comprises third parties, and, on the other hand, ordinary contracts where the intended audience is the parties themselves (even if third parties may become involved as assignees).

It is well-established that the contract must be read as a whole: *Chamber Colliery Co Ltd v Twyerould* (1893) [1915] 1 Ch 265n at 272 (per Lord Watson); and *Charter Reinsurance Co v Fagan* [1997] AC 313, 384 (per Lord Mustill).

14(2)

An acceptance of the modern objective and contextual approach to interpreting a contract contained in s 14(1) leaves open precisely how much weight is to be given to the words used as against other relevant factors including commercial common sense. Put another way, s 14(1) sets out the correct approach at quite a high level of generality and s 14(2) seeks to clarify how, in practice, that approach should be applied.

In *Rainy Sky SA v Kookmin Bank* [2011] UKSC 50, [2011] 1 WLR 2900, in applying what Lord Hoffmann had said in *Investors Compensation Scheme* (see especially his fifth principle), the Supreme Court indicated that, in a commercial context, where there is more than one plausible meaning, the commercially more sensible meaning is to be preferred. Lord Clarke at [43] said:

'if the language is capable of more than one construction, it is not necessary to conclude that a particular construction would produce an absurd or irrational result before having regard to the commercial purpose of the agreement.'

Earlier, at [21], he said:

'The language used by the parties will often have more than one potential meaning... the exercise of construction is essentially one unitary exercise in which the court must consider the language used and ascertain what a reasonable person, that is a person who has all the background knowledge which would reasonably have been available to the parties in the situation in which they were at the time of the contract, would have understood the parties to have meant. In doing so, the court must have regard to all the relevant surrounding circumstances. If there are two possible constructions, the court is entitled to prefer the construction which is consistent with business common sense and to reject the other.'

In applying these words in *Rainy Sky*, it has been stressed in subsequent cases (for example, *BMA Special Opportunity Hub Fund Ltd & Ors v African Minerals Finance Ltd* [2013] EWCA Civ 416 at [24] per Aikens LJ; *Cottonex Anstalt v Patriot*

Spinning Mills Ltd [2014] EWHC 236 (Comm), [2014] 1 Lloyd's Rep 615 at [52]–[58] per Hamblen J) that what constitutes the commercially more sensible meaning is often not obvious: it can therefore only be determinative where it can be ascertained by the court.

Moreover, in the latest Supreme Court decision on interpretation, *Arnold v Britton* [2015] UKSC 36, [2015] 2 WLR 1593, at [14]–[23] (which concerned the interpretation of a covenant to pay a service charge in a lease of a holiday chalet), there appears to have been a subtle move to steer interpretation back towards the words used as the primary factor of importance as against, for example, commercial common sense. Section 14(2) is an attempt to reflect the reasoning in [14]–[23] of the majority's judgment (Lord Neuberger with whom Lords Sumption and Hughes agreed) in that important case.

14(3)

This seeks to clarify the extent to which interpretation (contrast rectification: s 35 (6)) can operate so as, in effect, to 'amend' the words or syntax used.

The first half of the subsection, warning against the temptation to rewrite an improvident bargain, has been stressed many times and was emphasised again in *Arnold v Britton* [2015] UKSC 36, [2015] 2 WLR 1593, at [20]. Lord Neuberger said,

'The purpose of interpretation is to identify what the parties have agreed, not what the court thinks that they should have agreed. Experience shows that it is by no means unknown for people to enter into arrangements which are ill-advised, even ignoring the benefit of wisdom of hindsight, and it is not the function of a court when interpreting an agreement to relieve a party from the consequences of his imprudence or poor advice. Accordingly, when interpreting a contract a judge should avoid re-writing it in an attempt to assist an unwise party or to penalise an astute party.'

The second half directly reflects Lord Hoffmann's fourth principle (and see also his fifth principle) in *Investors Compensation Scheme* where he said, at 913, 'The background may not merely enable the reasonable man to choose between the possible meaning of words which are ambiguous, but even (as occasionally happens in ordinary life) to conclude that the parties must, for whatever reason, have used the wrong words or syntax'.

14(4)

This exclusion of the evidence of pre-contractual negotiations in interpreting a contract was accepted by Lord Hoffmann in *Investors Compensation Scheme Ltd* (see his third principle) and was confirmed after detailed analysis by Lord Hoffmann in *Chartbrook Ltd v Persimmon Homes Ltd* [2009] UKHL 38, [2009] 1 AC 1101. That exclusion is controversial because it conflicts with the normal way in which language is interpreted (which takes account of prior dealings) and Lord Hoffmann accepted that such evidence could be relevant. The exclusion was based on the grounds that to allow in such evidence would result in an unacceptable increase in the cost of dispute resolution and might encourage self-serving statements. While most practitioners appear to support this reasoning, the exclusion has been criticised by a number of commentators including McMeel, 'Prior Negotiations and Subsequent Conduct—the Next Step Forward for Contractual Interpretation' (2003) 119 LQR 272; and Lord Nicholls, 'My Kingdom for a Horse—The Meaning of Words' (2005) 121 LQR 577.

However, *Chartbrook Ltd v Persimmon Homes Ltd* recognised that pre-contractual negotiations may be taken into account in establishing that a background fact was known to the parties. It will be rare that a dispute on interpretation will turn on whether the parties did or did not know a particular background fact, but where pre-contractual negotiations are admissible under this exception they can include even 'without prejudice' pre-contractual negotiations: *Oceanbulk Shipping and Trading SA v TMT Asia Ltd* [2010] UKSC 44, [2011] 1 AC 662.

As regards (a) estoppel by convention and (b) rectification, Lord Hoffmann made clear in *Chartbrook*, at [47], that these are not exceptions to the general rule as such: '[b]oth . . . lie outside the exclusionary rule, since they start from the premise that, as a matter of construction, the agreement does not have the meaning for which the party seeking rectification or raising an estoppel contends.'

Turning to (a), the precise elements and scope of estoppel by convention are not easy to pin down and the wording in the text is not intended to be comprehensive. Rather it seeks to clarify how such an estoppel may work alongside interpreting a contract. Lord Hoffmann in *Chartbrook* said, at [47], 'If the parties have negotiated an agreement upon some common assumption, which may include an assumption that certain words will bear a certain meaning, they may be estopped from contending that the words should be given a different meaning.' Estoppel by convention was usefully discussed more generally in, for example, *Amalgamated Investment and Property Co Ltd v Texas Commerce Int Bank Ltd* [1982] QB 84, CA; *The Vistafjord* [1988] 2 Lloyd's Rep 343, CA; and *Prime Sight Ltd v Lavarello* [2013] UKPC 22, [2014] AC 436. In the last case, Lord Toulson said, at [29], 'The basis of estoppel by convention is that the parties expressly or impliedly agreed that a certain state of facts or law was to be treated as true for the purposes of the transaction, and that it would be unfair for one or other to resile from the basis on which the transaction had proceeded.' See also *Chitty on Contracts* (32nd edn, 2015) paras 4-108–4-115; Peel, *Treitel on the Law of Contract* (14th edn, 2015) paras 3-094–3-099.

Turning to (b), rectification (for mistake) is set out in s 35(6). Suffice it to say here that the fact that rectification is commonly pleaded as an alternative to interpretation tends to undermine the cost objection to allowing in pre-contractual negotiations as evidence (that is, it will have to be considered by the parties, and looked at by the court, in any event).

14(5)

That subsequent conduct cannot be taken into account in interpreting a contract was established in *James Miller & Partners Ltd v Whitworth Street Estates (Manchester) Ltd* [1970] AC 583, HL. The rationale for this is that one is concerned with what the contract meant at the time it was made and subsequent conduct is largely irrelevant to that. However, one can counter-argue that, provided one relates everything back to the objective intention of the parties at the time the contract was made, the subsequent conduct of the parties might be useful in determining the meaning of the contract at that time. For criticism of this restriction see, for example, the articles by McMeel and Lord Nicholls referred to in the commentary on the previous subsection.

14(6)

Although the modern approach to interpretation set out in s 14(1) means that many of the old rules of interpretation no longer apply—in Lord Hoffmann's words in the *Investors Compensation Scheme* case, at 912, 'almost all the old intellectual baggage of "legal" interpretation has been discarded'—it may remain the rule that an ambiguity will be construed *contra proferentem* ('against the person putting it forward'). Unfortunately, the precise meaning of that phrase is itself ambiguous because it might mean 'against the person who drew it up' or 'against the person relying on it'. The two may not necessarily be the same.

Example

A and B contract on terms drafted by A (that is, they are A's standard terms). B seeks to rely on a term that is ambiguous. It is unclear what interpreting the term *contra proferentem* here means. Certainly it would seem harsh that the ambiguity should be resolved against B, although B is the person relying on the term.

Given this central ambiguity in the *contra proferentem* idea, along with the modern general departure from the old rules of interpretation, it has been thought preferable in the Restatement simply to focus on the main practical application of the *contra proferentem* idea. This is that exclusion clauses will be interpreted 'strictly' so that clear words will be needed if a clause is to be interpreted as (a) excluding a party from (or indemnifying a party against) its own blameworthy conduct or (b) excluding its own serious breach.

As regards (a), in cases such as *Alderslade v Hendon Laundry Ltd* [1945] KB 189, CA, and *Canada Steamship Lines Ltd v R* [1952] AC 192, PC, the courts in the past have laid down that a generally worded exclusion (which does not expressly refer to negligence) will not cover negligence unless that is the only conceivable liability. The same approach was applied to interpreting an indemnity clause in *Smith v South Wales Switchgear Co Ltd* [1978] 1 WLR 165, HL. However, more recently in *HIH Casualty and General Insurance Ltd v Chase Manhattan Bank* [2003] UKHL 6, [2003] 2 Lloyd's Rep 61 (followed in, for example, *Lictor Anstalt Mir Steel UK Ltd v Morris* [2012] EWCA Civ 1397, [2013] 2 All ER (Comm) 54) it has been stressed that the *Canada Steamship* principles should be applied flexibly. They are helpful guidelines not statutory provisions.

Turning to (b) there used to be a rule of law to the effect that a party could not exclude a fundamental breach. That was departed from in *Photo Production Ltd v Securicor Transport Ltd* [1980] AC 827, HL, which made clear that there is merely a rule of construction that clear words will be needed if a clause is to be interpreted as excluding a party for its own fundamental breach. In the Restatement the word 'serious' has been preferred to 'fundamental' so as to avoid any suggestion of it now being necessary to define what is meant by a fundamental breach.

Two additional points are noteworthy. First, limitation clauses are less strictly construed than full exclusions of liability: *Ailsa Craig Fishing Co Ltd v Malvern Fishing Co Ltd* [1983] 1 WLR 964, HL; *George Mitchell (Chesterhall) Ltd v Finney Lock Seeds Ltd* [1983] 2 AC 803, HL.

Secondly, it has controversially been accepted by the Court of Appeal in *KG Bominflot Bunkergesellschaft fur Mineralole v Petroplus Marketing AG, The Mercini Lady* [2010] EWCA Civ 1145, [2011] 1 Lloyd's Rep 442 (cf *Air Transworld Ltd v Bombardier Inc* [2012] EWHC 243 (Comm), [2012] 1 Lloyd's Rep 349) that it remains good law that, if one is to exclude a condition implied under the Sale of Goods Act 1979, one must use words which expressly (or perhaps necessarily) refer to conditions. This approach appears to be a remnant of the 'old intellectual baggage' referred to by Lord Hoffmann and it is surprising that the Court of Appeal regarded itself as bound by the older cases to apply the rule it did: one would expect that, if given the opportunity, the Supreme Court will depart from it.

14(7)

By s 69 of the Consumer Rights Act 2015, 'if a term in a consumer contract . . . could have different meanings, the meaning that is most favourable to the consumer is to prevail'. It is clear that this is a class-protection measure that goes beyond the common law approach to interpretation (albeit that, in the past, *contra proferentem* interpretation of exclusion clauses may have produced the same results).

15 Implied terms

(1) Terms may be implied into a contract, or treated as included in a contract, by legislation (as, for example, the terms implied by sections 12 to 15 of the Sale of Goods Act 1979 and the terms treated as included in a consumer contract for the supply of goods, digital content or services by Part 1 of the Consumer Rights Act 2015).

(2) Apart from terms implied under subsection (1), terms may be implied into a contract—
  (a) by fact, or
  (b) by law,
but only if that is consistent with the express terms of the contract.

(3) A term implied by fact rests on the parties' intentions; and the underlying question to be asked in determining whether such a term should be implied is what the contract, viewed as a whole against the relevant background, would reasonably be understood to mean.

(4) In answering the question in subsection (3), it is helpful to apply one or both of the following tests—
  (a) whether, were an officious bystander to ask if the term was meant to be included, the parties would answer 'Of course' (commonly referred to as the 'officious bystander' test);
  (b) whether the term is necessary for the business efficacy of the contract (commonly referred to as the 'business efficacy' test).

(5) A term may be implied by law if the term is required by the type of contract or relationship in question (for example, there is an implied term not to destroy mutual trust and confidence in an employment contract).

(6) A term may be implied, whether by fact or law, requiring adherence to the custom or practice of the market, trade or locality relevant to the contract but such a term will only be implied if the custom or practice is certain, well-known, reasonable, regarded as intended to have legal consequences, and consistent with the express terms of the contract.

15(1)

The implication of terms by legislation is of great practical importance. Most contractual claims in respect of defective goods and services have been based on a breach of one of the terms implied by legislation. Terms have been implied by legislation into many different types of contract. As regards the sale of goods, by the Sale of Goods Act 1979 terms are implied as to, for example, title (s 12), correspondence with description (s 13), quality or fitness (s 14), and in respect of sales by sample (s 15). So, for example, by s 14(2) of the 1979 Act, 'Where the seller sells goods in the course of a business, there is an implied term that the goods supplied under the contract are of satisfactory quality.' And by s 14(3) of the 1979 Act, where the seller sells goods in the course of a business and the buyer makes known any particular purpose for which the goods are being bought, 'there is an implied term that the goods supplied under the contract are reasonably fit for that purpose' (except where the buyer does not rely on the seller's skill or judgment). Analogous terms are implied into contracts for the hire-purchase of goods by the Supply of Goods (Implied Terms) Act 1973, ss 8–11; into contracts for the hire of goods by the Supply of Goods and Services Act 1982, ss 7–10; and into contracts for work and materials, in relation to the materials supplied, by the Supply of Goods and Services Act 1982, ss 2–5. As regards services, terms are implied by the Supply of Goods and Services Act 1982 as to using reasonable care and skill in performing (s 13), performing within a reasonable time (s 14), and paying a reasonable charge (s 15).

In respect of implied terms in contracts for the supply of goods, digital content, or services by a trader to a consumer, Part 1 of the Consumer Rights Act 2015 has replaced the relevant provisions in the Sale of Goods Act 1979, the Supply of Goods (Implied Terms) Act 1973, and the Supply of Goods and Services Act 1982. This reform has not effected a significant change of substance to the law on implied terms. However, the statutory reference to an implied term in such a consumer contract is replaced by language which refers to the contract being 'treated as including a term...' This is the explanation for the inclusion of that alternative wording in this subsection of the Restatement.

It should be noted that, where terms are implied or treated as included under legislation, the legislation may rule out the implication of the same terms at common law (that is, under the rules for the implication of terms by fact or law set out in the rest of this section of the Restatement): see, for example, Sale of Goods Act 1979, s 14(1), and Consumer Rights Act 2015, s 18(1).

15(2)

In contrast to (some) terms implied by legislation, other types of implied term (sometimes referred to as terms implied by the courts or common law implied terms) cannot be implied if inconsistent with the express terms of the contract: see Lord Simon in *BP Refinery (Westernport) Pty Ltd v Shire of Hastings* (1977) 180 CLR 266, 283, PC (who also stressed that the implied term must be capable of clear formulation). This requirement for consistency need not apply to terms implied by legislation: so, for example, by reason of the Unfair Contract Terms Act 1977 s 6, the implied term in s 12 of the Sale of Goods Act 1979 is non-excludable as, under Part 1 of the Consumer Rights Act 2015, are the terms 'treated as included' in a consumer contract (see s 16(3)(d), 16(4)(a), and s 17(2)–(3) of the Restatement).

15(3)–(4)

The approach to implying terms by fact (which rest on the parties' objective intentions) was recast by Lord Hoffmann in *Attorney-General of Belize v Belize Telecom Ltd* [2009] UKPC 10, [2009] 1 WLR 1988, PC (but see above p xiii, n 13). Prior to that case the English courts tended to refer to one of two tests in implying terms by fact: the 'officious bystander' test as set out by MacKinnon LJ in *Shirlaw v Southern Foundries (1927) Ltd* [1939] 2 KB 206, 227; and, most commonly, the 'business efficacy' test established in *The Moorcock* (1889) 4 PD 64, CA. Lord Hoffmann in the *Belize* case explained, at [21], that those tests are underpinned by the single underlying question of 'what the [contract], read as a whole against the relevant background, would reasonably be understood to mean'. In subsequent cases (see, for example, *Mediterranean Salvage & Towage Ltd v Seamar Trading & Commerce Inc, The Reborn* [2009] EWCA Civ 531, [2009] 2 Lloyd's Rep 639) the courts have often continued to find it useful to refer to the business efficacy test but have indicated that that test must be seen as a help in answering Lord Hoffmann's underlying question; and the same can presumably be said of the 'officious bystander' test.

It is of importance to appreciate that, although English law does not impose a free-standing duty to perform a contract in good faith, it sometimes comes to the same result by implying a term that performance must be carried out in good faith: see, for example, *Yam Seng Pte Ltd v International Trade Corp Ltd* [2013] EWHC 111, [2013] 1 Lloyd's Rep 526; *Emirates Trading Agency v Prime Mineral Exports Pte Ltd* [2014] EWHC 2104 (Comm), [2015] 1 WLR 1145, at [51]. But the *Yam Seng* case has in general been given a rather lukewarm reception with the courts tending to stress that the context and type of contract are all-important: see, for example, *Mid Essex Hospital Services NHS Trust v Compass Group UK and Ireland Ltd* [2013] EWCA Civ 200, [2013] BLR 265 (although the issue there was how to construe an *express* term requiring performance in good faith); *Hamsard 3147 Ltd v Boots UK Ltd* [2013] EWHC 3251 (Pat) at [86]; *Greenclose Ltd v National Westminster Bank plc* [2014] EWHC 1156 (Ch), [2014] 2 Lloyd's Rep 169 , at [150]–[151]; *Acer Investment Management Ltd v Mansion Group Ltd* [2014] EWHC 3011 (QB) at [107]–[109].

In a number of cases it has been held that express contractual discretions are subject to an implied term that the discretion must be exercised in good faith and must not be exercised arbitrarily, capriciously, or irrationally: *Paragon Finance plc v Nash* [2001] EWCA Civ 1466, [2002] 1 WLR 685; *Lymington Marina Ltd v MacNamara* [2007] EWCA Civ 151, [2007] 2 All ER (Comm) 825; *Socimer International Bank Ltd v Standard Bank London Ltd* [2008] EWCA Civ 16, [2008] 1 Lloyd's Rep 558; *British Telecommunications plc v Telefonica O2 UK Ltd* [2014] UKSC 42, [2014] 4 All ER 907, at [37]; *Braganza v BP Shipping Ltd* [2015] UKSC 17, [2015] 1 WLR 1661. See generally Hooley, 'Controlling Contractual Discretion' [2013] CLJ 65.

15(5)

There is a separate category of common law implied terms—which, in line with common usage, are referred to in the Restatement as terms implied by law as opposed to terms implied by fact—where a term is implied where 'necessary' to the particular type of contract or relationship. Leading cases are *Liverpool CC v Irwin* [1977] AC 239, HL (term implied that a landlord should keep common parts of a block of flats in repair); *Scally v Southern Health and Social Services Board* [1992] 1 AC 294, HL (term implied that employer should inform employee of right to purchase 'added' pension years); and *Mahmud v Bank of Credit and Commerce International SA* [1998] AC 20, HL (implied term in an employment contract not to destroy mutual trust and confidence). In the last case, Lord Steyn, at 45, referred to this type of implied term as a 'standardised term implied by law' and said that such implied terms operate as 'default rules'. For that language, see also Lord Steyn in *Equitable Life Assurance Society v Hyman* [2002] 1 AC 408, 458–9 (albeit that that case concerned a term implied by fact, with Lord Steyn describing terms implied by fact as 'individual' and operating as 'ad hoc gap fillers').

In *Crossley v Faithful & Gould Holdings Ltd* [2004] EWCA Civ 293, [2004] 4 All ER 447, Dyson LJ said at [36] that 'rather than focus on the elusive concept of necessity, it is better to recognise that, to some extent at least, the existence and scope of standardised implied terms raise questions of reasonableness, fairness and the balancing of competing policy considerations: see Peden (2001) 117 LQR 459, 467–475'. Although this is controversial, because the House of Lords in *Liverpool CC v Irwin* earlier rejected the idea that terms could be implied if reasonable rather than necessary, Dyson LJ argued that, for example, the well-recognised implied term that an employer will take reasonable care with regard to the physical and mental health and safety of its employees is not a necessary feature of the employer/ employee relationship and is therefore best understood as based on wider policy grounds. See also Lord Denning MR's first category of implied term in *Shell UK Ltd v Lostock Garage Ltd* [1976] WLR 1187, CA.

The Restatement seeks to reflect Dyson LJ's insights by avoiding a strict test of necessity and talking instead of whether the implied term is 'required' by the type of contract or relationship in question (which leaves it open for the courts to take into account reasonableness and fairness in deciding whether the term is required).

15(6)

The five requirements here set out for custom or practice to be implied into a contract were most clearly laid down in *Cunliffe-Owen v Teather & Greenwood* [1967] 1 WLR 1421, 1438–9.

PART 4

LEGISLATIVE CONTROL OF EXEMPTION CLAUSES AND UNFAIR TERMS

It may be thought odd to include statutory law in a Restatement. Certainly one of the primary purposes of a Restatement is to make the law more accessible and that is less necessary where the law in question is already largely contained in legislation rather than being common law. Nevertheless, a Restatement that did not include the legislative control of exemption clauses and unfair terms would not be setting out what nearly all the books (cf the latest 32nd edition of *Chitty on Contracts*) agree is an important aspect of the general law of contract; and the view taken here is that it is helpful to summarise the main elements of the central legislation, *along with the relevant interpretative case law*, in as clear and accessible a manner as possible while stressing that *no attempt is here being made to replicate every detail of the legislation*. This Part of the Restatement should be read as a guide to, and not as a substitute for, reading the legislation.

Prior to the intervention of legislation, the unfair use of exemption clauses was a significant problem for the common law. As dealt with above (see the commentary to ss 13(6) and 14(6)), the two common law techniques for controlling exemption clauses are non-incorporation into the contract and a *contra proferentem* approach to interpretation of the clause. But those are plainly 'blunt' techniques and, while they are still applicable, they do not naturally discriminate between fair and unfair clauses. This deficiency of the common law led to the call for legislative intervention culminating in the Unfair Contract Terms Act 1977 ('UCTA'); and, under the influence of European law, intervention has been extended beyond the control of exemption clauses to the control of unfair terms generally in consumer contracts.

The Consumer Rights Act 2015 (which came into force on 1 October 2015 and applies to contracts made on or after that date) has consolidated (and modified) the relevant provisions on unfair terms, including exemption clauses, which protect consumers in consumer contracts. As a consequence, UCTA is concerned only with exemption clauses in non-consumer contracts and the Unfair Terms in Consumer Contracts Regulations 1999 (SI 1999/2083) have been repealed.

It should also be noted that there are provisions in specific legislation that invalidate contracting out of relevant legislative provisions: see s 5(3)(e) above.

16 Legislative control of exemption clauses in non-consumer contracts
(1) This section deals with legislation invalidating exemption clauses in a contract that is not a consumer contract, with subsections (3) to (5) and (7) referring to the Unfair Contract Terms Act 1977 and subsections (6) and (7) referring to section 3 of the Misrepresentation Act 1967.

(2) In this section, the party seeking to rely on the exemption clause is referred to as the defendant.

(3) If the liability of the defendant is business liability (for example, it arises while the defendant is acting in the course of a business)—

    (a) the defendant cannot by reference to a contract term exclude or limit liability for breach of a contractual obligation to use reasonable care, or breach of a duty of care in tort, causing death or personal injury;

    (b) the defendant cannot by reference to a contract term exclude or limit liability for breach of a contractual obligation to use reasonable care, or breach of a duty of care in tort, causing loss other than death or personal injury, unless the term satisfies the test of reasonableness;

    (c) if the claimant deals on the other's written standard terms of business, the defendant cannot by reference to a contract term exclude or limit liability for breach of contract (or claim to be entitled to render no performance or a substantially different performance than reasonably expected) unless the term satisfies the test of reasonableness;

    (d) in a contract for the sale of goods or hire-purchase, the defendant cannot by reference to a contract term exclude or limit liability for breach of the legislative implied term as to the title of the goods;

    (e) in a contract for the sale of goods or hire-purchase or hire or work and materials, the defendant cannot by reference to a contract term exclude or limit liability for breach of the legislative implied terms as to the goods' conformity with description or sample, satisfactory quality, or fitness for a particular purpose, unless the term satisfies the test of reasonableness.

(4) If the defendant is not acting in the course of a business so that the liability of the defendant is not business liability—

    (a) in a contract for the sale of goods or hire-purchase, the defendant cannot by reference to a contract term exclude or limit liability for breach of the legislative implied term as to the title of the goods;

    (b) in a contract for the sale of goods or hire-purchase, the defendant cannot by reference to a contract term exclude or limit liability for breach of the legislative implied term as to the goods' conformity with description or sample, unless the term satisfies the test of reasonableness.

(5) Subsections (3) and (4) do not apply to certain types of contract (even though not a consumer contract), including—

    (a) an international supply contract;

    (b) a contract of insurance;

    (c) a contract relating to the creation or transfer of an interest in land;

(d) a contract relating to the formation, dissolution, or constitution of a company;

(e) a contract relating to the creation or transfer of an intellectual property right;

(f) a contract relating to the creation or transfer of securities.

(6) A term in a contract that is not a consumer contract excluding or restricting liability for a misrepresentation by one party to the contract to the other before the contract was made is of no effect unless the term satisfies the test of reasonableness; but this subsection does not apply to an international supply contract.

(7) For the purposes of subsections (3), (4) and (6)—

(a) the test of reasonableness is whether the term is a fair and reasonable one to have been included having regard to the circumstances which were, or ought reasonably to have been, known to or in the contemplation of the parties when the contract was made;

(b) the burden of showing that the term is reasonable is on the defendant;

(c) factors that may be relevant in applying the test of reasonableness include—

(i) the bargaining power of the parties;

(ii) whether the claimant received an inducement to agree to the term or, in accepting it, had the opportunity to enter into a similar contract with someone else without that term (even if at a higher price);

(iii) whether the claimant knew or ought reasonably to have known of the term;

(iv) where the term excludes or limits liability if some condition is not complied with, whether it was reasonable at the time of the contract to expect that compliance with that condition would be practicable;

(v) whether the goods or services were sold or supplied to the special order of the claimant;

(vi) whether it is the practice in the trade for such a term to be enforced;

(vii) the insurance that the parties have taken out or could have taken out;

(viii) the nature of the breach, for example whether the breach is negligent;

(ix) the financial impact of the term.

16(1)–(2)

Section 16 deals with the legislative control of exemption clauses in a contract that is not made between a trader and a consumer. The primary relevant statute is therefore UCTA, as amended by the Consumer Rights Act 2015. The main impact of the 2015 Act on UCTA is to take out of UCTA the provisions invalidating exemption clauses in consumer contracts. UCTA is therefore now almost entirely confined to dealing with exemption clauses in business to business contracts (that is, subject to the exception in UCTA s 6(4): see Restatement s 16(4)).

Also included in this section (see s 16(6)) is s 3 of the Misrepresentation Act 1967, which controls the exemption of liability for misrepresentation in a contract that is not made between a trader and a consumer.

For convenience, the party seeking to rely on the exemption clause is referred to as the defendant.

For the meaning of 'consumer contract', 'exemption clause', and 'excluding or limiting' in relation to a liability, see s 6(2) of the Restatement.

16(3)

The need for the defendant's liability to be business liability, along with the full definition of what is meant by that liability, is set out in UCTA s 1(3). There is an exception to the need for there to be 'business liability' in a contract for the sale of goods or hire-purchase: UCTA s 6(4). However, that exception may be misleading because some of the terms implied by legislation in such contracts (for example, under the Sale of Goods Act 1979, s 14) are only implied where the seller is acting in the course of a business. To avoid misleading the reader, the Restatement (in s 16 (4)) deals separately with where the seller is not acting in the course of a business.

UCTA does not refer to the term being void and instead says that a person 'cannot' exclude etc, which is therefore the language used in the Restatement. This comes very close to saying that the term is void but it is possible that the protected party may wish to enforce other parts of the term.

16(3)(a)–(b)

These correlate to UCTA s 2(1)–(2).

16(3)(c)

This correlates to UCTA s 3. The words in brackets correlate to s 3(2)(b): that is, the wording of UCTA s 3 refers not only to the defendant excluding or limiting liability for breach but goes on, in s 3(2)(b), to refer to the reasonableness test applying to a term by which the defendant claims to be entitled—

'(i) to render a contractual performance substantially different from that which was reasonably expected of him, or

(ii) in respect of the whole or any part of his contractual obligation, to render no performance at all.'

It would appear that the sort of term that UCTA s 3(2)(b) is primarily directed at is a 'variation clause' under which a party is entitled to replace one performance with another inferior one (see, for example, *Anglo-Continental Holidays Ltd v Typaldos Lines (London) Ltd* [1967] 2 Lloyd's Rep 61, CA). One view is that such a clause is not an exemption clause as such and that s 3(2)(b) therefore extends the scope of UCTA beyond exemption clauses. Another view is that the underlying concept is always the exemption of liability and that what s 3(2)(b) seeks to make clear is that all forms of exemption clause (including what one may label 'disguised exemption clauses') are covered (a point reinforced by UCTA s 13 which is headed 'varieties of exemption clause'). Certainly the apparently wide words of s 3(2)(b) have not given rise to an expansive interpretation by the courts.

16(3)(d)

This correlates to UCTA s 6(1). The relevant implied term as to title is laid down in s 12 of the Sale of Goods Act 1979 and in s 8 of the Supply of Goods (Implied Terms) Act 1973. (For the exemption of analogous implied terms in other contracts where goods pass, see UCTA s 7(3A) (unexcludable) and 7(4) (unexcludable unless reasonable) which are not reflected in the Restatement.)

16(3)(e)

This correlates to UCTA s 6(1A) and s 7(1A). The relevant implied terms are laid down in ss 13–15 of the Sale of Goods Act 1979, ss 9–11 of the Supply of Goods (Implied Terms) Act 1973, and ss 3–5, 8–10 of the Supply of Goods and Services Act 1982.

16(4)

This subsection reflects UCTA s 6(1), (1A), and (4), plus the point made at the start of the commentary on the last subsection, namely that the exception to the need for business liability is narrower than may at first sight appear. The relevant implied terms referred to here are therefore the ones that are implied into contracts for the sale of goods or hire-purchase (for example, under the Sale of Goods Act 1979, ss 12–13, 15) even if the seller is not acting in the course of a business.

16(5)

The exclusion from the controls in UCTA of international supply contracts is contained in UCTA s 26 (which also defines what an international supply contract is for these purposes). The other examples of exclusions here set out ((b)–(f)) are in para 1 of UCTA Schedule 1 (where it is made clear that the exclusions apply only to certain sections of UCTA). For the full list of other exclusions, see UCTA Schedule 1 (for example, s 16(3)(b)–(c) of the Restatement do not apply to a charterparty or a contract for the carriage of goods by sea; and s 16(3)(a)–(b) do not apply to a contract of employment, except in favour of the employee).

16(6)

The law on misrepresentation is set out in s 36 of the Restatement. As regards the legislative control of an exemption of liability for misrepresentation, the relevant provision in a non-consumer contract is s 3 of the Misrepresentation Act 1967 (as substituted by s 8 of UCTA). The legislative control of such a clause in a consumer contract falls within the general control of unfair terms in such a contract in the Consumer Rights Act 2015 (see s 17 of the Restatement).

Section 3(1) of the Misrepresentation Act 1967 lays down that a term that would exclude or restrict any liability for a misrepresentation by one party to the other before the contract was made:

'shall be of no effect except in so far as it satisfies the requirement of reasonableness as stated in section 11(1) of the Unfair Contract Terms Act 1977; and it is for those claiming that the term satisfies that requirement to show that it does.'

That test, and the main factors that the courts have considered relevant in applying it (although not all the factors listed are applicable to an exemption for misrepresentation) are set out in s 16(7) below. For cases deciding that a clause excluding rescission for misrepresentation was not a fair and reasonable one to have been included, see *Walker v Boyle* [1982] 1 WLR 495; *Cleaver v Schyde Investments Ltd* [2011] EWCA Civ 929, [2011] 2 P & CR 21.

It was decided in *Trident Turboprop (Dublin) Ltd v First Flight Couriers Ltd* [2009] EWCA Civ 290, [2010] QB 86 that the exclusion of international supply contracts in UCTA also applied to s 3 of the Misrepresentation Act 1967.

It is an important practical point that, as explained in the commentary to s 13(4), an 'entire agreement clause' is, strictly speaking, not a clause excluding or limiting liability for misrepresentation and therefore falls outside s 3 of the 1967 Act. Also outside s 3 is a term by which a principal limits the authority of its agent to make representations: *Overbrooke Estates Ltd v Glencombe Properties Ltd* [1974] 1 WLR 1335. In contrast, a 'no reliance' or 'no representation' clause may be an exemption of liability for misrepresentation and may therefore fall within s 3: *Government of Zanzibar v British Aerospace (Lancaster House) Ltd* [2000] 1 WLR 2333 (as regards 'clause C'); *Springwell Navigation Corp v JP Morgan Chase* [2010] EWCA Civ 1221 at [180]–[181] ('no representation' and 'no reliance' clauses held to be reasonable exclusions under s 3 of the Misrepresentation Act 1967). In *Raiffeisen Zentralbank Osterreich AG v Royal Bank of Scotland plc* [2010] EWHC 1392 (Comm), [2011] 1 Lloyd's Rep 123, Christopher Clarke J at [314] said that the key question in deciding whether the 'no reliance' or 'no representation' clause is an exemption clause, so as to fall within the scope of s 3 of the 1967 Act, is 'whether the clause attempts to rewrite history or parts company with reality'.

The explanation for the validity of a 'no reliance' or 'no representation' clause has been said to turn on a 'contractual estoppel': for discussion of this and 'contractual estoppel' generally, see the end of the commentary to s 12.

For the rule of public policy that one cannot exclude liability for one's own fraudulent misrepresentation, see s 44(5).

16(7)(a)

This is the test of reasonableness set out in UCTA s 11(1). As laid down in *Stewart Gill Ltd v Horatio, Myer & Co Ltd* [1992] QB 600, CA, a court cannot sever the reasonable from the unreasonable parts even though the claimant is seeking to rely only on the reasonable parts. Cf *Watford Electronics Ltd v Sanderson CFL Ltd* [2001] EWCA Civ 317, [2001] 1 All ER (Comm) 696 (severance possible where two separate terms albeit in a single clause).

16(7)(b)

This correlates to UCTA s 11(5).

16(7)(c)

This paragraph sets out the main factors that have been considered relevant by the courts in applying the reasonableness test. It should be stressed that this paragraph reflects not only what is set out in the statute but also the most important case law interpreting the statutory test.

The first five factors, (i)–(v), correlate to the five 'Guidelines for the Application of the Reasonableness Test' in UCTA Schedule 2. Although those guidelines are required to be considered, if relevant, only where assessing reasonableness under, for example, UCTA s 6(1A) and 7(1A) (that is, in this Restatement s 16(3)(e) and 16(4)(b)), they have been considered to be guidelines of general application: *Stewart Gill Ltd v Horatio Myer & Co Ltd* [1992] QB 600, CA; *St Albans City and DC v International Computers Ltd* [1995] FSR 686; *Avrora Fine Arts Investment Ltd v Christie, Manson & Woods Ltd* [2012] EWHC 2198 (Ch), [2012] PNLR 35, at [149].

Factors (vi), (vii), and (viii), as well as (i), (ii), and (iii), were taken into account in *George Mitchell (Chesterhall) Ltd v Finney Lock Seeds Ltd* [1983] 2 AC 803, HL (although that case was dealing with an earlier, and slightly differently worded, reasonableness test). For an illustration of the application of factor (iv), see *Stag Line Ltd v Tyne Ship Repair Group Ltd* [1984] 2 Lloyd's Rep 211, 223; and for an illustration of the application of (v), see *Watford Electronics Ltd v Sanderson CFL Ltd* [2001] EWCA Civ 317, [2001] 1 All ER (Comm) 696, at [52]. The availability of insurance (see factor (vii)) is expressly mentioned as a relevant factor in UCTA s 11 (4) where the exemption clause limits liability to a specified sum. As mentioned in *Phillips Products Ltd v Hyland* [1987] 1 WLR 659, CA, factor (viii) (the nature of the breach) must be related back to having been in the contemplation of the parties at the time the contract was made. The same temporal point applies in relation to factor (ix). Factor (ix) was taken into account in, for example, *Balmoral Group Ltd v Borealis (UK) Ltd* [2006] EWHC 1900 (Comm), [2006] 2 Lloyd's Rep 629, where the drastic effect of the limitation would have been to restrict the claimant buyer (who was claiming damages of £50m) to a repayment of the price of the goods; in contrast in *Avrora Fine Arts*, the exclusion clause was held reasonable where the claimant was, in any event, entitled to a refund of the price paid for a forged painting.

Of all these factors, the first is of most importance. In general, the courts will not intervene to strike down a clause as unreasonable where negotiated between parties of equal bargaining power: *Watford Electronics Ltd v Sanderson CFL Ltd* [2001] EWCA Civ 317, [2001] 1 All ER (Comm) 696; *Granville Oil and Chemicals Ltd v Davies Turner and Co Ltd* [2003] EWCA Civ 570, [2003] 1 All ER (Comm) 819; *Regus (UK) Ltd v Epcot Solutions Ltd* [2008] EWCA Civ 361, [2009] 1 All ER (Comm) 586.

17   Legislative control of exemption clauses and unfair terms in consumer contracts

(1) This section deals with the provisions in the Consumer Rights Act 2015 (the '2015 Act') invalidating exemption clauses and unfair terms in a consumer contract.

(2) In a contract for the supply of goods or digital content by a trader to a consumer, a term is not binding on the consumer to the extent that it would exclude or limit the trader's liability for breach of a term (which the 2015 Act treats as being included in such a contract) that, for example—

　　(a) the goods or digital content are of satisfactory quality, fit for a particular purpose made known to the trader by the consumer, and as described;

　　(b) the trader has the right to supply the goods or digital content;

but, as regards paragraph (b), special provision applies in relation to a contract for the hire of goods.

(3) In a contract for the supply of services by a trader to a consumer, a term is not binding on the consumer to the extent that it would exclude or limit the trader's liability for breach of a term (which the 2015 Act treats as being included in such a contract) that, for example, the trader must perform the service with reasonable care and skill.

(4) A trader cannot exclude or limit liability in a consumer contract for breach of a contractual obligation to use reasonable care, or breach of a duty of care in tort, causing death or personal injury.

(5) A term of a consumer contract that is unfair is not binding on the consumer.

(6) A term is unfair for the purposes of subsection (5) if, contrary to the requirement of good faith, it causes a significant imbalance in the parties' rights and obligations under the contract to the detriment of the consumer.

(7) Factors that may be relevant in applying the test in subsection (6) include—
  (a) the bargaining power of the parties;
  (b) whether the consumer had an inducement to agree to the term;
  (c) whether the goods or services were sold or supplied to the special order of the consumer;
  (d) the extent to which the trader has dealt fairly and equitably with the consumer.

(8) But, provided that it is transparent and prominent (and not a term listed in Part 1 of Schedule 2 to the 2015 Act), a term cannot be assessed for fairness to the extent that—
  (a) it specifies the main subject matter of the contract; or
  (b) the assessment is of the appropriateness of the price payable under the contract by comparison with the goods, digital content or services supplied under it.

(9) A term is transparent if it is expressed in plain and intelligible language and (in the case of a written term) is legible; and a term is prominent if it is brought to the consumer's attention in such a way that an average consumer would be aware of the term.

(10) Where there are proceedings before a court which relate to a term of a consumer contract, the court must consider whether the term is fair even if not raised by the parties unless the court considers that it has insufficient legal and factual material to do so.

(11) Some of the above subsections do not apply to certain types of consumer contract so that, for example—
  (a) subsection (2) does not apply to a contract for a trader to supply coins or notes to a consumer for use as currency or to a contract for the supply of goods to a consumer that is intended to operate as a security;
  (b) subsections (3) and (5) do not apply to a contract of employment or apprenticeship;
  (c) subsection (4) does not apply to a contract of insurance or a contract relating to the creation or transfer of an interest in land.

17(1)

Part 1 of the Consumer Rights Act 2015 deals with consumer contracts for goods, digital content, and services and automatically invalidates (that is, irrespective of applying a fairness test) certain exemption clauses in such contracts. Some of that law was previously in the Unfair Contract Terms Act 1977, but that Act no longer applies to consumer contracts. Part 2 of the 2015 Act deals with unfair terms (including unfair exemption clauses) in consumer contracts: with the exception of automatically invalidating an exemption of liability for negligently caused personal injury and death, it applies a test of fairness to determine whether the term binds the consumer or not. For the meanings of 'consumer', 'trader', and 'consumer contract' (which derive from the 2015 Act, ss 2(2), 2(3), and 61(3)), see s 6 of the Restatement. Part 2 of the 2015 Act is similar, but not identical, to the Unfair Terms in Consumer Contracts Regulations 1999 (SI 1999/2083) which have been repealed.

Note also that, outside the law of contract as conventionally understood, the Consumer Rights Act 2015, s 70 and Schedule 3 provides for the Competition and Markets Authority (and other regulators) to apply for an injunction to restrain the use of unfair (or non-transparent) terms. See also generally the Enterprise Act 2002, Part 8.

17(2)

This correlates to the 2015 Act, ss 31 and 47. These provisions automatically invalidate the exemption clauses specified. Terms as to satisfactory quality, fitness for purpose, description, and the trader's right to supply are 'treated as included in the contract' by reason of the 2015 Act, ss 9–11 and 17 (as regards goods) and ss 34–36 and 41 (as regards digital content). The words 'for example' have been used because ss 31 and 47 also automatically invalidate the exemption of other terms treated as included in the contract (for example, as to pre-contract information, the delivery of goods, and the passing of risk). The special provision referred to, as regards the trader's right to supply in a contract for the hire of goods, is contained in s 31(5)–(6) of the 2015 Act.

17(3)

This correlates to the 2015 Act, s 57. This automatically invalidates the exemption clauses specified. A term requiring the service to be performed using reasonable care and skill is 'treated as included in the contract' by reason of the 2015 Act, s 49. The words 'for example' have been used because s 57 also automatically invalidates the exemption of other terms treated as included in the contract (for example, that the service be performed within a reasonable time for a reasonable price—although, by s 57(3), the invalidity in this instance applies only if the exemption prevents the consumer recovering the price paid—or that information given about the trader is binding).

17(4)

This automatic invalidation provision correlates to s 65 of the 2015 Act.

17(5)

This correlates to s 62(1) of the 2015 Act. This comes very close to saying that the term is void but it is possible that the consumer may wish to enforce other parts of the term.

17(6)

This definition of an unfair term is set out in s 62(4) of the 2015 Act. By s 63, guidance as to the type of terms which *may* be regarded as unfair is given in 'an indicative and non-exhaustive' list in Schedule 2 to the 2015 Act. Part 1 of that Schedule lists 20 types of term which may be unfair; Part 2 of that Schedule then modifies that list by excluding some types of term from it.

The leading English cases on the approach to this test as to whether a term is unfair are *Director General of Fair Trading v First National Bank plc* [2001] UKHL 52, [2002] 1 AC 481, HL (applying the now repealed Unfair Terms in Consumer Contracts Regulations 1994, SI 1994/3159) and *ParkingEye Ltd v Beavis* [2015] UKSC 67 at [102]–[114] and [200]–[213] (applying the now repealed Unfair Terms in Consumer Contracts Regulations 1999, SI 1999/2083).

17(7)

These four factors are mentioned in explaining the requirement of 'good faith' in Recital 16 of the preamble to the 1993 Directive on Unfair Terms in Consumer Contracts (93/13/EEC of 5 April 1993). The Directive was initially implemented in the UK by the Unfair Terms in Consumer Contracts Regulations 1994 (SI 1994/3159) and these factors were copied out in Schedule 2. Although those factors have not been included in the 2015 Act, the 2015 Act is designed to implement the 1993 Directive and those factors therefore remain useful indicators in applying the test as to whether a term is unfair. In the light of the decision of the Court of Justice in *Aziz v Caixa d'Estalvis de Catalunya, Tarragona i Manresa* (C-415/11) [2013] 3 CMLR 89, it would appear that, in assessing good faith, the last of those factors is especially significant. The Court of Justice there laid down, at [69], that 'the national court must assess for those purposes [that is, assessing good faith] whether the seller or supplier, dealing fairly and equitably with the consumer, could reasonably assume that the consumer would have agreed to such a term in individual contract negotiations'. For application of that approach, see *ParkingEye Ltd v Beavis* [2015] UKSC 67 at [108]–[109].

Although not particularly revealing, it should be added that by s 62(5) of the Consumer Rights Act 2015:

'Whether a term is fair is to be determined—(a) taking into account the nature of the subject-matter of the contract, and (b) by reference to all the circumstances existing when the term was agreed and to all of the other terms of the contract or of any other contract on which it depends.'

17(8)

This correlates to s 64(1)–(2) and (6) of the 2015 Act. Applying the previous version of this exclusion (in the Unfair Terms in Consumer Contracts Regulations 1999 reg 6 (2)) it was controversially decided in *Office of Fair Trading v Abbey National plc* [2009] UKSC 6, [2009] 3 WLR 1215, that bank charges for unauthorised overdrafts were part of the price in the contract between the bank and its customer and, provided in plain intelligible language, could not therefore be assessed for fairness. In contrast in other cases (for example, *Office of Fair Trading v Ashbourne Management Service Ltd* [2011] EWHC 1237 (Ch)) a narrow construction of the 'core exclusion' was taken which then allowed the court to assess the fairness of the term. It is not absolutely clear what difference, if any, has been made by the differently formulated exclusion in the 2015 Act. Certainly subsequent to *Abbey National*, the Court of Justice has taken a narrow view of the 'core exclusion' in cases such as *Kásler v OTP Jelzálogbank Zrt* (C-26/13) [2014] 2 All ER (Comm) 443 and *Matei v SC Volksbank România SA* (C-143/13) [2015] 1 WLR 2385.

17(9)

This correlates to s 64(3)–(5) of the 2015 Act. For the meaning of 'average consumer', see s 6(2) of the Restatement (which correlates to s 64(5) of the 2015 Act).

17(10)

This correlates to s 71 of the Consumer Rights Act 2015. This was the law initially laid down in interpreting the Unfair Terms Directive (93/13/EEC) by the European Court of Justice in *Océano Grupo Editorial SA v Quintero* (C-240–244/98) [2002] 1 CMLR 43. Normally of course it is for a party, not the court, to raise the issue in question. But this exception is a consumer protection measure. See also s 44(6) of the Restatement. For the linked question of the burden of proof in relation to fairness, see *Chitty on Contracts* (32nd edn, 2015) paras 38-307–38-310, 38-362.

17(11)

The exclusions from the 2015 Act are a ragbag and are not neatly found in one place. Some of the main examples are set out here. Paragraph 17(11)(a) correlates to s 3(3)(a) and (c) of the 2015 Act. Paragraph 17(11)(b) correlates to ss 48(2) and 61(2) of the 2015 Act. Paragraph 17(11)(c) correlates to s 66(1) of the 2015 Act.

The end of this section appears to be the most appropriate point in the commentary to mention that, in respect of many consumer contracts, there are other important legislative consumer protection measures. See, in particular, Part 3 of the Consumer Contracts (Information, Cancellation and Additional Charges) Regulations 2013 (SI 2013/3134) which allows a consumer to cancel within certain time limits a 'distance' or 'off-premises' contract, for example a contract made at a place other than the trader's business premises (and the 2013 Regulations also deal with the consequences, including the restitutionary consequences, of cancellation). These provisions are not concerned with the fairness of otherwise of the terms as such but are rather designed to guard against procedural unfairness by giving the consumer a 'cooling-off' period.

PART 5

BREACH OF CONTRACT AND REMEDIES FOR BREACH

18 Breach of contract

(1) A party commits a breach of contract by failing to perform the contract in accordance with its terms.

(2) An anticipatory repudiation may also constitute a breach of contract (see sections 19(10) and (11)(b)).

(3) A party may commit a breach of contract without being at fault unless the terms of the contract impose merely an obligation to use reasonable care (or an equivalent standard requiring proof of fault).

(4) The rest of this Part deals with the remedies available to one party (the 'innocent party' or 'claimant') for a breach of contract by the other party (the 'other party' or 'defendant') (but, except in sections 19(13) and 26(4), it does not deal with the special remedies for a consumer in Part 1 of the Consumer Rights Act 2015).

18(1)–(2)

Leaving aside anticipatory breach, the concept of breach in English law is a straightforward one which is adequately captured by referring to a failure to perform as the terms of the contract require (s 18(1)). Although one could elaborate on 'failing to perform' by talking of, for example, a refusal to perform or defective performance, it would appear that 'failing to perform' is a sufficiently wide notion to cover these situations. Furthermore, 'failing to perform' embraces not only the breach of a positive obligation but also the breach of a promise not to do something. It can also be taken to cover where the breach is of a promise that a particular state of affairs exists.

More difficult is s 18(2), which deals with anticipatory repudiation (sometimes referred to as 'anticipatory breach'). This is explained further in s 19(11)(b). The important point for the concept of breach is that an anticipatory repudiation (for example, making clear in advance that one is not going to perform) entitles the innocent party to terminate now—and to recover damages immediately—by choosing to 'accept' the repudiation.

The Restatement does not separate out as a distinct form of breach where a party disables itself from performing. 'Disablement' is embraced either by s 18(1) as a failure to perform or by s 18(2) as an anticipatory repudiation. (Cf the difficult analysis in *Universal Cargo Carriers v Citati* [1957] 2 QB 401, 436–8 per Devlin J, discussed in *Chitty on Contracts* (32nd edn, 2015) para 24-031, Peel, *Treitel on the Law of Contract* (14th edn, 2015) para 17-077.)

Some of the further details on breach (for example, what is meant by, and the significance of, the term broken being a condition, a warranty, or an innominate term) are best dealt with in discussing the remedy of termination (s 19).

Most contract books have a separate section on 'performance'. It has been thought unnecessary to have such a Part or section in the Restatement. This is because 'performance' is a mirror image of breach or relates to the remedy of the award of an agreed sum (see s 24) so that what is discussed in the books under 'performance' merely replicates what is here said about breach or is later said about the award of an agreed sum. In any event, the essential simple point is that performance turns on what the contract requires. So, for example, the law on the order of performance—which may be crucial in determining which party is in breach—turns on the terms of the contract and their interpretation. One party's performance may be a condition precedent to the other party's performance, but whether that is so depends on the terms and the standard rules of interpretation. Similarly, the terms of the contract and their interpretation will determine whether a party must perform personally or whether, in contrast, the performance may be carried out vicariously (that is, through another person). For discussion of vicarious performance, see *Chitty on Contracts* (32nd edn, 2015) paras 19-82–19-85, Peel, *Treitel on the Law of Contract* (14th edn, 2015) paras 17-007–17-013.

18(3)

Civilian lawyers may be surprised to discover that there is no added requirement for breach that the party is at fault for its failure to perform. Whether a contract imposes a strict obligation or one to use reasonable care depends on the terms of the contract (including implied terms) and their interpretation. Most contractual obligations are strict, but some (for example, some obligations undertaken by a professional in relation to services for a client) impose merely an obligation to use reasonable care; and it is very common for there to be both types of obligation in a single contract. For an excellent discussion, see Peel, *Treitel on the Law of Contract* (15th edn, 2015) paras 17-065–17-071.

18(4)

The practical importance of establishing a breach of contract is that various remedies are made available to the innocent party for breach. Although some of these—notably an action for the agreed sum and specific performance (see *Hasham v Zenab* [1960] AC 316, *Zucker v Tyndall Holdings plc* [1992] 1 WLR 1127)—may in theory be awarded simply because the contract requires performance, without the need to establish a breach, in practice it is very unlikely that even those remedies will be sought or granted unless there is at least a threatened breach of contract.

This is the appropriate point to make clear that, consistently with the focus on the general law (see s 1(b) above), the Restatement does not set out the special remedies in Part 1 of the Consumer Rights Act 2015. Part 1 of the Act deals with consumer contracts for the supply of goods, digital content, or services. Under ss 19–26 and 28 (in respect of goods), ss 42–45 (in respect of digital content), and ss 54–56 (in respect of services), special remedies are provided for a consumer in respect of a trader's breach of contract covered by the 2015 Act. So, in respect of non-conforming goods, a consumer has a short-term right to reject, the right to repair or replacement, and the right to a price reduction or the final right to reject (s 19(3) of the 2015 Act). As regards non-conforming digital content, a consumer has the right to repair or replacement and the right to a price reduction. Again, in respect of services, a consumer has the right to require repeat performance and the right to a price reduction (s 54(3)). These special remedies are, in general, additional to the common law and equitable remedies, such as damages and specific performance, that the consumer might in any event have (see, for example, ss 19(9)–(11), 42(6)–(7), and 54(5)–(6) of the 2015 Act), although the consumer cannot combine remedies so as to produce double recovery as made clear by s 19(10)(a) and s 42(6) of the 2015 Act.

However, in two important respects (concerning termination and specific performance respectively) the general law of remedies for breach of contract set out in this Part of the Restatement may be regarded as having been amended by provisions within Part 1 of the Consumer Rights Act 2015. It has therefore been thought appropriate to include subsections dealing with those amendments in ss 19(13) and 26(4) of the Restatement.

It has to be said that the remedies provisions in the Consumer Rights Act 2015 are excessively complex and poorly drafted. They must be read with great care and a clear head. For invaluable help, see *Chitty on Contracts* (32nd edn, 2015) paras 38-477–38-488, 38-517–38-522, 38-540–38-544.

19   Termination

(1) The innocent party has the right to terminate the contract for breach by the other party in the situations set out in subsection (8).

(2) Termination of a contract for breach depends on the election of the innocent party and does not occur automatically as a matter of law.

(3) Termination is effected by the innocent party making clear to the other party, by words or conduct, that it is treating the contract as at an end.

(4) Termination of the contract means that, subject to contrary agreement, the parties are discharged from their obligations under the contract which would arise after termination but not those which have arisen before.

(5) If a benefit has been obtained by one party from the other under a contract that has been terminated for breach, the right to restitution in respect of that benefit is governed by the law of unjust enrichment.

(6) An innocent party elects not to terminate, and thereby affirms, the contract, so that it cannot then change its mind and terminate the contract for the same breach, if, with knowledge of the facts constituting the breach and of the legal right to terminate, it unequivocally manifests an intention to continue with the contract.

(7) Under the Sale of Goods Act 1979, a buyer of goods (who is not a consumer buying from a trader) loses the right to terminate the contract of sale for breach of a condition by the seller if the buyer accepts the goods (as defined in section 35 of that Act) even though the acceptance does not constitute an affirmation.

(8) The situations referred to in subsection (1) are as follows—

  (a) there is the breach by the other party of a term that is a condition (rather than being a warranty or an innominate term);

  (b) there is the breach by the other party of an innominate term and the consequences of the breach are such as to deprive the innocent party of substantially the whole benefit of the contract; or

  (c) the other party repudiates the contract.

(9) For the purposes of subsection (8)(a) and (b)—

  (a) a term is a condition if it is such an important term of the contract that any breach of it would deprive the innocent party of substantially the whole benefit of the contract or if it is otherwise clear that the intention of the parties is that any breach of it should give the innocent party the right to terminate the contract;

  (b) a term is a warranty if it is such a minor term of the contract that no breach of it would deprive the innocent party of substantially the whole benefit of the contract;

  (c) an innominate term is a term that is neither a condition nor a warranty;

  (d) subject to legislation (for example, sections 12 to 15A of the Sale of Goods Act 1979), the intentions of the parties determine whether a term is a condition or a warranty or an innominate term but the fact that the contract refers to the term as a 'condition' is not conclusive.

(10) For the purposes of subsection (8)(c), the other party repudiates the contract if it makes clear to the innocent party, by words or conduct, that—

  (a) it is not going to perform the contract at all;

  (b) it is going to commit a breach of a condition; or

> (c) it is going to commit a breach of an innominate term and the consequences of the breach will be such as to deprive the innocent party of substantially the whole benefit of the contract.
>
> (11) The repudiation may occur—
>   (a) on or after the due date of performance; or
>   (b) prior to the due date for performance (an 'anticipatory repudiation') in which case the innocent party, without waiting for the due date for performance, can elect to accept the repudiation thereby terminating the contract and becoming immediately entitled to damages for breach.
>
> (12) The parties may include a term in the contract that provides for termination of the contract on an event other than a breach allowing termination under subsection (8).
>
> (13) Subsection (8) is subject to provisions in Part 1 of the Consumer Rights Act 2015 (for example, sections 19, 20, and 42) which, in some circumstances, govern a consumer's right to terminate a contract for breach by a trader of a consumer contract for the supply of goods or digital content.

19(1)

The law as to when an innocent party can terminate for breach is set out in subsection (8) below, which is then further explained in subsections (9)–(11).

19(2)

In contrast to frustration of a contract (see Part 6), which terminates a contract automatically, termination for breach is dependent on the innocent party choosing to terminate the contract. After doubts raised in some cases, it was made clear in *Geys v Société Générale, London Branch* [2012] UKSC 63, [2013] 1 AC 523, that the standard election approach applies even to the breach of contracts of employment.

19(3)

Termination is a self-help remedy so that there is no need to come to court. All that is required is that one makes clear to the other party that one is treating the contract as at an end: *Vitol SA v Norelf Ltd, The Santa Clara* [1996] AC 800, HL.

19(4)

That termination (sometimes referred to as 'discharge') for breach is different from rescission for, for example, misrepresentation was made clear in *Johnson v Agnew* [1980] AC 367, HL, and *Photo Productions Ltd v Securicor Transport Ltd* [1980] AC 827, HL. Rescission wipes away the contract from the start; termination wipes away only future obligations. That is why one can both terminate for breach of contract and be awarded damages for breach whereas one cannot both rescind (for misrepresentation) and be awarded damages for breach. To avoid confusion, it is preferable never to talk of rescission for breach.

However, it is important to appreciate that the parties may intend some clauses to apply even after termination. This will commonly be the case in respect of, for example, jurisdiction and arbitration clauses and, in contracts of employment, restraint of trade and confidentiality clauses.

Lord Diplock in a number of cases (for example, *Photo Production Ltd v Securicor Transport Ltd* [1980] AC 827 at 848–9) set out an analysis whereby, on termination, primary obligations are discharged while secondary obligations, principally the obligation to pay damages, continue to apply. This may be considered over-elaborate and, in particular, the right to damages is a remedy imposed by law for breach so that it is far from clear that it is helpful to see it as somehow contained within the contract.

19(5)

It has been explained above (see commentary to s 3(1)) that this Restatement takes a conceptual, rather than a contextual, approach to what falls within the law of contract. Restitution where a contract has been terminated for breach is best viewed as a remedy for unjust enrichment with the unjust factor being failure of consideration. The details of the relevant law are to be found in *A Restatement of the English Law of Unjust Enrichment* (2012) (see especially s 15 of that Restatement).

19(6)

An innocent party who elects not to terminate is said to affirm the contract (also sometimes referred to as a 'waiver' of one's right to terminate). For a recent careful consideration and application of the test for affirmation, see *White Rosebay Shipping SA v Hong Kong Chain Glory Shipping Ltd, The Fortune Plum* [2013] EWHC 1355 (Comm), [2013] 2 All ER (Comm) 449. Once it has affirmed, the innocent party cannot change its mind and terminate (for the same breach). In *Peyman v Lanjani* [1985] Ch 457, CA, it was controversially held that the innocent party must know of its legal right to terminate before it can be held to have affirmed a transaction (although there must surely be an exception to this where the innocent party makes clear that it is affirming irrespective of its lack of knowledge). Perhaps because the default position is that the contract continues, it would appear that affirmation does not require communication from the innocent party to the party in breach (but for a contrary view, see O'Sullivan, Elliott, and Zakrzewski, *The Law of Rescission* (2nd edn, 2014) para 23.57).

In contrast to rescission for, for example, misrepresentation, there is no delay or laches bar to termination for breach (and nor is there any limitation period in the Limitation Act 1980). However, a delay by the innocent party in terminating may constitute affirmation. Note also that, in contrast to rescission, it is not a bar to termination for breach that a bona fide purchaser has acquired the title to the property transferred under the contract. That is because termination does not revest title in property that has already been transferred under the contract.

19(7)

Section 19(7) is included to draw attention to the statutory modification of the law on affirmation under the Sale of Goods Act 1979 (although, under s 19(3), (4), (6), and (12) and ss 20–22 of the Consumer Rights Act 2015, a different regime applies in respect of consumer contracts). By ss 35 and 35A of the 1979 Act, a buyer who has the right to terminate the contract and/or to reject the goods ('rejection' is the statutory language in s 30 of the 1979 Act) for delivery of defective goods or delivery of the wrong quantity or late delivery may lose that right by 'acceptance' of those goods. Although 'acceptance' is clearly similar to 'affirmation', it is not identical.

19(8)

This makes clear that the right to terminate a contract for breach is triggered in one of three ways: the defendant commits a breach of condition; or the defendant's breach is of an innominate term that has sufficiently serious consequences for the innocent party in the sense that, as explained by Diplock LJ in *Hongkong Fir Shipping Co Ltd v Kawasaki Kisen Kaisha Ltd* [1962] 2 QB 26, 70, it deprives the innocent party of substantially the whole benefit of the contract (see commentary to s 19(9) below); or the defendant repudiates the contract. All three are commonly referred to as a 'repudiatory breach'.

If the innocent party has a right to terminate, the prima facie position is that it does not matter that it terminates the contract for a reason that is incorrect in fact or law: *Boston Deep Sea Fishing & Ice Co v Ansell* (1888) 39 Ch D 339. However, this is probably subject to the innocent party being estopped (by promissory estoppel) from later using the 'good' reason for termination by having led the other party to believe that it would not invoke that reason: see *Chitty on Contracts* (32nd edn, 2015) para 24-014.

19(9)

The distinction between conditions, warranties, and innominate terms—first set out in the seminal judgment of Diplock LJ in *Hongkong Fir Shipping Co Ltd v Kawasaki Kisen Kaisha Ltd* [1962] 2 QB 26, CA—is often presented in the books as part of the examination of the terms of the contract. However, as the practical importance of this distinction is in deciding whether the innocent party can terminate the contract for breach, it is more illuminating to focus on it here within the context of termination as a remedy for breach.

A condition is a major term of the contract any breach of which entitles the innocent party to terminate the contract. Although in practice one rarely needs to distinguish a warranty from an innominate term, a warranty is, in contrast, a minor term of the contract such that no breach will entitle the innocent party to terminate the contract.

An innominate term (sometimes referred to as an 'intermediate term') is neither a condition nor a warranty; and it would appear that most terms are now regarded as innominate. Where a term is innominate, the question as to whether the contract can be terminated turns on the seriousness of the consequences of the breach (judged at the time of the termination taking into account what has happened and is likely to happen: see *Ampurius Nu Homes Holdings Ltd v Telford Homes (Creekside) Ltd* [2013] EWCA Civ 577, [2013] 4 All ER 377 esp at [64]) rather than on the importance of the term broken. In deciding whether the consequences are sufficiently serious, Diplock LJ's test from the *Hongkong Fir Shipping* case is whether the innocent party is being deprived of substantially the whole benefit of the contract. He said, at 70:

'There are...many contractual undertakings of a more complex character which cannot be categorised as being "conditions" or "warranties"...Of such undertakings all that can be predicated is that some breaches will and others will not give rise to an event which will deprive the party not in default of substantially the whole benefit which it was intended that he should obtain from the contract.'

See also Sellers LJ at 63–4 who spoke of whether the breach goes 'to the root of the contract'. For further helpful discussions, see *Cehave NV v Bremer Handelsgesell-schaft mbH, The Hansa Nord* [1976] QB 44, CA; *Ampurius Nu Homes Holdings Ltd v Telford Homes (Creekside) Ltd* [2013] EWCA Civ 577, [2013] 4 All ER 377, at [44] and [64]; *Urban I (Blonk St) Ltd v Ayres* [2013] EWCA Civ 816, [2014] 1 WLR 756, esp at [44].

That the classification of a term turns on the intention of the parties (which must, as usual, be objectively construed) was made clear in, for example, *Bentsen v Taylor Sons & Co* [1893] 2 QB 274, 281 (per Bowen LJ) and *Bunge Corporation v Tradax Export SA* [1981] 1 WLR 711, 725 (per Lord Roskill). However, as shown particularly clearly in *L Schuler AG v Wickman Machine Tool Sales Ltd* [1974] AC 235, HL, the fact that a term is labelled a condition in the contract does not necessarily mean that the term is in law a condition rather than being an innom-inate term (or even a warranty).

Moreover, some implied terms are classified by statute as being conditions or warranties. Most obviously, the Sale of Goods Act 1979, first enacted in 1893 and codifying the common law, has long drawn a distinction between conditions and warranties. By what are now ss 12(5A), 13(1A), 14(6), and 15(3) of the 1979 Act the implied terms in a contract for the sale of goods (which is not a consumer contract) as to the goods' title, description, quality, fitness for purpose, and correspondence with sample are all specified to be conditions. By section 12(5A), the implied terms as to freedom from encumbrances and quiet enjoyment are warranties. However, s 15A of the 1979 Act lays down that, where the buyer does not deal as a consumer, and subject to a contrary intention, the implied terms in ss 13–15 are not conditions where 'the breach is so slight that it would be unreasonable for the [buyer] to reject [the goods]'. One can argue that, in effect, this comes close to applying an innominate term approach. Section 11(3) of the Sale of Goods Act 1979 explains the effect of the distinction between conditions and warranties.

The advantage of a term being classified as a condition is that the innocent party knows for certain that it can terminate on breach. This desire for certainty no doubt explains why, in commercial contracts, 'time clauses' are often conditions: see *Maredelanto Compania Naviera SA v Bergbau-Handel GmbH, The Mihalis Angelos* [1971] 1 QB 164, CA; *Bunge Corporation v Tradax Export SA* [1981] 1 WLR 711, HL; *BS & N Ltd (BVI) v Micado Shipping Ltd (Malta), The Seaflower* [2001] 1 Lloyd's Rep 341, CA; *Kuwait Rocks Co v AMN Bulkcarriers Inc, The Astra* [2013] EWHC 865 (Comm), [2013] 2 All ER (Comm) 689. However, the default position is that 'time is not of the essence' in contracts for the sale of land (Law of Property Act 1925, s 41) or for clauses requiring payment in a contract for the sale of goods (Sale of Goods Act 1979, s 10).

Example 1

By the terms of a contract, A, a seller of goods is contractually bound to load the goods on board a ship to be nominated by B, the buyer. B must give notice of the probable readiness of the ship for loading by 13 June. In breach of contract, B does not give notice until 17 June. A terminates the contract and seeks damages. A is entitled to do so because the breach by B is the breach of a condition. (This example is based on *Bunge Corporation v Tradax Export SA*.)

Example 2

B, the owner of a ship, lets out the ship under a two-year time charterparty to A. By a term of the charterparty, the ship is to be 'in every way fitted for ordinary cargo service'. In fact, the members of the crew are too few and too incompetent to deal with the ship's old-fashioned machinery. This leads to a delay in the first voyage undertaken by A. Although a new crew is to be substituted which is competent to deal with the machinery, A terminates the charterparty for breach with 17 months still to run. A is not entitled to do so (and is itself committing a repudiatory breach by refusing to go ahead with the contract). The relevant term broken is not a condition but an innominate term and the consequences of the breach of that term are not so serious as to justify termination. (This example is based on *Hongkong Fir Shipping Co Ltd v Kawasaki Kisen Kaisha Ltd*.)

Many contractual disputes turn on a 'race' to termination: that is, on which of the two parties was entitled to terminate the contract for the other's repudiatory breach.

This is a convenient point to mention that, although there is some uncertainty on this, it would appear that English law does not qualify the right to terminate by giving the party in breach a right to cure its defective performance. So while a buyer of goods may be bound to accept a good tender that follows a bad tender within the time fixed for performance (see *Borrowman Phillips & Co v Free & Hollis* (1878) 4 QBD 500), the buyer is entitled to terminate if the first bad tender is a repudiatory breach (see, for example, Peel, *Treitel on the Law of Contract* (14th edn, 2015) para 17-004).

19(10)–(11)

A repudiation (sometimes referred to as a 'renunciation') occurs where the defendant makes clear (and this may be by conduct as well as words: see *Chitty on Contracts* (32nd edn, 2015) para 24-018) that it is not going to perform at all or that it is not going to perform a condition or that it is not going to perform an innominate term such that the innocent party will be deprived of substantially the whole benefit of the contract: see *Federal Commerce and Navigation Ltd v Molena Alpha Inc, The Nanfri* [1979] AC 757, HL; *Geden Operations Ltd v Dry Bulk Handy Holdings Inc, The Bulk Uruguay* [2014] EWHC 885 (Comm), [2014] 2 Lloyd's Rep 66; *Chitty on Contracts* (32nd edn, 2015) para 24-018.

Commonly, repudiation occurs prior to the due time for performance. This is known as 'anticipatory repudiation' (see s 18(2) above). The importance of there being an anticipatory repudiation (sometimes referred to as 'anticipatory breach') is that the claimant does not need to await the due date for performance in order to terminate the contract and claim damages for breach. Rather the anticipatory repudiation can be accepted immediately as terminating the contract and as giving an immediate entitlement to damages. So the innocent party is entitled to terminate *at once*—and to recover damages *at once*—by 'accepting' the anticipatory repudiation: there is no need to wait for a failure to perform at the due date of performance. Classic cases illustrating this include *Hochster v De La Tour* (1853) 2 E & B 678; and *Frost v Knight* (1872) LR 7 Ex 111.

Example 3

In April, A agrees to engage B as a tour guide starting in June. In May, A changes his mind and informs B that he will not require those services. B is immediately entitled to terminate the contract for A's anticipatory repudiation and to claim damages for breach without waiting until the due date for performance in June. (This example is based on *Hochster v De La Tour*.)

As with repudiation on or after the date of performance, the innocent party has an election whether to accept the anticipatory repudiation as terminating the contract. If the repudiation is not accepted, the contract remains on foot which may ultimately mean that the innocent party ends up worse off than if it had accepted the repudiation. This may be, for example, because the contract becomes frustrated so that the right to damages is lost (as in *Avery v Bowden* (1855) 5 Ex B 714) or because the innocent party commits a breach of its own obligations so that the party who had committed the anticipatory repudiation is itself entitled to terminate the contract and to recover damages (as in *Fercometal SARL v Mediterranean Shipping Co SA* [1989] AC 788, HL).

English law's theoretical approach to anticipatory repudiation—and, in particular, to when there is a breach of contract—is opaque. It may be thought fictional to say that there is an implied obligation not to renounce the contract. But if there is no such implied obligation, it would appear that the innocent party can choose whether to treat the anticipatory repudiation as a breach (by accepting it or not) which is an odd idea. As Lord Mustill has written in '*The Golden Victory*—Some Reflections' (2008) 124 LQR 569, 579, 'a breach is a breach however the promisee reacts'. The apparent truth is that, while the rules on anticipatory repudiation are clear—the innocent party can choose to terminate immediately and thereby become entitled to damages at once (and with the 'duty to mitigate' being triggered at the same time)—the precise rational explanation for these rules is elusive. See Lord Sumption, citing Lord Mustill's article, in *Bunge SA v Nidera BV* [2015] UKSC 43, at [12]–[13].

19(12)

Commonly in commercial contracts the parties will include a termination clause which may entitle a party to terminate the contract in a situation where there would otherwise be no right to terminate. So, for example, there may be an express right to terminate on the occurrence of an event that does not constitute a breach (let alone a repudiatory breach). The parties may also deal expressly with what the consequences of that termination will be. Where there is termination under an express clause for an event that is not a repudiatory breach there is no right to damages for the future but there is a right to damages for past breaches: *Financings Ltd v Baldock* [1963] 2 QB 104, CA; *Lombard North Central plc v Butterworth* [1987] QB 527, CA.

There can be difficult questions of interpretation as to whether an express termination clause does oust what would otherwise be the law applicable to termination for breach: see, for example, *Rice v Great Yarmouth BC* (2001) 3 LGLR 4, CA, where it was controversially held that the express termination clause did not oust the general law. In consumer contracts, termination clauses that are unfair to consumers may be struck down under the Consumer Rights Act 2015: see s 17(5)–(11) of the Restatement.

19(13)

Among the special remedies given to a consumer by Part 1 of the Consumer Rights Act 2015 for breach of the rights conferred by the Act are a short-term right to reject, and a final right to reject, goods (s 19(3) of the 2015 Act). The short-term right to reject is explained in ss 20 and 22 of the Act and the long-term right to reject in ss 20 and 24. Both entitle the consumer 'to reject the goods and to treat the contract as at an end' (s 20(4)) (and note that, by s 19(13) of the Act, 'treating a contract as at an end means treating it as repudiated'). They can therefore be regarded as a special form of 'termination' provided by the legislation and as sitting directly alongside, and to some extent outflanking, the common law on termination. Certainly, one can regard the provisions as amending the common law on termination for breach in a contract for the supply of goods in the sense that the Act allows termination even though the terms in question are not classified as conditions and without any innominate term analysis. Moreover, by s 19(12) of the Act, where the consumer has a right to reject, and so to terminate, for breach of the rights conferred by the Act, then the consumer cannot terminate other than by the special remedies of rejection. But by s 19(11)(e) of the Act there can be termination at common law for breach of an *express* term (which may overlap with the terms which the Act treats as included so that, for example, it appears that there can be termination at common law for breach of an *express* term as to the quality of the goods). As regards a contract for digital content, s 42(8) of the Act lays down that it is not open to a consumer to terminate for breach of the rights conferred by the Act (although this presumably leaves open termination at common law for breach of express terms). (Cf s 28 of the Act, which deals with the consumer in certain circumstances 'treating the contract as at an end' because of non-delivery or late delivery but does not lay down that termination under the Act for breach of the 'treated as included' term as to the delivery or time of delivery is in any sense exclusive of the common law on termination.) See on these complex provisions, *Chitty on Contracts* (32nd edn, 2015) paras 38-486, 38-489, 38-521, 38-522.

---

20 Compensatory damages

(1) Where there has been a breach of contract, the claimant has a right to compensatory damages which—
    (a) have the purpose of providing a monetary equivalent to the claimant's loss caused by the breach;
    (b) are measured in accordance with the aim in subsection (2) (unless compensatory damages are being awarded as hypothetical release damages under section 22(4)(a)); and
    (c) are subject to the limits in section 21.

(2) The aim of compensatory damages for breach of contract is to put the claimant into as good a position as if the contract had been performed.

(3) In applying the aim in subsection (2), gains obtained by the claimant as a result of the breach will normally be deducted unless too far removed from the breach.

(4) In applying the aim in subsection (2), there is sometimes a choice between awarding—

    (a) the difference in value between the claimant's position after breach and the position the claimant would have been in had the contract been performed (the 'difference in value' measure); or

    (b) what it will, or has, cost the claimant to be put into as good a position as if the contract had been performed (the 'cost of cure' measure).

(5) If the cost of cure measure is higher than the difference in value measure, the former will not be awarded unless—

    (a) the claimant has incurred the cost of cure or intends to do so; and

    (b) it was, or will be, reasonable for the claimant to incur the cost of cure.

(6) The difference in value and cost of cure measures are usually assessed at the date of the breach of contract (the 'breach date' rule) but this is not an inflexible rule and may be departed from if, on the facts known at the date of assessment and taking into account section 21(1)(c), that rule would under-compensate or over-compensate the claimant.

(7) In applying the aim in subsection (2), the claimant can choose (as an alternative to a direct assessment of the position it would have been in if the contract had been performed) to be compensated for the wasted expenses, or other losses, incurred in reliance on, or in anticipation of, the contract; but by making this choice the claimant should not be put into a better position than if the contract had been performed (and the defendant has the burden of proving that the claimant would be put into that better position).

(8) In applying the aim in subsection (2), the claimant must prove the loss (applying the normal standard of proof on the balance of probabilities) subject to the following—

    (a) if the uncertainty relates not to a past fact but to a future or hypothetical event, other than the hypothetical conduct of the claimant, and the claimant has lost a substantial chance of making a gain or of avoiding a loss, damages can be awarded that are proportionate to the lost chance;

    (b) where the defendant had a choice under the contract as to the way in which the contract would be performed, damages will usually be assessed on the assumption that the defendant would have performed in the way most favourable to itself;

    (c) in some rare situations, special rules apply to proving the causation of personal injury;

    (d) in some rare situations, loss is presumed (for example, loss of credit is presumed where a bank in breach of contract fails to honour the claimant's cheque).

(9) In applying the aim in subsection (2), if the claimant is an individual who suffers a non-pecuniary loss as a result of the breach, damages may be awarded for that loss only—

    (a) if it comprises loss of satisfaction (such as enjoyment or peace of mind) or distress and it was an important object of the contract that the claimant should have satisfaction or should not suffer distress;

    (b) if it comprises physical inconvenience or discomfort or distress consequent on that inconvenience or discomfort; or

    (c) if it comprises pain, suffering, or loss of amenity consequent on the claimant's personal injury.

20(1)

Although some commentators (most notably Stevens, *Torts and Rights* (2007) ch 4; and 'Damages and the Right to Performance: *A Golden Victory* or Not?' in *Exploring Contract Law* (eds Bronaugh, Neyers, and Pitel, 2009) 171–98) have advocated radical new approaches to understanding damages for torts and breach of contract, the Restatement adheres to the traditional view that damages are usually concerned to compensate the claimant for the loss caused by the breach of contract. That is, damages are usually compensatory. Hypothetical release damages (that is, '*Wrotham Park* damages'), which may or may not be compensatory, are dealt with in s 22 as is an account of profits.

As made clear in s 20(1)(a), the loss in question must have been caused by the breach. This is a reference to what is often termed 'factual causation', which is usually determined by applying a 'but for' test (and indeed the standard 'as if' formulation of the aim of compensatory damages in s 20(2) is a synonym for the 'but for' test). In contract, the controversial issues on causation have tended to turn on the question of whether the chain of (factual) causation has been broken—which is usually referred to as 'legal causation'—and this is dealt with in s 21(1)(b).

It should perhaps be stressed at the outset that, while the Restatement attempts to set out the rules applicable to the assessment of damages as precisely as possible, some judges would choose to make clear that the assessment of damages requires flexibility and is not an exact science: see, for example, Upjohn LJ in *Charterhouse Credit Co Ltd v Tolly* [1963] 2 QB 683, 712: 'the assessment of damages has never been an exact science; it is essentially practical'.

20(2)

As regards breach of contract (and leaving aside hypothetical release damages), the loss in question is measured by reference to the performance that the claimant was entitled to under the contract. Hence the classic formulation by Baron Parke in

Robinson v Harman (1848) 1 Exch 850, 855, that the aim of (compensatory) damages for breach of contract is to put the claimant into as good a position as if the contract had been performed. This has often been described as the protection of the claimant's expectation or performance interest.

20(3)

That gains obtained by the claimant as a result of the breach must normally be deducted has been referred to in various ways. For example, one can talk of compensating the claimant's 'net loss' only; or of not compensating 'loss avoided'; or of not compensating loss that has been 'mitigated'. In the leading case of *British Westinghouse Electric and Manufacturing Co Ltd v Underground Electric Rlys Co of London Ltd* [1912] AC 673, HL, the greater efficiency of replacement turbines was deducted in assessing the damages for breach of contract in supplying defective turbines.

However, it would appear that, where the gain obtained is too far removed from the breach (that is, the benefit is completely collateral to the breach) it will not be taken into account: see, for example, *Lavarack v Woods of Colchester Ltd* [1967] 1 QB 278, CA (as regards the profit on the shares in Ventilation). There may also be policy reasons for particular benefits not to be deducted (for example, insurance proceeds are not deducted).

There is inconsistency in the cases as to whether, on a breach by a seller, sub-sales by the buyer which reduce the loss are taken into account. In principle, in line with the compensatory aim, they ought to be deducted, and that was the approach taken by the majority in *Bence Graphics Int Ltd v Fasson UK Ltd* [1998] QB 87, CA. For the contrary approach see, for example, *Slater v Hoyle and Smith Ltd* [1920] 2 KB 11, CA. See also in relation to sub-sales by a seller, following breach by a buyer in failing to pay for goods, *AKA Jamal v Moolla Dawood Sons & Co* [1916] 1 AC 175, PC, in which a resale of shares on a rising market was ignored even though this contradicted the compensatory aim. Lord Wrenbury said, at 179: '[T]he speculation as to the way the market will subsequently go is the speculation of the seller, not of the buyer; the seller cannot recover from the buyer the loss below the market price at the date of the breach if the market falls, nor is he liable to the purchaser for the profit if the market rises.'

20(4)–(5)

In seeking to put the claimant into as good a position as if the contract had been performed, there is sometimes a choice between awarding a 'difference in value' measure or a 'cost of cure' measure. In general terms, the lower of the two measures will be awarded. But this is not necessarily the case. Even though the cost of cure is higher, it will be awarded if the twin requirements in s 20(5) are satisfied as has been discussed in several well-known cases involving contracts to build, or to do other work, on another's land. See *Tito v Waddell (No 2)* [1977] Ch 106; *Radford v de Froberville* [1977] 1 WLR 1262; *Ruxley Electronics and Construction Ltd v Forsyth* [1996] AC 344, HL.

Example 1

In breach of contract, B fails to construct a swimming pool for A to the required depth, that is, it is nine inches too shallow at the deep end. The pool is perfectly safe for swimming and diving. It will cost £21,560 (which is nearly a third of the total price of the pool) for the pool to be rebuilt to the specified depth. The difference in value between A's land with and without the increased depth is zero. A is not intending to have the pool rebuilt to the required depth. A is not entitled to cost of cure damages of £21,560. (This example is based on *Ruxley Electronics and Construction Ltd v Forsyth*.)

Note, however, that in the *Ruxley* case the House of Lords did not confine the compensatory damages to the zero difference in value. Rather, £2,500 was awarded as 'loss of amenity' damages. The precise explanation for those damages is contro-versial, but one view is that they were compensating for non-financial loss (and therefore fell within s 20(9)(a) of the Restatement).

The interplay between factors (a) and (b) in s 20(5) is also controversial. On one view, if the claimant in *Ruxley* had already rebuilt the pool, or clearly intended to do so, he would have been entitled to the higher cost of cure damages so that reasonableness has a relatively limited role to play.

20(6)

It is often said that one assesses damages for breach of contract as at the date of the breach of contract: see, for example, the prima facie measure of damages for breach of a contract for the sale of goods laid down in Sale of Goods Act 1979, s 50(3) (damages for non-acceptance) and s 51(3) (damages for non-delivery), which refer to the market value of the goods at the date when they should have been accepted or should have been delivered, respectively. However, it is clear that a court is not precluded from taking into account events that are known about at the date of trial. For example, a loss of profit, or an expense, incurred after the breach can obviously be taken into account albeit that it may not be recoverable because ruled out by one of the limiting principles in s 21. Moreover, it was accepted by the House of Lords in *Johnson v Agnew* [1980] AC 367 that assessment at the date of breach, even in a contract of sale, is 'not an absolute rule' and that 'the court has power to fix such other date as may be appropriate in the circumstances' (per Lord Wilberforce at 401).

The best interpretation, therefore, is that the breach date rule applies to the basic measure of loss reflected in the difference in value or cost of cure measures and is not intended to apply to consequential losses (or gains). Even then, it is not an inflexible rule and should not contradict the compensatory aim. Indeed, it may merely reflect the idea that, usually, the 'duty to mitigate' (as set out in s 21(1)(c)) will mean that, as soon as there has been a breach, or very shortly after, the claimant must take reasonable steps to avoid the loss. So, for example, the references to the market value of the goods at the date of breach in the Sale of Goods Act 1979 reflect the fact that, at that date, the seller or buyer can reasonably avoid further loss by selling the goods to another buyer (where the buyer is in breach) or by buying replacement goods from another seller (where the seller is in breach).

The leading case of *Golden Strait Corp v Nippon Yusen Kubishika Kaisha, The Golden Victory* [2007] UKHL 12, [2007] 2 AC 353 (which, despite criticism by some academics, was followed in *Bunge SA v Nidera BV* [2015] UKSC 43, [2015] 3 All ER 1082) shows that the breach date rule will be departed from where it would contradict the compensatory aim.

Example 2

After three years of a seven-year charterparty between A (the charterer) and B (the owner), there is a repudiatory breach by A which is accepted by B. Some 15 months later, the Second Gulf War breaks out which, under a war clause in the charterparty, would have entitled A to cancel the contract in any event and it is assumed that A would have done so. Damages for B should be assessed at the date of trial on the basis of a 15-month remaining charterparty and not at the date of breach on the basis of a four-year remaining charterparty. (This example is based on *The Golden Victory*.)

20(7)

There has been considerable confusion about the role of so-called 'reliance damages' in contract. This confusion stems from the famous article by Fuller and Perdue, 'The Reliance Interest in Contract Damages' (1936) 46 Yale LJ 453, which has fuelled the belief that, in contract, 'reliance damages' are an alternative aim of damages to the normal expectation aim. At least as far as English law is concerned, it is now clear that that is a myth. Putting to one side *Wrotham Park* damages (see s 22), there is one overall aim of compensatory damages (seeking to protect the expectation or performance interest) and so-called 'reliance damages' are merely a method of achieving that single aim. A claimant, instead of directly seeking its lost profits, can alternatively claim its reliance loss, but, as the aim is still to put the claimant into as good a position as if the contract had been performed, two features follow: (i) a claimant cannot escape from what the defendant proves to be a bad bargain and (ii) even pre-contractual expenses may be recoverable. The formulation in the Restatement stressing losses 'in anticipation of the contract' and that 'the claimant should not be put into a better position than if the contract had been performed (and the defendant has the burden of proving this)' covers both these features. The most important case clarifying the correct understanding of 'reliance damages' is *Omak Maritime Ltd v Mamola Challenger Shipping Co, The Mamola Challenger* [2010] EWHC 2026 (Comm), [2011] 1 Lloyd's Rep 47. Other relevant cases are *Anglia TV v Reed* [1972] 1 QB 60, CA; *C & P Haulage v Middleton* [1983] 1 WLR 1461, CA; *CCC Films (London) Ltd v Impact Quadrant Films Ltd* [1985] QB 16.

Example 3

A, the owner of a ship, enters into a charterparty with B. Even though the market rate is higher than the charter rate (that is, the bargain is a good one for B), B repudiates the contract. A accepts the repudiation and enters into a substitute charterparty at the higher rate. A claims 'reliance damages' to cover the expenses it incurred in preparing to perform the charterparty with B. A's claim fails. Leaving aside *Wrotham Park* damages, the single aim of compensatory damages in contract is to put the claimant into as good a position as if the contract had been performed and, applying that aim, A has suffered no loss (on the contrary, A is significantly better off as a result of the breach). (This example is based on *Omak Maritime Ltd v Mamola Challenger Shipping Co, The Mamola Challenger*.)

In most contracts (where the aim is financial gain) it is helpful to think of the claimant who seeks 'reliance damages' as having the benefit of a presumption, rebuttable by the defendant, that reliance expenses (including pre-contractual expenses) would have been recouped had the contract been performed. But this is unhelpful where profit is not the aim.

Example 4

A enters into a contract with B, a musician, for B to perform at a concert held in memory of a friend of A's. A incurs expenses of £2,000 for the hire of a hall. In breach of contract, B fails to turn up. In seeking to put A into as good a position as if the contract had been performed, A is entitled to 'reliance damages' of £2,000. This is so even though one cannot sensibly talk of A recouping those expenses had the contract been performed because this is not a commercial contract.

20(8)(a)

The vexed question of when one can award compensatory damages in contract (and similar issues arise in tort) for 'loss of a chance' is best approached by recognising that damages for loss of a chance are an exception to the usual all-or-nothing standard of proof in civil law, which is proof by the claimant on the balance of probabilities. That usual standard applies to the assessment of damages where the uncertainty relates to a past fact as opposed to where the uncertainty is as to a future or hypothetical event: *Mallett v McMonagle* [1970] AC 166, 176, HL (albeit that that was not a contract case but a tort case dealing with the assessment of damages in respect of a fatal accident). Even where the uncertainty does relate to a hypothetical event, a balance of probabilities all-or-nothing approach applies, rather than a proportionate loss of a chance approach, if the uncertainty is as to the hypothetical conduct *of the claimant*: see *Allied Maples Group Ltd v Simmons & Simmons* [1995] 1 WLR 1602, CA (a solicitor's negligence case). It follows from this that it is where the uncertainty in assessing damages relates to a future event or to the hypothetical conduct of a third party, and provided not entirely speculative, that the courts award damages that are proportionate to the chances of gain (or the chances of avoiding a loss). The classic example is *Chaplin v Hicks* [1911] 2 KB 786, CA (uncertainty of winning a competition where the 'prizes' were jobs in a theatre company); and an assessment of lost profits is often dependent on uncertainty about the future or about the hypothetical conduct of third parties (for example, the damages, diminishing over time, awarded for loss of profits in *Jackson v Royal Bank of Scotland plc* [2005] UKHL 3, [2005] 1 WLR 377).

Example 5

A runs a national singing competition where the first prize (a recording contract) is judged by an independent panel. According to the rules of the competition, those who make it through the initial rounds will be informed by e-mail or phone and told of the arrangements for the final round. B makes it though the initial rounds but in breach of contract is not informed, as she should have been, of the final round, which goes ahead in her absence. B is entitled to damages assessed according to the chances that she would have won the competition.

Consistently with the *Allied Maples* case, in aiming to put the claimant into as good a position as if the contract had been performed, there is no assumption that the claimant would have been able to perform. Rather, if in issue, that must be proved by the claimant on the balance of probabilities. For confirmation of this, in the context of breach of a contract for the carriage of goods by sea, see *Flame SA v Glory Wealth Shipping PTE Ltd, The Glory Wealth* [2013] EWHC 3153 (Comm), [2014] QB 1080.

20(8)(b)

The law is not entirely clear as to how one assesses damages where the defendant has a choice of how to perform. It would seem, however, that one must first ascertain whether there is any choice and, if so, the scope of that choice, by interpretation of the contract. In some cases, the issue has been resolved at this initial stage because it was decided that what appeared to be a choice was, as a matter of interpretation, not a choice at all: see, for example, *Lion Nathan Ltd v C-C Bottlers Ltd* [1996] 1 WLR 1438, PC. Where, as a matter of interpretation, there is a choice, the usual approach is to assume that the defendant would have performed in the way most favourable to itself, that is, which would reduce the damages payable to the minimum (sometimes referred to as the 'minimum obligation' principle): *Re Thornett & Fehr and Yuills Ltd* [1921] 1 KB 219; *Lavarack v Woods of Colchester Ltd* [1967] 1 QB 278 at 294, CA; *Paula Lee Ltd v Robert Zehil & Co Ltd* [1983] 2 All ER 390; *Horkulak v Cantor Fitzgerald International* [2004] EWCA Civ 1287, [2005] ICR 402; *Durham Tees Valley Airport Ltd v Bmibaby Ltd* [2010] EWCA Civ 485, [2011] 1 Lloyd's Rep 68.

Example 6

A contracts with B to buy beef tallow, with the quantity specified to be '200 tonnes, 5% more or less'. In breach of contract, B fails to deliver the tallow. A's damages for breach of contract are assessed on the basis that B would have delivered the minimum amount, that is, 190 tonnes. (This example is based on *Re Thornett & Fehr and Yuills Ltd.*)

In principle, an alternative approach would be to look at the defendant's most likely performance on the balance of probabilities. Indeed, it is arguable that the 'minimum obligation principle' is merely a default rule that, in general, corresponds to the defendant's most likely performance (that is, parties do not generally exceed their minimum legal obligations) but which may be departed from where the claimant can establish on the balance of probabilities that the defendant would have exceeded its minimum obligation. A further alternative in principle would be to apply an approach that assesses damages in proportion to the chances that the defendant would have exceeded its minimum obligation.

20(8)(c)

It is not appropriate in a Restatement of Contract to deal with the tangled law on the causation of personal injury (which includes disease) given that all the leading cases have been tort cases. Suffice it to recognise that, while the usual civil standard of proof by the claimant on the balance of probabilities normally applies to causation of personal injury (so that one cannot generally recover for the lost chance of avoiding a particular injury: see *Gregg v Scott* [2005] UKHL 2, [2005] 2 AC 176) the line of cases on an employer materially increasing the risk of an employee contracting mesothelioma (which includes *Fairchild v Glenhaven Funeral Services Ltd* [2005] UKHL 20; and *Barker v Corus (UK) plc* [2002] UKHL 20, [2003] 1 AC 32, which prompted the Compensation Act 2006, s 3) represents a departure from that usual standard. In principle, the same approach as that taken in the tort cases ought to apply even if the cause of action were breach of contract (although there is some tantalising obiter dicta that may be regarded as suggesting the contrary in *Rothwell v Chemical and Insulating Co Ltd* [2007] UKHL 39, [2008] 1 AC 281, at [74] (per Lord Scott)).

20(8)(d)

In rare situations, the claimant does not have to prove a loss. Rather it will be presumed. The classic example in the context of breach of contract is that the claimant is presumed to suffer, and need not prove, a pecuniary loss of reputation where a bank, in breach of contract, fails to honour the claimant's cheque: *Kpohraror v Woolwich BS* [1996] 4 All ER 119, CA.

20(9)

The general rule remains that compensatory damages in contract law are concerned to compensate pecuniary loss and not non-pecuniary loss so that, in general, damages cannot be awarded for 'mental distress' (using that as an umbrella term) caused by the breach: *Addis v Gramophone Co Ltd* [1909] AC 488, HL (which concerned a wrongful dismissal); *Johnson v Gore Wood & Co* [2002] AC 1, 37–8, HL. However, apart from personal injury caused by a breach of contract (for which damages for pain, suffering, and loss of amenity can be awarded albeit that the claim is almost always brought in tort), there are two major exceptions which are set out as s 20(9)(a) and (b). Both were recognised, and applied, in the leading case of *Farley v Skinner* [2001] UKHL 49, [2002] 2 AC 732, where a surveyor negligently failed to report on aircraft noise.

The first exception (s 20(9)(a)) has its origins in the ruined holiday case of *Jarvis v Swans Tours Ltd* [1973] QB 233, CA, and, as regards relief from distress, *Heywood v Wellers* [1976] QB 446, CA (solicitor's failure to obtain injunction to stop molestation of the claimant by her former boyfriend). That the satisfaction or relief from distress should be an important object of the contract, rather than the predominant object, was made clear in *Farley v Skinner*. This exception appears also to be the best explanation of the award of 'loss of amenity' damages in the *Ruxley Electronics* case (see commentary to s 20(4)–(5) above).

Where the second exception (s 20(9)(b)) applies, the claimant can recover damages for the physical inconvenience and discomfort caused by the breach and for the mental distress directly consequent on it: *Perry v Sidney Phillips & Son* [1982] 1 WLR 1297, CA; *Watts v Morrow* [1991] 1 WLR 1421, CA (both negligent survey cases). Physical inconvenience was widely construed in *Farley v Skinner* to include inconvenience from noise.

As non-pecuniary loss is, by definition, only capable of being experienced by humans it cannot be recovered by a company (hence the words in the Restatement 'if the claimant is an individual').

Two points are worth adding at the end of this subsection because they are significant if one is considering how far the general rule against the recovery of non-pecuniary loss laid down in *Addis v Gramophone Co Ltd* continues to be relevant. The first is that, while no special rules apply as regards pecuniary loss consequent on a loss of reputation caused by a breach of contract (see *Mahmud v Bank of Credit and Commerce International SA* [1998] AC 20, HL), it is not clear what the law is on non-pecuniary loss consequent on a loss of reputation. In principle, as such a non-pecuniary loss is similar to mental distress, one would expect a similar approach to s 20(9)(a) to be applied. The second is that, although not part of the general law on damages, wrongful dismissal has recently been treated as requiring special restrictions on damages so as to avoid undermining the statutory regime of unfair dismissal: *Johnson v Unisys Ltd* [2001] UKHL 13, [2003] 1 AC 518; *Eastwood v Magnox Electric plc* [2004] UKHL 35, [2005] 1 AC 503; and *Edwards v Chesterfield Royal Hospital NHS Foundation Trust* [2011] UKSC 58, [2012] 2 AC 22.

21   Limits on compensatory damages

(1)   The following rules limit compensatory damages for breach of contract—

    (a)   the loss must not be too remote from the breach (see subsections (2) and (3));

    (b)   an intervening action of the claimant or a third party or a natural event must not break the chain of causation between the breach and the loss;

    (c)   the claimant cannot recover for loss that it should reasonably have avoided;

    (d)   if there has been the breach of a contractual obligation to use reasonable care, and there is concurrent liability in the tort of negligence, damages may be proportionately reduced for any contributory negligence of the claimant.

(2)   The general rule is that loss is too remote if that type of loss could not reasonably have been contemplated by the defendant as a serious possibility at the time the contract was made assuming that, at that time, the defendant had thought about the breach.

(3)   Irrespective of the general rule in subsection (2)—

    (a)   loss is too remote if the defendant did not assume responsibility for that loss;

    (b)   loss is not too remote if the defendant assumed responsibility for that loss.

21

This section deals with the principles that limit compensatory damages. In other words, these principles cut back the extent to which the claimant is entitled to be put into as good a position as if the contract had been performed. So, if one views s 20 as setting out the basic aim and important elements in applying that basic aim, s 21 contains the limits on that aim.

It would appear that the burden of proving all these limits is on the defendant: see, for example, *Philco Radio and Television Corpn of Great Britain Ltd v Spurling Ltd* [1949] 2 KB 33 (intervening cause); and, as regards the 'duty to mitigate', *Roper v Johnson* (1873) LR 8 CP 167, *Garnac Grain Co Inc v Faure & Fairclugh Ltd* [1968] AC 1130n, and *Geest plc v Lansiquot* [2002] UKPC 48, [2002] 1 WLR 3111.

21(1)(a), (2), and (3)

The law on remoteness in contract has been much discussed. The remoteness restriction is based on the view that it is unfair to a defendant, and imposes an unwarranted burden, to hold the defendant responsible for losses however unusual and however far removed from the breach of contract.

The traditional test for remoteness in contract was laid down in two rules (dealing with ordinary and exceptional loss respectively) in the best-known of all English contract cases, *Hadley v Baxendale* (1854) 9 Exch 341. It has since been refined, and commonly expressed as one rule, in cases such as *Victoria Laundry (Windsor) Ltd v Newman Industries Ltd* [1949] 2 KB 528, CA; *Koufos v Czarnikow Ltd, The Heron II* [1969] 1 AC 350, HL; *Parsons v Uttley Ingham & Co Ltd* [1978] QB 791, CA; and *Brown v KMR Services Ltd* [1995] 4 All ER 598, CA. The rule set out in s 21(2) is a synthesis of those cases.

Section 21(3) reflects the departure from the traditional test heralded by the judgment of Lord Hoffmann (see also Lord Hope) in the House of Lords in *Transfield Shipping Inc v Mercator Shipping Inc, The Achilleas* [2008] UKHL 48, [2009] 1 AC 61. What Lord Hoffmann focused on was whether the defendant had assumed responsibility for the loss. As subsequently explained in *Supershield Ltd v Siemens Building Technologies FE Ltd* [2010] EWCA Civ 7, [2010] 1 Lloyd's Rep 349, the 'assumption of responsibility' (or 'scope of duty undertaken') can override the traditional 'reasonable contemplation' test—which remains the general test—in two ways. First, as in *The Achilleas* itself, it may have an 'exclusionary' effect by making loss that would be recoverable under the traditional test too remote. This is reflected in s 21(3)(a). Secondly, it may have an 'inclusionary' effect, as on the facts of the *Supershield* case, by making loss that would be non-recoverable under the traditional test not too remote. This is reflected in s 21(3)(b).

It is unclear how one determines whether a loss is within or outside the assumption of responsibility and hence whether the general test will be overridden. Lord Hoffmann indicated that this all turns on the construction of the contract. But it seems more helpful to try to articulate the factors that appear relevant. So in *The Achilleas* itself it would appear that the general understanding of the law in the shipping industry was thought crucial; and in *Sylvia Shipping Co Ltd v Progress Bulk Carriers Ltd, The Sylvia* [2010] EWHC 542 (Comm), [2010] 2 Lloyd's Rep 81, at

[40], Hamblen J referred not only to 'clear evidence that such a liability would be contrary to market understanding and expectations' but also to where the application of the general test may lead to an 'unquantifiable, unpredictable, uncontrollable or disproportionate liability'. Another relevant factor appears to be whether the whole purpose of the duty was to guard against the risk that has eventuated, however unlikely.

Example 1

B contracts with A to carry a machine part to repairers to arrive the next day. What B does not know, because not informed, is that A's business has to shut down until the machine part is repaired and returned. Normally a business would have a spare part for the machine. The price for the carriage is a standard price. In breach of contract, B is late by several days in delivering the part. A's loss of profits during the closure are too remote from the breach and are therefore irrecoverable. (This example is based on *Hadley v Baxendale*.)

Example 2

B, in breach of a time charterparty, redelivers a ship to A, the shipowner, nine days late. A has entered into a follow-on time charter but, because of the breach by B, A is forced to renegotiate that follow-on charter. The market rate for hire has fallen since the follow-on charter was concluded and A has to accept a reduced rate, by $8,000 a day, on the follow-on charter. A claims as damages the loss of $8,000 a day for the whole of the period of the follow-on charter. These were the facts in *The Achilleas*. According to the House of Lords, that loss was too remote because B had not assumed responsibility for that loss; and it would appear that that was largely thought to be because of the understanding in the shipping industry as to the extent of liability (as well perhaps as the fact that that loss was unpredictable and uncontrollable). All that was held recoverable was the difference between the market rate and the charter rate for the nine-day overrun period.

Example 3

B, in breach of contract with A, the owner of a building, fails properly to install a float valve in a fire-sprinkler water storage system. Normally that breach would not have caused the building to flood because the drains would have taken away the overflow water. But on this occasion when the valve fails, the drains are blocked, so that A's building is flooded. These were the facts in *Supershield Ltd v Siemens Building Technologies FE Ltd*. According to the Court of Appeal, A's loss by reason of the flooding was not too remote because, although that type of loss was not reasonably contemplatable as a serious possibility at the time of the contract, B had assumed responsibility for that loss. This would appear to be because the very purpose of B's duty to fit the valve properly was to stop there being excess water and hence flooding.

21(1)(b)

Even though the defendant's breach of contract is a cause of the claimant's loss, the claimant will not recover damages for the loss where an intervening cause (whether a natural event or a third party's conduct or the claimant's conduct) is so much more responsible for the loss that it breaks the chain of causation. In other words, although the breach of contract may be a factual cause of the loss, it must also be a legal cause. No clear test or set of principles has emerged from the contract cases to determine whether the chain of causation has been broken or not. Indeed in some cases (the best-known being *Galoo Ltd v Bright Grahame Murray* [1994] 1 WLR 1360, 1375, CA) the courts have resorted to saying that it is simply a matter of 'common sense'. It is probably accurate to say the following: that it will be rare for a natural event to break the chain of causation; that, in the context of intervention by a third party, the courts will tend to ask whether or not the defendant had a duty to prevent the third party's intervention (*Stansbie v Troman* [1948] 2 KB 48, CA); and that, as regards the claimant's own conduct, it will be important to decide how unreasonable the conduct has been (so, for example, the chain of causation was broken in *Quinn v Burch Bros (Builders) Ltd* [1966] 2 QB 370 but was not broken in *Borealis AB v Geogas Trading SA* [2010] EWHC 2789 (Comm), [2011] 1 Lloyd's Rep 482). In the last situation, the statutory proportionate defence of contributory negligence may be available to reduce damages, but this defence does not apply where the contractual duty broken is a strict one: see s 21(1)(d).

Example 4

B, in breach of contract, fails to supply a step-ladder to A. A instead uses an unfooted trestle to climb up the side of a building and falls and injures himself when the trestle gives way. A's own unreasonable conduct breaks the chain of causation so that A cannot recover damages for his injury. (This example is based on *Quinn v Burch Bros (Builders) Ltd.*)

21(1)(c)

The claimant has a so-called 'duty to mitigate' whereby it must take all reasonable steps to minimise its loss and must not take unreasonable steps to increase the loss. Although very commonly used, the language of a 'duty' is here misleading because the claimant's failure to comply with that 'duty' does not constitute a wrong. All that is meant is that loss is irrecoverable where it should reasonably have been avoided by the claimant (that is, where it is unreasonable for the loss to be allocated to the defendant). For that reason, the Restatement has steered clear of using the language of a 'duty to mitigate'.

The classic exposition of the rule was by Viscount Haldane LC in *British Westinghouse Electric and Manufacturing Co Ltd v Underground Electric Rlys Co of London Ltd* [1912] AC 673, 689. Clearly what should *reasonably* have been avoided is fact-specific, but certain principles have emerged from past cases. For example, the claimant need not take action which will put its commercial reputation at risk (*James Finlay & Co Ltd v Kwik Hoo Tong* [1929] 1 KB 400, CA); the claimant need not take steps which would involve it in complicated litigation (*Pilkington v Wood* [1953] 1 Ch 770); the claimant need not make a claim against a third party who, in addition to the defendant, is also liable to the claimant (*The Liverpool (No 2)* [1963] P 64, CA; *Peters v East Midlands Strategic Health Authority* [2009] EWCA Civ 145, [2010] QB 48); and it will generally be unreasonable for the claimant to turn down an offer of alternative performance of a contract of sale, if acceptance would reduce its loss (*Payzu Ltd v Saunders* [1919] 2 KB 581, CA).

21(1)(d)

The law on contributory negligence (where the claimant has been at fault for its own loss) rests on the Law Reform (Contributory Negligence) Act 1945. Although contributory negligence is well-established as a defence for most torts, its applicability to contract has been unclear essentially because the definition of 'fault' in the 1945 Act is geared towards tort and not contract. The position reached in the cases, as a matter of statutory interpretation, is that set out in s 21(1)(d): see obiter dicta in *Forsikringsaktieselskapet Vesta v Butcher* [1989] AC 852, CA (affirmed on a different point [1989] AC 880, HL); *Barclays Bank plc v Fairclough Building Ltd* [1995] QB 214, CA; *UCB Bank plc v Hepherd Winstanley & Pugh* [1999] Lloyd's Rep PN 963, CA. This is hardly a rational position for the law to take, but the hands of the courts appear to be tied by the unsatisfactory wording in the 1945 Act.

In practice, it will almost always be the case that the breach of a contractual duty of care gives rise to a concurrent liability in the tort of negligence (see *Henderson v Merrett Syndicates Ltd* [1995] 2 AC 145, HL) so that one is largely left with contributory negligence being inapplicable to where the breach has been the breach of a strict contractual duty. So contributory negligence would not be applicable, so as to reduce damages, in Example 4 above: the contractual obligation to supply the ladder in that type of situation is a strict obligation.

If contributory negligence applies, then under s 1(1) of the 1945 Act, it leads to a reduction in damages 'to such extent as the court thinks just and equitable having regard to the claimant's share in the responsibility for the damage'. This is therefore a proportionate defence in contrast to the 'duty to mitigate' and intervening cause, which are all-or-nothing restrictions: that is, if one focuses on a particular loss, a failure in the 'duty to mitigate' that loss or a break in the causal chain to that loss means that no damages will be awarded for it; whereas contributory negligence in relation to a loss means that damages are reduced, not eliminated, for that loss.

22   Hypothetical release damages or an account of profits

(1) As an alternative to compensatory damages assessed in accordance with the aim in section 20(2), a court may award—
   (a) hypothetical release damages (commonly referred to as '*Wrotham Park* damages'); or
   (b) an account of profits.
(2) Hypothetical release damages are assessed according to the price which the claimant could reasonably have charged the defendant for releasing the defendant from the obligation that has been broken had the defendant approached the claimant immediately before committing the breach.
(3) Hypothetical release damages will be advantageous to a claimant where, for example, damages assessed in accordance with the aim in section 20(2) would be nominal because no loss can be proved or the loss is otherwise irrecoverable.
(4) The purpose of hypothetical release damages may be—
   (a) to compensate the claimant for, for example, the loss of the claimant's opportunity to bargain with the defendant;
   (b) to reverse a benefit acquired by the defendant from the breach; or
   (c) to value the contractual right that has been infringed by the defendant.
(5) An account of profits is assessed according to the profits made by the defendant from the breach and the purpose of such an award is to remove those profits; but such an award will be made only in very exceptional circumstances where all other remedies for breach (including hypothetical release damages) are inadequate.
(6) Punitive or exemplary damages, which have the purpose of punishing the defendant, cannot be awarded for breach of contract.

22

This section deals with two exceptional monetary awards: hypothetical release damages (commonly referred to as '*Wrotham Park* damages') and an account of profits.

22(1)(a), (2)–(4)

A very difficult and topical question in the law on contractual damages is the availability and purpose of '*Wrotham Park* damages'. In *Wrotham Park Estate Co Ltd v Parkside Homes Ltd* [1974] 1 WLR 798, houses had been built in breach of a restrictive covenant. Brightman J refused to grant a mandatory injunction ordering the houses to be pulled down. Damages assessed in the normal way (looking at what the claimant's position would have been had the houses not been built) would have been nominal because the claimant's land had not been diminished in value. Nevertheless substantial damages were awarded based on what the claimant could reasonably have demanded for releasing the defendant from the restrictive covenant. In fixing that reasonable sum the defendant's anticipated profit was taken into account.

In several contract (as well as tort) cases since then, damages assessed according to a hypothetical release have been awarded, irrespective of any claim for an injunction. In nearly all the cases, one can interpret the contractual obligation broken as being negative rather than positive, but the penultimate case of those listed below shows that that is not a necessary restriction. See, for example, *Amec Developments Ltd v Jury's Hotel Management (UK) Ltd* (2000) 82 P & CR 286 (breach of restrictive covenant); *Experience Hendrix LLC v PPX Enterprises Inc* [2003] EWCA Civ 323, [2003] 1 All ER (Comm) 830 (breach of obligation to hand over, and not to use, certain master tapes); *Lane v O'Brien Homes Ltd* [2004] EWHC 303 (QB) (breach of obligation not to build more than three houses); *Lunn Poly Ltd v Liverpool and Lancashire Properties Ltd* [2006] EWCA Civ 430, [2006] 2 EGLR 29 (landlord's breach of covenant of quiet enjoyment); *Pell Frishmann Engineering Ltd v Bow Valley Iran Ltd* [2009] UKPC 45, [2011] 1 WLR 2370 (breach of obligations in joint venture); *Vercoe v Rutland Fund Management Ltd* [2010] EWHC 424 (Ch) (breach of obligation to purchase a company jointly); *Van der Garde v Force India Formula One Team Ltd* [2010] EWHC 2373 (QB) [499]–[559], esp at [505]–[507] (breach of obligation to allow driving time); *Primary Group (UK) Ltd v Royal Bank of Scotland* [2014] EWHC 1082, [2014] 2 All ER (Comm) 1121 (breach of contractual, and equitable, obligations of confidentiality).

It is not clear from the authorities whether the claimant has a free choice to claim *Wrotham Park* damages or whether it is a requirement that damages assessed in the normal way (that is, to put the claimant into as good a position as if the contract had been performed) must first be shown to be inadequate. The better view, reflected in s 22(3), is that there is no such requirement albeit that, in practice, a claimant is unlikely to choose this mode of assessment (and hence *Wrotham Park* damages are in practice secondary) unless damages assessed in the normal way are small or nominal (as where no loss can be proved or any loss is irrecoverable because it is non-pecuniary and outside the limits in s 20(9)). To insist on inadequacy being a pre-condition would not only produce uncertainty at the margins as to what inadequacy means in this context but would also appear to produce the oddity that, the greater the loss the claimant can prove, the less likely it would be that *Wrotham Park* damages would be available.

In relation to any particular breach, *Wrotham Park* damages are an alternative to, and cannot be added to, damages assessed in the normal way: hence the opening words of s 22(1) ('As an alternative to ...'). This is because the assumption underpinning the damages is that the defendant has been released from the obligation in question so that it would be inconsistent then to add on damages as if the defendant had not been released.

Much academic ink has been spilt in trying to clarify the precise purpose of *Wrotham Park* damages. Are they compensatory, gain-based (sometimes referred to as 'restitutionary' or 'disgorgement' damages), or neither? While the courts have generally referred to them as compensatory, much of the reasoning in the cases seems more concerned with requiring payment for the value of a benefit obtained (including stripping away some of the defendant's profits from breach). It may also be thought artificial to think of the damages as compensating for, for example, a lost opportunity to bargain when the claimant would never have bargained away that right. Another approach (that is neither compensatory nor gain-based) is to say that the courts are here concerned to value the right that was infringed (that is, that these are damages 'substituting' for the right) and again there is language of the courts that supports this: for that approach, see Stevens, *Torts and Rights* (2007) ch 4. The Restatement (see s 22(4)) takes the view that all three are possible explanations.

22(1)(b), (5)

Section 22(1)(b) and (5) seek to reflect the law laid down in the much-discussed decision of the House of Lords in *Attorney-General v Blake* [2001] 1 AC 268. In that case, it was recognised for the first time in English law that an account of profits (sometimes referred to as 'restitutionary' or 'disgorgement' damages) can be awarded, in exceptional circumstances, to strip away a contract-breaker's profits. In the case itself, the notorious spy, George Blake, was held accountable to the Crown for the profits on the book he had written, in breach of his contractual undertaking to the Crown, about his life and work as a spy. Lord Nicholls stressed (at 265) that, in contract, such an award would be appropriate only in exceptional circumstances where all other remedies for breach would be inadequate. Lord Nicholls recognised that an account of profits is a standard award for the equitable wrongs of breach of fiduciary duty or breach of confidence and Blake's conduct had been close to constituting those wrongs.

However, in the light of the flexibility already given by hypothetical release damages (one purpose of which may be to strip a proportion of the defendant's profits), one can argue that there are very few situations in which an account of profits for breach of contract is justified. Indeed there has been only one case subsequent to *Blake* in which an account of profits has been awarded for breach of contract and the reasoning in that case is unconvincing (*Esso Petroleum Co Ltd v Niad*, 22 November 2001, unreported). It is therefore clear, more than a decade after *Blake*, that such an award will be made only in *very* exceptional circumstances. Moreover, given the dearth of cases, it is not possible to specify what those circumstances are, although, in addition to the inadequacy of all other remedies, it would appear that a minimum requirement is that the defendant has committed the breach deliberately calculating that it would be profitable to do so. Note also that, while in other areas in which an account of profits has been awarded, there has sometimes been an allowance for the defendant's work and skill (see, for example, *Boardman v Phipps* [1967] 2 AC 46, HL, breach of fiduciary duty), no such allowance was given in *Blake*.

22(6)

Under English law, punitive or exemplary damages cannot be awarded for breach of contract: *Addis v Gramophone Co Ltd* [1909] AC 488, HL; *Perera v Vandiyar* [1953] 1 WLR 672, CA. This can be criticised as marking an unnecessary contrast with tort, where such damages can be awarded if the facts fall within the categories set out in the leading case of *Rookes v Barnard* [1964] AC 1129, HL. The arguments for and against punitive damages continue to divide opinion and some would favour their abolition in tort let alone their expansion to contract. It is noteworthy that even the Law Commission, *Aggravated, Exemplary and Restitutionary Damages*, Report No 247 (1997), which favoured expanding the scope of punitive damages in tort so as to put the law on a more principled basis, did not recommend their being made available in contract. The recognition that an account of profits can be awarded, albeit very exceptionally, for breach of contract in *A-G v Blake* may be regarded as having filled part of the gap left by there being no possible punitive damages albeit that removing profit is distinct from, and less drastic than, punishment.

23 Agreed damages, penalties and forfeiture

(1) The parties may include a term in the contract by which a stipulated sum is agreed to be the damages payable in the event of breach.
(2) But the agreed damages will be payable (as 'liquidated damages') instead of damages assessed by the court only if the stipulated sum is not a penalty (which is unenforceable).
(3) The stipulated sum is not a penalty if, judged at the time of the making of the contract, it is not out of all proportion to a legitimate interest of the claimant in the performance of the contract (so that, in particular, a genuine pre-estimate of the claimant's loss from the breach is not a penalty).
(4) A term which requires a sum to be paid on an event other than breach cannot be a penalty.

(5) Although not concerning agreed damages, subsection (3) is also applicable to determine whether a term is unenforceable for being a penalty if in the event of breach the term—

    (a) requires the defendant to do something other than to make a stipulated payment (for example, to transfer shares); or

    (b) allows the claimant not to pay the defendant a sum that would otherwise be owed.

(6) Where a term allows the claimant, in the event of the defendant's breach, to take away ('forfeit') from the defendant—

    (a) a personal right to the repayment of money, or

    (b) a proprietary or possessory right,

that term may be unenforceable or the defendant may otherwise be granted relief against forfeiture (for example, by being given further time for payment).

23(1)–(3)

Parties commonly include a term in the contract setting out the amount of damages that will be payable in the event of breach. Provided the amount set out is 'liquidated damages' and is not a penalty, the courts will give effect to it rather than awarding damages assessed by the court in the normal way. The term 'penalty clause' is often a neutral description used to refer to an agreed damages clause without meaning to suggest that the clause is a penalty rather than liquidated damages.

In deciding whether the agreed damages constitute liquidated damages or a penalty, the classic test, as laid down by Lord Dunedin in *Dunlop Pneumatic Tyre Ltd v New Garage and Motor Co Ltd* [1915] AC 79, HL, is whether the sum is a genuine pre-estimate of the claimant's loss from the breach. That test should be flexibly applied in accordance with Lord Dunedin's additional point, at 87, that a sum is a penalty if it is 'extravagant and unconscionable in amount in comparison with the greatest loss that could conceivably be proved'. As Lord Dunedin also made clear, the parties' own use of the label 'liquidated damages' or 'penalty' is not conclusive.

The Supreme Court has recently reconsidered the law on penalties in the conjoined appeals in *Cavendish Square Holding BV v Talal El Makdessi* ('*Makdessi*') and *ParkingEye Ltd v Beavis* ('*ParkingEye*') [2015] UKSC 67. The Supreme Court made clear that, even though a stipulated sum is not a genuine pre-estimate of loss, it is not a penalty if it protects a legitimate interest of the claimant (in the performance of the contract) and is not out of all proportion in doing so. In other words, the traditional focus on (non-excessive) compensation is only one of the legitimate interests that the claimant may protect. Lords Neuberger and Sumption, at [32], formulated the test as follows: 'The true test is whether the impugned provision is a secondary obligation which imposes a detriment on the contract-breaker out of all proportion to any legitimate interest of the innocent party in the enforcement of the primary obligation.' See the similar formulations of Lord Mance at [152] and Lord Hodge at [255] supported by Lord Toulson at [293]. So, for example, on the facts of the cases, the legitimate interests included maintaining the goodwill of the company (in *Makdessi*) and encouraging the prompt turnover of car parking space and funding the claimant's business as car park managers (in *ParkingEye*). As the detriment on the defendant imposed by the clauses was not out of all proportion to those legitimate interests the clauses were not penalties and were therefore enforceable. In clarifying the law in this way, the Supreme Court may be regarded as having built on the approach articulated in *Lordsvale Finance plc v Bank of Zambia* [1996] QB 752, 764 (and followed in a number of subsequent cases) where Colman J said that a clause would be upheld if it was 'commercially justifiable, provided always that its dominant purpose was not to deter the other party from breach'. However, the Supreme Court stressed that it is unhelpful to regard deterrence as objectionable; and the notion of 'commercial justification' has been replaced by the emphasis on protecting a legitimate interest and doing so proportionately. The modern trend is of a reluctance by the courts, as regards commercial parties, to decide that a clause is a penalty; and note that where the defendant is a consumer the term may in any event be invalid if it is unfair under the Consumer Rights Act 2015, Part 2 (see s 17(5)–(11) above) although, on the facts of *ParkingEye*, it was decided that the term was fair (applying the Unfair Terms in Consumer Contracts Regulations 1999).

Lord Dunedin's classic test will no doubt continue to be useful at least in simple damages clauses in standard contracts (see [2015] UKSC 67 at [22]); hence its retention in the words in brackets in s 23(3). But the important step taken by the Supreme Court is to make it clear that the underpinning wider principle is one of legitimate interest and proportionality as set out in s 23(3).

Example 1

A enters into a contract with B (the operator of the car park) when A parks his car in a retail park car park. There is a clearly displayed parking charge of £85 if a motorist exceeds the two hours free parking time. A exceeds the two hours and is charged £85 by B. B is entitled to the £85 as 'liquidated damages'. It is not a penalty because B has a legitimate interest to protect and the sum charged is not out of all proportion in protecting that interest. (This example is based on *ParkingEye*.)

An agreed damages clause that is a penalty is unenforceable (or, arguably, void) and there is no question of partial enforcement. Instead, the standard law on (unliquidated) damages applies. See *Makdessi* [2015] UKSC 67 at [83]–[87].

It is worth adding that the recognition of the principle set out in s 23(3) makes it unnecessary to deal separately with what have been termed 'underliquidated damages'. It is clear that, even though not a genuine pre-estimate of loss, a clause that fixes a sum that seeks to limit the claimant's damages is not a penalty: *Cellulose Acetate Silk Co v Widnes Foundry Ltd* [1933] AC 20, HL; *Suisse Atlantique Société d'Armement Maritime SA v Rotterdamsche Kolen Centrale NV* [1967] 1 AC 361, 421, HL. This sort of clause is similar to, but different from a standard limitation clause, because the sum is payable even if the actual loss turns out to be lower than the sum stipulated.

23(4)

Although this has sometimes been criticised, it is clear that the law on penalties cannot be applied other than to payments payable on breach: *Alder v Moore* [1961] 2 QB 57, CA; *Export Credits Guarantee Department v Universal Oil Products Co* [1983] 2 All ER 205, HL. This was recently strongly confirmed by the Supreme Court in *Cavendish Square Holding BV v Talal El Makdessi* and *ParkingEye Ltd v Beavis* [2015] UKSC 67, at [12]–[13], [40]–[43], [239]–[241], rejecting the controversial decision of the High Court of Australia in *Andrews v Australia and New Zealand Banking Group Ltd* [2012] HCA 30, (2012) 247 CLR 205, which departed from the breach requirement. Indeed in *Makdessi*, Lords Neuberger and Sumption (with whom Lord Carnwath agreed) thought that the clauses were in any event primary, not secondary, obligations so that they fell outside the penalty jurisdiction. But a majority (Lords Mance, Hodge, Clarke, and Toulson) took a different, or neutral, view on this point.

It would appear that, on the present law, there is not only a breach requirement but also a formal approach to what constitutes a breach. It can be argued—and there is support for this in obiter dicta in *Makdessi* [2015] UKSC 67 esp at [258]— that, while retaining the breach requirement, the question as to whether there has been a breach should be approached as one of substance rather than form. If so, 'disguised penalties' (to use the terminology of Bingham LJ in *Interfoto Picture Library Ltd v Stiletto Visual Programmes Ltd* [1989] QB 433, 439, 445–6) would be within the law on penalties. Consider the following two examples:

Example 2

A agrees to construct a building for B for £2m. As a term of the contract, A promises to complete the building by 1 June 2015 and agrees to pay B £250,000 for each month by which the completion is delayed.

Example 3

A agrees to construct a building for B for £2m. A makes no promise as such about the date of completion. But by the terms of the contract, A is to be paid

£2m if the building is completed on 1 June 2015, £1.75m if it is completed on 1 July, £1.5m if it is completed on 1 August, and so on.

It is clear that the courts can strike down the late payment clause as a penalty in Example 2 because that is indisputably triggered by A's breach in completing the building late.

In contrast, the present law would appear to be that one cannot strike down the deduction clause in Example 3 because there is no breach. It would require a move to applying a substantive, rather than a formal, approach to breach if such a clause were to be struck down as a penalty.

23(5)

Section 23(5)(a) is inserted in the light of the decision in *Jobson v Johnson* [1989] 1 WLR 1026, which extended the law on penalties to a clause to transfer shares. This has been confirmed, and applied to the facts, in *Makdessi* [2015] UKSC 67, at [16], [157]–[159], [170], [230]–[233].

As regards s 23(5)(b), until recently there continued to be some controversy as to whether a clause allowing the claimant to withhold a sum owed to the defendant in the event of the defendant's breach could be struck down as a penalty. However, both in terms of authority and principle, the better view is that it can be: see, for example, *Gilbert-Ash (Northern) Ltd v Modern Engineering (Bristol) Ltd* [1974] AC 689, HL, at 698, 703, 711, 723; *General Trading Company (Holdings) Ltd v Richmond Corp Ltd* [2008] EWHC 1479 (Comm), [2008] 2 Lloyd's Rep 557. This has now been confirmed and applied to the facts in *Makdessi* [2015] UKSC 67, at [69]–[73], [154], [170], [226]–[228]. Certainly it is hard to see the substantive difference between a term that requires B to pay A £1,000 on breach and a term that, on breach, allows A to withhold £1,000 that it would otherwise have owed to B.

In applying s 23(3) in this context, as there is no stipulated sum, it is the detriment to the claimant under the clause that must not be out of all proportion to the legitimate interest.

There are obiter dicta in *Makdessi* [2015] UKSC 67, at [16]–[18], [156], [234]–[238], suggesting that a clause allowing the innocent party to retain a pre-payment by a contract-breaker may be a penalty as well as falling within the law on relief against forfeiture (see the next subsection).

23(6)

Although a forfeiture clause with which this subsection is concerned is different from a standard liquidated damages or penalty clause—and it is therefore incorrect to think, for example, that the 'genuine pre-estimate of loss' test has any role to play—this is the most convenient place in the Restatement to cover relief against forfeiture. This is not only because, like penalty clauses, forfeiture clauses are agreed sanctions against breach but also because the courts have the power (irrespective of any legislation) to strike down the forfeiture clause or otherwise to grant relief against the forfeiture (for example, by giving the contract-breaker more time to perform).

It has been thought helpful to consider in this one subsection, clauses dealing with the forfeiture of money paid and clauses dealing with the forfeiture of proprietary or possessory rights.

As regards the forfeiture of money paid (for example, where the contract refers to the payment as a 'non-refundable deposit'), it was held in *Workers Trust and Merchant Bank Ltd v Dojap Investment Ltd* [1993] AC 573, PC, that the forfeiture clause was unenforceable as a 'penalty' (although, traditionally, that language of 'penalty' has been thought misleading in this context) applying a test of whether the clause was reasonable. It was indicated that in a contract for the sale of land, repudiated by the buyer, the standard forfeiture of 10 per cent of the purchase price paid was reasonable: in contrast, the actual clause in question was to the effect that a deposit of 25 per cent of the purchase price was to be forfeited. It was therefore unreasonable and unenforceable. For other cases on the forfeiture of money paid, see *Stockloser v Johnson* [1954] 1 QB 476, CA (Somervell and Denning LJJ indicating that repayment would have been required if unconscionable for the money to be forfeited); *Amble Assets LLP v Longbenton Foods Ltd* [2011] EWHC 3774 (Ch), [2012] 1 All ER (Comm) 764, at [62]–[82] (Andrew Sutcliffe QC, sitting as a Deputy High Court Judge, regarding the test as being whether it was unconscionable to allow the forfeiture to take effect): cf, for a different, more restrictive, view of the courts' power to relieve against forfeiture of money paid, Romer LJ in the *Stockloser* case and Sachs J in *Galbraith v Mitchenall Estates Ltd* [1965] 2 QB 473.

There are obiter dicta in *Makdessi* [2015] UKSC 67, at [16]–[18], [156], [160]–[161], [230], [291], which suggest that: (i) both the law on penalties and the law on relief against forfeiture may be applied to the same clause albeit that the relationship between the two is 'not entirely easy'; (ii) a case like *Workers Trust v Dojap* may be best rationalised as applying the law on penalties (looking at legitimate interest and proportionality) rather than the law on relief against forfeiture.

For the power to relieve against the forfeiture of a proprietary or possessory right see, in particular, *Shiloh Spinners Ltd v Harding* [1973] AC 691, HL (power to relieve against a landlord's termination of a lease but not exercised on the facts); *Scandinavian Trading Tanker Co AB v Flota Petrolera Ecuatoriana, The Scaptrade* [1983] 2 AC 694, HL (no power to relieve against a shipowner's withdrawal of a ship in a time charterparty because a time-charterer has no proprietary or possessory right in the ship). For further decisions that there was no power to relieve, see *Sport International Bussum BV v Inter-Footwear Ltd* [1984] 1 WLR 776 (contractual licence) and *Celestial Aviation Trading 71 Ltd v Paramount Airways Private Ltd* [2010] EWHC 185, [2011] 1 Lloyd's Rep 9 (aircraft operating lease). For an example of the exercise of the power, see *BICC plc v Burndy Corp* [1985] Ch 232; and for the recognition that relief would have been granted had the relevant goods not been sold, see *On Demand Information plc v Michael Gerson (Finance) plc* [2002] UKHL 13, [2003] 1 AC 368.

Note also that, in a consumer contract, a term allowing forfeiture may be unfair and not binding on the consumer under the Consumer Rights Act 2015: see s 17(5) above.

See generally on this difficult topic of forfeiture (although written before *Makdessi*), *Chitty on Contracts* (32nd edn, 2015) paras 26-205–26-216; Peel, *Treitel on the Law of Contract* (14th edn, 2015) paras 18-065–18-067, 20-147–20-155.

24   The award of an agreed sum

(1) Subject to section 23, the claimant is entitled to the award of an agreed sum, by which the defendant is required to pay the sum that it contracted to pay, provided that the agreed sum is due under the contract.

(2) Subject to legislation (in particular, section 49(1) of the Sale of Goods Act 1979) the terms of the contract determine whether the sum is due or not.

(3) Subject to subsection (2), the following rules apply—

    (a) where the obligation or contract is interpreted as being 'entire', this means that substantial performance of it is required before payment is due;

    (b) where the obligation or contract is interpreted as being 'severable', this means that payment is due once there has been substantial performance of a specified part of it.

(4) Where the contract has been repudiated by the defendant, the claimant is normally entitled to hold the contract open, to perform (where it is possible to do so without the defendant's co-operation), and to be awarded the agreed sum due for that performance; but, as a rare exception to that normal rule, a claimant is not so entitled where to hold the contract open, to perform, and to claim the agreed sum would be wholly unreasonable.

24(1)–(3)

The award of an agreed sum is the commonest remedy for breach of contract. It directly enforces the debt owed under the contract. The sum owed may be the price of goods or land sold, or remuneration for work or services, or rent payable by a tenant to a landlord, or the repayment of a loan. It differs from liquidated damages in that the agreed sum is payable as a primary duty under the contract and does not represent the parties' agreed damages for breach of a primary contractual duty.

The simple and essential requirement for the award of an agreed sum is that the sum is due under the contract. Whether the sum is due is normally determined by the terms of the contract. But in general, and in the absence of any express provision as to advance payment, an agreed price for goods is not due until property in the goods has passed to the buyer (as laid down in s 49(1) of the Sale of Goods Act 1979); and a builder is not entitled to remuneration until it has completed the work or there has been 'substantial performance' of the work, or the stage of the work, to which the payment relates. For the emphasis on 'substantial performance' in a contract for work to a building, see *Dakin v Lee* [1916] 1 KB 566, CA, *Hoenig v Isaacs* [1952] 2 All ER 176, CA (in both of which there was held to be substantial performance), and *Bolton v Mahadeva* [1972] 1 WLR 1009 (no substantial performance). Where there has been substantial performance but incomplete or defective performance, the person performing the work is entitled to the agreed sum subject to a counterclaim (or set-off) by the other party for damages for breach.

A distinction is often drawn, especially in considering whether an agreed sum is due in the context of building and analogous contracts, between entire and severable obligations or contracts. This distinction appears merely to rest on recognising that an entire obligation or contract is one that requires substantial performance of the whole of the work (rather than a part) by the relevant party before the agreed sum is due. Most building contracts are severable/contain severable obligations requiring stage payments for parts of the work.

Note, however, the view expressed in Peel, *Treitel on the Law of Contract* (14th edn, 2015) para 17-040 that, in respect of an entire obligation, all the performance must be rendered before the money is due: that is, that the doctrine of substantial performance does not apply to entire obligations. So if the painting of a house is an entire obligation, Treitel's view is that the whole house must have been painted, even if defectively, in order for the agreed sum to be due. But this appears not to be the conventional interpretation of cases such as *Dakin v Lee* and *Hoenig v Isaacs*.

If the agreed sum is not specified, but is rather a reasonable sum, one may hesitate to refer to the remedy as the award of an agreed sum. Certainly, where the price or remuneration has not been fixed, the action has commonly been referred to as one for a (contractual) quantum meruit (in the case of services) or quantum valebat (in the case of goods). But in principle it is better to regard those contractual awards as covered by the action for, and the award of, an agreed sum. This is not least because the terminology of a quantum meruit and a quantum valebat is more commonly used to describe *non-contractual* restitutionary awards in the law of unjust enrichment (see *A Restatement of the Law of Unjust Enrichment* (2012) pp 32, 154–9).

24(4)

The first part of this subsection rests on the leading case of *White and Carter (Councils) Ltd v McGregor* [1962] AC 413, HL (Sc). It is sometimes expressed by saying that the 'duty to mitigate' that applies to compensatory damages does not apply to this remedy.

Example 1

A supplies to local authorities litterbins, on which it lets advertising space. B contracts to pay A for displaying adverts for a three-year period but, later the same day, B repudiates the contract. A refuses to accept the repudiation and displays the adverts for B for the three years and then claims the agreed price. A is entitled to the agreed price. (This example is based on the *White and Carter* case, although in that case the claimant, without actually performing for the three years, became entitled to the full payment, on repudiation, because of an accelerated payment clause.)

Lord Reid made clear that this principle can only apply factually where the claimant is able to carry on with its performance without the defendant's cooperation. Some subsequent cases have distinguished *White and Carter* by giving a wide interpretation to this restriction: see, for example, *Hounslow London Borough v Twickenham Garden Developments Ltd* [1971] Ch 233; *Attica Sea Carriers v Ferostaal, The Puerto Buitrago* [1976] 1 Lloyd's Rep 250, 256, CA.

The last part of this subsection deals with the exception to *White and Carter* which Lord Reid expressed as being where the claimant has 'no legitimate interest' in holding the contract open. Other judges have subsequently expressed this— hence the wording in the Restatement—as being where the claimant is acting 'wholly unreasonably': for example, *Gator Shipping Corp v Trans-Asiatic Oil Ltd SA, The Odenfeld* [1978] 2 Lloyd's Rep 357. However, whatever the terminology preferred, it is important to appreciate that, although *White and Carter* has been heavily criticised (see, for example, Burrows, *Remedies for Torts and Breach of Contract* (3rd edn, 2004) 440), the exception only applies in extreme cases (of which *White and Carter* itself was not one) so that the first part of s 24(4) is very much the normal rule: see *Ocean Marine Navigation Ltd v Koch Carbon Inc, The Dynamic* [2003] EWHC 1936 (Comm), [2003] 2 Lloyd's Rep 693, esp at [22]–[23]; *Reichman v Beveridge* [2006] EWCA Civ 1659, (2007) 1 P & CR 20; *Isabella Shipowner SA v Shagang Shipping Co Ltd, The Aquafaith* [2012] EWHC 1077 (Comm), [2012] 2 All ER (Comm) 461.

Example 2

A charters a ship from B for 17 months on terms that A is bound to carry out any necessary repairs during the charter. The ship develops engine trouble. It would cost four times more to repair the ship than the difference in value between the ship with and without the engine trouble. A repudiates the contract and accepts liability to pay for most of that difference in value. B refuses to accept the repudiation, insists that the ship is repaired by A, and claims the continuing agreed hire. B is not entitled to the agreed hire. This is an extreme case where B's conduct is wholly unreasonable because repairing the ship would have been so economically wasteful. (This example is based on *Attica Sea Carriers v Ferostaal, The Puerto Buitrago*.)

(Note the controversial decision of Leggatt J in *MSC Mediterranean Shipping Co SA v Cottonex Anstalt* [2015] EWHC 283 (Comm), [2015] 1 Lloyd's Rep 359, that holding open a contract, so as to claim continuing demurrage in excess of income lost, was wholly unreasonable. Leggatt J also reasoned that the 'wholly unreasonable' or 'no legitimate interest' qualification was an aspect of good faith in contractual dealings and is analogous to the idea that an express contractual discretion must be exercised in good faith and not arbitrarily, capriciously, or irrationally: see commentary to s 15(4) above.)

There is a final general point on the award of an agreed sum. The Restatement does not set out the law on set-off. That is because the relevant principles applicable to set-off, while very commonly concerning cross-claims *in contract* (especially for agreed sums, that is, contractual debts), extend beyond contract. Moreover, the law cannot be fully understood without examining set-off in insolvency and insolvency is a specialist topic outside the scope of this Restatement. Nevertheless, this seems the most appropriate place in the commentary to point out that, leaving to one side insolvency set-off, the general position on set-off is as follows:

(i) Legal set-off is applicable (so that there is a defence to the extent of the set-off) where there are cross-claims between the same parties for liquidated sums even if the cross-claims are unconnected: *Axel Johnson Petroleum AB v MG Mineral Group AG, The Jo Lind* [1992] 2 All ER 163, CA.

(ii) Equitable set-off is applicable (so that there is a defence to the extent of the set-off) where there are monetary cross-claims (whether for liquidated sums or not) between the same parties provided that there is such a close connection between the cross-claims that it would be manifestly unjust to enforce payment without taking into account the cross-claim: *Federal Commerce and Navigation Ltd v Molena Alpha Inc, The Nanfri* [1978] 1 QB 927, CA (affd [1979] AC 757, HL); *Geldof Metaalconstructie NV v Simon Carves Ltd* [2010] EWCA Civ 667, [2011] 1 Lloyd's Rep 517.

For a detailed examination of the law on set-off, see Derham, *The Law of Set-Off* (4th edn, 2010).

Alongside set-off, there is also the common law doctrine of 'abatement of price' whereby a person can set up, in diminution or extinction of the price for goods or work done, damages for defects in those goods or that work: *Mondel v Steel* (1848) 8 M & W 858; *Gilbert-Ash (Northern) Ltd v Modern Engineering (Bristol) Ltd* [1974] AC 689; Sale of Goods Act 1979 s 53(1)(a). See also the consumer's 'right to a price reduction' for breach by a trader of a consumer contract for goods, digital content, or services in Consumer Rights Act 2015, ss 19, 24, 42, 44, 54, 56.

25 Interest

(1) Under section 17 of the Judgments Act 1838, simple interest of 8 per cent per annum is payable from the date of judgment on a judgment debt such as the award of an agreed sum or damages.

(2) A term of a contract may specify the interest that is payable on an agreed sum or damages.

(3) Under the Late Payment of Commercial Debts (Interest) Act 1998 (the '1998 Act'), there is an implied term in a commercial contract (other than an excepted contract) that simple interest is payable on an agreed sum—

    (a) at base rate plus 8 per cent per annum,

    (b) for the period from the day after the relevant day (as defined in the 1998 Act) and prior to there being a judgment debt,

but the interest may be remitted, wholly or in part, because of the creditor's conduct and, subject to exceptions, the implied term may be ousted or varied by the agreement of the parties.

(4) For the purposes of subsection (3), a commercial contract is a contract for the supply of goods and services where both parties are acting in the course of a business.

(5) Under section 35A of the Senior Courts Act 1981, the courts may award simple interest on an agreed sum or damages from the date of the breach of contract until the date of judgment or, if earlier, the date of payment; but no interest can be awarded under that section if the payment was made prior to the commencement of proceedings.

(6) Interest, including compound interest, may be awarded as damages for breach of contract (or in an account of profits) in accordance with the rules in sections 20 to 22.

25(1)

Under s 17(1) of the Judgments Act 1838, interest automatically runs on a 'judgment debt' at a rate of, what since 1993 (see the Judgment Debts (Rate of Interest) Order 1993 (SI 1993/564)) has been, 8 per cent. By the relevant rules of court (CPR 40.8) the interest on a judgment debt runs from the date of the judgment unless the court orders otherwise. There is no discretion for a court to award judgment debt interest at a different rate than 8 per cent (other than where the award is being made in a currency other than sterling as provided for by s 44A of the Administration of Justice Act 1970). In county courts, judgment debt interest is governed by the County Courts (Interest on Judgment Debts) Order 1991 (SI 1991/1184).

25(2)

Where the claim is for a contractual debt (or damages for breach of contract) there is commonly a contractual term requiring the debtor to pay interest if the debt is not paid on time. The relevant rate of interest may also be set out in the contract. Such contractually agreed interest is, and always has been, enforceable in the same way as any other contractually agreed sum.

25(3)–(4)

The Late Payment of Commercial Debts (Interest) Act 1998, albeit dealing with a narrow subject-matter, is a (needlessly) complex statute and the usual warning about legislation given in this Restatement applies: to understand the statute properly, one must read it. What is contained in the Restatement is intended merely as an overall guide to the legislative provisions. See generally Peel, *Treitel on the Law of Contract* (14th edn, 2015) para 20-063; *Chitty on Contracts* (32nd edn, 2015) paras 26-232–26-235).

The contracts to which the Act applies are defined in s 2; the 'excepted contracts' in s 2(7) are a consumer credit agreement and a contract intended to operate by way of security. The rate of interest has been laid down by the Secretary of State in the Late Payment of Commercial Debts (Rate of Interest) (No 3) Order 2002 (SI 2002/1675), under the powers conferred in s 6. The period from when the statutory interest runs—which turns on the definition of the 'relevant day'—is extremely complex. It is principally laid down in s 4 (and for advance payments in s 11), but complexity has been added by the amendments to s 4 by the Late Payment of Commercial Debts Regulations 2013 (SI 2013/395) and the Late Payment of Commercial Debts (Amendment) Regulations 2015 (SI 2015/1336). By s 4 it appears that where no date for payment has been agreed, the interest normally runs from 30 days after the date (which, for shorthand, may be referred to as the 'performance/notice date') on which the creditor performed or on which the debtor had notice of the amount of the debt, whichever is the later; but if the parties have agreed a date for payment, interest runs from the day after that date or, if earlier than the agreed payment date, 60 days from the performance/notice date (or, if the debtor is a public authority, 30 days from the performance/notice date). By reason of s 3(2), interest under this Act does not run after there is a judgment debt because then the Judgments Act 1838, s 17, applies. The power to remit interest is contained in s 5: it applies 'where, by reason of any conduct of the supplier, the interests of justice require [it]'. Sections 8–9 deal with the circumstances where the parties cannot oust or vary the right to interest under the Act, in particular where the contract would not otherwise provide a substantial remedy for late payment.

25(5)

Under s 35A(1) and (3) of the Senior Courts Act 1981, the courts have a discretion (rarely, if ever, not exercised) to award simple interest at such rate as the court thinks fit, where a judgment is being given for a debt or damages, for all or any part of the period between when the cause of action arose and the date of judgment; and the same applies (with the relevant period being up to the date of payment) where there has been payment after proceedings have been commenced but before judgment. Note, however, that the 1981 Act does not apply, so that no interest can be awarded, if the debtor pays before the creditor has commenced proceedings to recover the debt (or damages). Under s 35A(2), the courts must award simple interest in relation to a judgment given for damages for personal injuries or death which exceed £200 unless the court is satisfied that there are special reasons to the contrary. The equivalent powers in the county courts are set out in s 69 of the County Courts Act 1984.

It is unsatisfactory that the courts under s 35A of the 1981 Act (and s 69 of the 1984 Act) have no power to award compound, rather than simple, interest. This is not least because arbitrators have such a power under s 49 of the Arbitration Act 1996. However, by reason of the *Sempra Metals* case (see the next subsection), compound interest may now be awarded *as* damages (rather than *on* damages).

25(6)

The old common law rule, laid down in *London Chatham and Dover Railway v South Eastern Railway* [1893] AC 429, HL, was that one could not award damages for non-payment of money owing. This was departed from in *Sempra Metals Ltd v Commissioners of Inland Revenue* [2007] UKHL 34, [2008] 1 AC 561. Although the actual decision in *Sempra Metals* concerned restitution for unjust enrichment, it was accepted that compensatory damages can be awarded for a proved loss of interest (including compound interest) subject to normal limiting principles, such as remoteness and the 'duty' to mitigate. In *JSC BTA Bank v Ablyazov* [2013] EWHC 867 (Comm) it was made clear by Teare J that, to recover compound interest as damages, that loss had to be specifically pleaded and proved; but a different approach, applying a conventional compound interest rate of borrowing, without the need for specific evidence, was subsequently applied by Males J in *Equitas Ltd v Walsham Brothers & Co Ltd* [2013] EWHC 3264 (Comm), [2014] PNLR 8. As regards an account of profits, it has long been recognised that interest (including compound interest) can be awarded within the court's equitable jurisdiction at least for claims for fraud and breach of fiduciary duty (see, for example, *Wallersteiner v Moir (No 2)* [1975] QB 373); in the light of *Sempra Metals*, that must surely also be true in the very rare case where an account of profits is awarded for a breach of contract.

26 Specific performance

(1) A court may make an order of specific performance which requires the defendant to perform a positive contractual obligation.

(2) A court will not order specific performance if, as will usually be the case, damages (or the award of an agreed sum) are adequate unless the contract is for the sale, or other disposition, of an interest in land.

(3) Even if (applying subsection (2)) specific performance would otherwise be ordered, it will not be ordered where any of the following applies—

    (a) the contract is one of employment or for personal services and the order is sought against—

        (i) the employee or person required to perform personal services; or

        (ii) the employer or person entitled to receive personal services unless the employer or that person retains trust and confidence in the employee or person required to perform personal services;

    (b) there would be a lack of mutuality in the sense that the defendant would have an inadequate remedy against the claimant if the claimant in turn failed to perform;

    (c) the order would require constant supervision;

    (d) performance would be physically or legally impossible;

    (e) performance would entail severe hardship for the defendant;

    (f) the order would be too uncertain;

    (g) the contract was not supported by consideration or, if there was consideration, it was merely nominal;

    (h) the defendant's consent to the contract was unfairly obtained;

    (i) after the making of the contract, the conduct of the claimant has been such that the order should not be granted;

    (j) the doctrine of laches applies (see section 30(7)).

(4) By reason of section 58 of the Consumer Rights Act 2015, some of the above bars (for example, the bar in subsection (2)) do not apply where an order of specific performance is sought enforcing a consumer's legislative right against a trader to the repair or replacement of goods or digital content or the repeat performance of a service.

(5) Specific performance may be ordered on terms.

(6) Specific performance is a final and not an interim order so that it can only be ordered at trial although a court can grant an interim mandatory injunction requiring performance of a positive contractual obligation.

26(1)–(2)

Specific performance is an equitable, rather than a common law, remedy (that is, it historically derives from the Court of Chancery rather than the common law courts). It orders the defendant to perform its positive contractual obligations. In English law, in contrast to some civilian systems, specific performance is thought of as a secondary remedy to compensatory damages (for criticism of this see, for example, Schwartz, 'The Case for Specific Performance' (1979) 89 Yale LJ 271). This links in to the important initial hurdle that a claimant must overcome, namely that, as set out in s 26(2), specific performance will not be ordered if damages (or the award of an agreed sum) are adequate. In a contract of sale, the major determinant of inadequacy is the uniqueness of the subject-matter so that specific performance is conventionally ordered in contracts for the sale, or other disposition, of an interest in land because historically each piece of land has been thought of as unique. Nowadays contracts for the sale of land are best viewed as an exception to the adequacy bar in the sense that specific performance is the primary remedy for both parties in such a contract without the need to establish on the facts that damages would be inadequate. On the basis that, on the facts, damages were inadequate, specific performance has been ordered of contracts to sell physically unique goods (*Falcke v Gray* (1859) 4 Drew 651) and even (through an interim injunction amounting to temporary specific performance) of contracts to sell goods which may be described as 'commercially unique' because buying substitutes would involve such difficulty or delay that the claimant's business would be severely disrupted (*Sky Petroleum Ltd v VIP Petroleum Ltd* [1974] 1 WLR 576; cf *Société des Industries Metallurgiques SA v Bronx Engineering Co Ltd* [1975] 1 Lloyd's Rep 465, CA).

It is worth pointing out here that there has been very little discussion in the cases of a contract in which the parties stipulate that specific performance should be the remedy for breach. It is likely that the courts would apply the law that would in any event apply and would treat such a contract as invalidly ousting their jurisdiction and as therefore contrary to public policy.

26(3)

There are a number of additional bars to specific performance which apply even if damages are inadequate or the contract is one for the sale, or other disposition, of an interest in land.

26(3)(a)

This bar to specific performance against an employee reflects the common law (*De Francesco v Barnum* (1890) 45 Ch D 430) and is embodied in the Trade Union and Labour Relations (Consolidation) Act 1992, s 236.

In contrast, there is no absolute bar to specific performance being ordered against an employer. An exception applies where the employer retains trust and confidence in the employee: see, for example, *Powell v Brent London Borough Council* [1988] ICR 176, CA; *Ashworth v Royal National Theatre* [2014] EWHC 1176 (QB), [2014]

4 All ER 238. However, in the latter case, it was held that specific performance would not be granted at trial requiring the National Theatre to carry on employing musicians in the performance of the play *War Horse* because 'loss of confidence is fact-specific' [23] and there was 'clearly an absence of personal confidence on the part of the National Theatre, which considered that the musicians could not contribute positively to the play' [25]. Cranston J thought it additionally important that such an order would interfere with the National Theatre's right of artistic freedom (protected by Article 10 of the European Convention on Human Rights and s 12 of the Human Rights Act 1998).

26(3)(b)

This seeks to reflect the decision and reasoning in the leading case of *Price v Strange* [1978] Ch 337, CA.

26(3)(c)

The traditional view derived from *Ryan v Mutual Tontine Westminster Chambers Assoc* [1893] 1 Ch 116, CA, and recently authoritatively confirmed in *Cooperative Insurance Society Ltd v Argyll Stores (Holdings) Ltd* [1998] AC 1, HL, is that specific performance is barred where the order would require constant supervision. It is not obvious that this should be so and a number of cases have supported the view that, provided the order would not be too uncertain (see s 26(3)(f)), there is no separate constant supervision objection: see, for example, *Wolverhampton Corpn v Emmons* [1901] 1 KB 515, CA; *Tito v Waddell (No 2)* [1977] Ch 106, 322; *Rainbow Estates Ltd v Tokenhold Ltd* [1999] Ch 64, 73. After all, defendants can be expected to comply with court orders that are backed up, as specific performance is, by the law of contempt so that the problem of constant supervision may be more theoretical than real. In any event, if specific performance is otherwise the appropriate remedy, one can argue that that should not be outweighed by the mere fear of extra costs in enforcement. However, in *Cooperative Insurance Society Ltd v Argyll Stores (Holdings) Ltd* [1998] AC 1 the House of Lords reaffirmed the constant supervision objection in overturning an order for specific performance of a covenant in a 35-year lease to keep premises open for retail trade during usual hours of business. Lord Hoffmann drew a difficult distinction between orders to carry on activities (as on the facts) to which the constant supervision bar was relevant and orders to achieve results (his Lordship treated building contracts as falling within the latter category) to which the bar was irrelevant. It was in any event thought that the order could not be drawn up with sufficient precision. Irrespective of that, one can argue that the more convincing reason than constant supervision for denying specific performance was that, to comply with the order, the defendant would be forced to carry on with a business that was losing money: and that can be seen as an aspect of the severe hardship bar (see s 26(3)(e)).

26(3)(d)

Authorities on this bar include *Ferguson v Wilson* (1866) Ch App 77 and *Warmington v Miller* [1973] QB 877.

26(3)(e)

See, for example, *Wroth v Tyler* [1974] Ch 30 and *Patel v Ali* [1984] Ch 283.

26(3)(f)

Authorities on this bar include *Joseph v National Magazine Co* [1959] Ch 14; and *Co-operative Insurance Society Ltd v Argyll Stores (Holdings) Ltd* [1998] 1 AC 1, 13–14, 16.

26(3)(g)

A contract may be valid even though there is no valuable consideration as where it is made by deed or for nominal consideration. However, applying the maxim 'equity will not assist a volunteer' (this maxim applies because specific performance is an equitable remedy), specific performance will not be ordered of such a contract: see, for example, *Cannon v Hartley* [1949] Ch 213.

26(3)(h)

In many situations a contract will be voidable where it has been unfairly obtained as, for example, by misrepresentation or duress. Even if the contract is not voidable, specific performance may be denied because of the claimant's unfair conduct in obtaining the contract: see, for example, *Walters v Morgan* (1861) 3 De G F & J 718; *Webster v Cecil* (1861) 30 Beav 62.

26(3)(i)

This falls within the maxims 'he who comes to equity must come with clean hands' or 'he who seeks equity must do equity': *Lamare v Dixon* (1873) LR 6 HL 414; *Chappell v Times Newspapers Ltd* [1975] 1 WLR 482, CA. These maxims apply because specific performance is an equitable remedy. They perform a similar role to, for example, the law on illegality (which is a common law doctrine).

26(3)(j)

The doctrine of laches is dealt with at s 30(7). Examples of its application to bar specific performance include *Milward v Earl of Thanet* (1801) 5 Ves 720n; and *Lazard Bros & Co Ltd v Fairfield Properties Co (Mayfair) Ltd* (1977) 121 Sol Jo 793. There is no limitation period for specific performance directly laid down in the Limitation Act 1980 and, in the important decision in *P & O Nedlloyd BV v Arab Metals Co* [2006] EWCA Civ 1717, [2007] 2 All ER (Comm) 401, it was held that the standard six-year period for contract claims under s 5 of the 1980 Act does not apply to specific performance by analogy under s 36(1) of the 1980 Act. This means that only laches, and not a statutory limitation period, is applicable to specific performance (and, by similar reasoning, the same applies to injunctions).

26(4)

There are special remedies provided for a consumer in Part 1 of the Consumer Rights Act 2015(see commentary to s 18(4) above). By ss 19 and 23 and ss 42–43 of the Consumer Rights Act 2015, these include that a consumer, who has a contract for the supply of goods or digital content by a trader, has a right to the repair or replacement, within a reasonable time, of goods or digital content which do not conform to the contract terms (as defined in s 19(1)–(2) and s 42(1)) unless repair or replacement is impossible or disproportionate (compared to the other of those two rights). Similarly, by ss 54–55 of the 2015 Act a consumer, who has a contract for the supply of a service by a trader, has a right to require repeat performance, within a reasonable time and unless impossible, where the performance has not been in conformity with the contract terms (as defined in s 54(2)). By section 58 of the 2015 Act (which is headed 'powers of the court'), the courts are expressly given the power to enforce these special remedies—the right to repair or replacement, or the right to repeat performance—by an order of specific performance.

It is important to appreciate that s 58 of the 2015 Act on specific performance, enforcing a consumer's legislative right to repair or replacement, or the right to repeat performance, represents a move away in this area from the normal require-ment for specific performance that damages must be inadequate (see s 26(2) of the Restatement). It appears that (subject to the court's discretion to decide that another relevant special remedy is appropriate under s 58(3) of the 2015 Act) a court should only refuse specific performance (ordering repair or replacement of goods or digital content or ordering the repeat performance of services) if impos-sible or, as between repair and replacement, disproportionate to the other (ss 23(3), 43(3), 55(3) of the 2015 Act). Hence s 26(4) of the Restatement should be seen as an exception to s 26(2) of the Restatement. Indeed the law on specific performance under the 2015 Act can be seen as departing not only from the adequacy of damages requirement but also, on the face of it, from several other of the bars set out in s 26 (3) of the Restatement (for example, the bars concerning personal services, mutu-ality, constant supervision, and severe hardship to the defendant).

26(5)

A common example of this is where the vendor of land seeks specific performance against the purchaser and there is some non-substantial defect in the property. Specific performance may be ordered 'with compensation' (that is, subject to the vendor paying compensation to the purchaser to cover the defect): *Re Fawcett and Holmes' Contract* (1889) 42 Ch D 150; *Shepherd v Croft* [1911] 1 Ch 521.

26(6)

A court cannot make an order of specific performance pre-trial. An interim mandatory injunction can be awarded requiring the defendant to perform a positive contractual obligation (for an example, see *Astro Exito Navegacion SA v Southland Enterprise Co Ltd, The Messiniaki Tolmi* [1982] QB 1248, CA); but, not least because the claimant's right has not been established at trial, the courts are reluctant to grant such an injunction (see, generally, *Zockoll Group Ltd v Mercury Communications Ltd* [1998] FSR 354, CA).

27 Injunction

(1) A court may grant a prohibitory injunction which orders the defendant not to break a negative contractual obligation.

(2) A prohibitory injunction ordering the defendant not to break a negative contractual obligation will readily be granted so that, even if the adequacy of damages is a reason to refuse such an injunction, it will be a rare case in which, in this context, damages will be regarded as adequate.

(3) Equivalent bars to those set out for specific performance in section 26(3)(e) to (j) apply to bar a prohibitory injunction.

(4) A prohibitory injunction ordering the defendant not to break a negative contractual obligation will not be granted if its indirect practical effect would be to order the defendant to perform a positive contractual obligation in respect of which a court would not order specific performance (for example, because it would require performance of personal services).

(5) A court may grant a mandatory restorative injunction which orders the defendant to undo what it has done in breach of contract.

(6) An injunction may be a final or an interim order.

27(1)

The prohibitory injunction is the appropriate remedy for restraining the breach of a negative contractual obligation. It therefore belongs on the reverse side of the coin from the remedy of specific performance, which orders the performance of positive contractual obligations. Like specific performance, an injunction is an equitable remedy (and, although no example of this has been found in the cases, it is presumably correct that, like specific performance, an injunction can be ordered on terms: see s 26(5)).

27(2)

In contrast to specific performance in respect of positive contractual obligations, a prohibitory injunction is the primary remedy for breach of a negative contractual obligation. This is because, although it is conventional to think of there being an adequacy of damages bar, it is very rare for damages to be thought adequate in this negative obligation context. See, for example, Lord Cairns LC in *Doherty v Allman* (1878) 3 App Cas 709, 720; *Araci v Fallon* [2011] EWCA Civ 668; *AB v CD* [2014] EWCA Civ 229, [2015] 1 WLR 771. This is presumably because it is considered less of an infringement of individual liberty to be ordered not to do something than to do something. Indeed so rare is it for damages to be adequate in this context, that it may be better to regard there as being no such bar (see Elias LJ in *Araci v Fallon* at [70]).

27(3)

To say that the prohibitory injunction is the primary remedy does not mean that it will never be refused. It would appear that bars equivalent to the last six set out in relation to specific performance also apply to an injunction. For one example (equivalent to s 26(3)(i) concerned with the claimant's reprehensible conduct) resulting in the refusal of a prohibitory injunction to restrain a breach of contract, see *Telegraph Despatch and Intelligence Co v McLean* (1873) LR 8 Ch App 658, CA.

27(4)

In the famous case of *Lumley v Wagner* (1852) 21 LJ Ch 898, it was decided that an injunction restraining Johanna Wagner from singing at a rival's theatre should be ordered because that did not constitute indirect specific performance of her contractual obligation to sing at the claimant's theatre (which would not have been ordered). This was followed in *Warner Bros Pictures Ltd v Nelson* [1937] 1 KB 209 although a different approach was taken in *Page One Records v Britton* [1968] 1 WLR 157. In *Warren v Mendy* [1989] 1 WLR 853, 865, CA, the approach in the latter case was preferred on the grounds of 'realism and practicality' and *Warner Bros* was disapproved. *Lumley v Wagner* was distinguished because of the short contract period involved.

Example

B is employed by A as a professional footballer. There is a restrictive covenant in B's employment contract whereby, without A's consent, B is not to play for any other team while employed by A or within one year of leaving A. In breach of contract, B leaves A and starts to play for C. A seeks an injunction to restrain B from playing for C. Even if the restrictive covenant is valid, A will not be granted the injunction because it would indirectly amount to specific performance, against an employee, of a contract of employment.

However, matters have been thrown into doubt by *LauritzenCool AB v Lady Navigation Inc* [2005] EWCA Civ 579, [2005] 1 WLR 3686. In upholding the grant of an injunction to restrain a shipowner from breaking a time charter by employing the ship with any other charterer, the Court of Appeal drew a controversial distinction between a prohibitory injunction that *juristically* would amount to specific performance and one that *as a practical matter* would amount to specific performance. Bars to specific performance were thought applicable to the former but not the latter. Yet surely it is the practical effect that is important. If the injunction would in practice force the defendant to perform, and yet specific performance would be barred, the injunction should not be granted. It may be, therefore, that what was driving this decision was a doubt as to the correctness of the traditional rule that specific performance cannot be ordered of a time charter because it requires the performance of personal services.

27(5)

A mandatory restorative injunction can be ordered for breach of contract. The most common example that has arisen in the cases is where there has been building in breach of a restrictive covenant. The court may order the building to be pulled down or modified. The principles applicable to this type of injunction are far from clear although, because of the positive conduct required and the often drastic consequences for the defendant, such an injunction is far more difficult to obtain than a prohibitory injunction. A mandatory restorative injunction was refused in *Shepherd Homes Ltd v Sandham* [1971] Ch 340 (although the injunction sought there was interim), *Wrotham Park Estate Co Ltd v Parkside Homes Ltd* [1974] 1 WLR 798, and *Gifford v Graham* [1999] 3 EGLR 75, CA; but was granted in *Charrington v Simons & Co Ltd* [1971] 1 WLR 598, *Wakeham v Wood* (1982) 43 P & CR 40, and *Mortimer v Bailey* [2004] EWCA Civ 1514, [2005] 2 P & CR 9.

27(6)

Where an interim prohibitory injunction is sought, the standard approach of the courts (and there is no reason to think that this is not also applied in respect of breach of contract) is that laid down in *American Cyanamid Co v Ethicon Ltd* [1975] AC 396, HL. According to this, the claimant must show that there is a serious question to be tried and that the balance of convenience favours the grant of the interim injunction. However, as has been mentioned under s 26(6), the courts are reluctant to order an interim mandatory injunction and, in respect of that type of injunction, it would appear that *American Cyanamid* is not applied.

28 Damages in substitution for specific performance or an injunction

(1) Under section 50 of the Senior Courts Act 1981, a court may award damages in substitution for specific performance or an injunction.

(2) Subject to subsection (3), the purpose and assessment of such damages is governed by sections 20 to 22 above.

(3) Such damages can be awarded even though the claimant does not have a cause of action for breach of contract because, for example, a breach of contract is anticipated but has not yet occurred.

28

The damages that are almost invariably granted for breach of contract are common law damages. So-called 'equitable damages', which can be awarded in substitution for an injunction or specific performance under the Senior Courts Act 1981, s 50 (originally Lord Cairns's Act), offer no advantage over common law damages in the sense that they are assessed in the same way: *Johnson v Agnew* [1980] AC 367, HL. However, there is one major practical advantage, which is that a claimant can be awarded damages under s 50 even though it has no action for breach of contract: see *Tulk v Moxhay* (1848) 18 LJ Ch 83 (equitable damages awarded even though, at common law, third party had no action for breach of a restrictive covenant); *Oakacre Ltd v Claire Cleaners (Holdings) Ltd* [1982] Ch 197 (equitable damages for anticipated breach even though no action at common law); *English Private Law* (ed Burrows, 3rd edn, 2013) paras 21.141–21.142.

29 Declaration and nominal damages

(1) A court may make a declaration as to a party's contractual rights or remedies.

(2) Where there has been a breach of contract and no other monetary award is being made, the claimant has a right to nominal damages which have the purpose of recognising formally that there has been a breach of contract.

29(1)

While all judicial remedies impliedly declare what the parties' rights are, a declaration is a remedy, generally regarded as statutory albeit with equitable roots, by which a court pronounces on, without altering, the rights (or the remedies) of the parties. The power to make a declaration is contained in Civil Procedure Rules (CPR) 40.20 and, under CPR 25.1(1)(b), there is now power to grant an interim declaration. A declaration is available in relation to any kind of legal right and is readily granted. Normally, however, there must be a dispute between the parties. For example, in *Meadows Indemnity Co Ltd v Insurance Corpn of Ireland Ltd* [1989] 2 Lloyd's Rep 298, CA, a declaration sought by a reinsurer as to the invalidity of a claim made under the head insurance was refused on the ground that there was no contested issue between the reinsurer and the head-assured. For examples of declarations in the context of contract, see *Louis Drayfus et Cie v Parnaso Cia Naviera SA* [1959] 1 QB 498, revsd [1960] 2 QB 49 (declaration that defendants were in breach of contract granted at first instance but refused on appeal); and *Rajbenbach v Mamon* [1955] 1 QB 283 (tenant granted declaration of landlord's contractual obligations to tenant following landlord's anticipatory repudiation).

29(2)

Nominal damages—and, in past cases, courts have awarded nominal damages of £2 up to £20—operate as a form of declaration that there has been a breach of contract by the defendant. They are not compensatory and must therefore be distinguished from a small sum of compensatory damages. They are available for breach of contract (and for torts actionable per se). For an example of nominal damages being awarded for breach of contract, see *C and P Haulage v Middleton* [1983] 1 WLR 1461, CA.

30 Limitation of actions

(1) The rules set out in subsections (2) to (6) are largely derived from the Limitation Act 1980.

(2) Subject to the exceptions in subsections (3) to (8), there is a limitation period of 6 years, or 12 years if the contract has been made by deed, to bring a claim for a monetary remedy for breach of contract which runs from when the cause of action accrues; and the cause of action for breach of contract accrues on the date of the breach.

(3) The limitation period does not run while the claimant is under 18 or lacks mental capacity; but once the period has started to run, it will not be suspended by reason of a supervening lack of mental capacity.

(4) If any fact relevant to the claim has been deliberately concealed from the claimant by the defendant, the limitation period does not start to run until the claimant has discovered, or could reasonably have discovered, the concealment.

(5) Where the defendant acknowledges a claim for the award of an agreed sum or liquidated damages, or makes any part payment in respect of such a claim, the limitation period (unless it has already expired) starts to run afresh from the date of the acknowledgement or part payment.

(6) There are legislative provisions (for example, where the damages are in respect of personal injury or the agreed sum is payable under certain types of loan) that displace the 6 or 12 year limitation period running from the date of the accrual of the cause of action.

(7) Under the doctrine of laches, an equitable remedy (for example, specific performance or an injunction) may be barred where there has been such unreasonable delay by the claimant in commencing the claim that to grant the remedy would be unjust to the defendant; but there can be no such unreasonable delay until the claimant has discovered, or could reasonably have discovered, that it has a claim against the defendant.

(8) In general (but subject, for example, to subsections (3) and (4)) the terms of a contract may govern—

    (a) the limitation period; and

    (b) when that period starts to run.

30

The law on limitation of actions and laches ensures that, after a fixed period of time or where there has been unreasonable delay by the claimant in commencing its claim, an action or remedy is barred. Somewhat oddly, the legal burden of proving that a claim falls within a limitation period is on the claimant (cf the doctrine of laches) albeit that the defendant must plead limitation: see *Chitty on Contracts* (32nd edn, 2015) paras 28-62, 28-108.

30(1)

The relevant law is largely contained in legislation with the main statute being the Limitation Act 1980. It may therefore be thought unnecessary to include in the Restatement legal rules which are already in statutory form. However, it has been thought helpful—while stressing that this is a guide to, and not a substitute for, reading the legislation—to summarise the main elements of the central legislation along with the relevant interpretative case law. The 1980 Act is not comprehensive so that, for example, the non-statutory equitable doctrine of laches may apply (s 30(7)).

30(2)

By s 5 of the Limitation Act 1980, 'An action founded on simple contract shall not be brought after the expiration of six years from the date on which the cause of action accrued.' The reference to 'simple contract' is to be contrasted with a contract made by deed, which is a 'specialty' under s 8(1) of the Act. Section 8(1) reads: 'An action upon a specialty shall not be brought after the expiration of twelve years from the date on which the cause of action accrued.' These provisions most obviously apply to damages and the award of an agreed sum but, by reason of s 23 of the Act, they also apply to an account of profits for breach of contract albeit that laches also applies to that remedy (see commentary to s 30(7) below). There is no limitation period applicable (and nor does laches apply) to termination for breach (although the claimant must elect whether to terminate or not: see s 19(2) above).

The cause of action for breach of contract accrues on the date of the breach of the contract even if no loss has been suffered at that date: see *Chitty on Contracts* (32nd edn, 2015) para 28-32. In contrast, a cause of action for the tort of negligence only accrues once the breach of a duty of care has caused loss or damage and, in addition to legislative rules on latent damage in the tort of negligence, this explains why a claimant may have a longer limitation period in tort than in contract.

The limitation period of 6 or 12 years from the date of the accrual of the cause of action is the general position. It is subject to numerous exceptions, which are set out in the Restatement in s 30(3)–(8). Of these, s 30(3)–(6) are set out in statute, s 30(7) refers to the equitable doctrine of laches, and s 30(8) deals with contractually agreed limitation periods.

30(3)

By reason of s 28 of the Limitation Act 1980, time does not run if, at the date when the cause of action accrues, the claimant is under a 'disability'; and by s 38 of the 1980 Act a person is treated as under a disability if he or she is 'an infant, or lacks capacity within the meaning of the Mental Capacity Act 2005 to conduct legal proceedings'. The wording of s 28 of the 1980 Act means that a supervening lack of capacity does not suspend the running of time.

30(4)

The postponement of the running of time for deliberate concealment is set out in s 32(1)(b) of the Limitation Act 1980 and may be just as relevant to breach of contract as to any other claim. Where there has been deliberate concealment after the limitation period has started to run, the limitation period starts to run again from the date when the claimant has discovered, or could reasonably have discovered, the concealment: *Sheldon v RHM Outhwaite (Underwriting Agencies) Ltd* [1996] AC 102, HL.

In contrast, it has been thought unnecessary to include in the Restatement the postponement for mistake or fraud also set out in s 32 of the 1980 Act (because it is difficult to think of a situation where they will operate in respect of breach of contract given that, following *Test Claimants in the Franked Investment Income Group Litigation v HMRC* [2012] UKSC 19, [2012] 2 AC 337, the mistake, and analogously the fraud, must be an essential element of the cause of action).

30(5)

The fresh accrual of a cause of action from the date of the defendant's acknowledgement or part payment of a 'debt or liquidated pecuniary claim' (which in contract means a claim for the award of an agreed sum or liquidated damages) is embodied in s 29(5) of the Limitation Act 1980. By s 29(6) there is an exception for the part payment of rent or interest. Once the limitation period has expired, it cannot be revived by a subsequent acknowledgement or part payment (s 29(7)). By s 30(1) of the 1980 Act, the acknowledgement 'must be in writing and signed by the person making it' (and s 30(2) of the 1980 Act deals with agents).

30(6)

This makes clear that the Restatement is merely intended to set out the main relevant limitation provisions for monetary remedies for breach of contract. Exceptions in the Limitation Act 1980 include s 6 (special time limit for actions to recover certain loans) and s 11 (special time limit in respect of personal injuries).

30(7)

By the flexible doctrine of laches (sometimes referred to as the 'lapse of time bar') equitable remedies may be barred where there would be injustice to the defendant caused by the unreasonable delay of the claimant in commencing its claim. Although in principle mere delay can constitute laches, the defendant will almost invariably have to establish that it has suffered, or will suffer, prejudice consequent on the delay, whether in defending the claim or in complying with the remedy. In the context of breach of contract, the equitable remedies are specific performance, injunction, declaration, and an account of profits. It is also convenient to mention here, albeit not remedies for breach, rescission (in equity) of contracts for innocent misrepresentation or undue influence and rectification of contracts for mistake. For a classic formulation of the laches doctrine, see *Lindsay Petroleum Co v Hurd* (1874) LR 5 PC 221, 239–40, PC. For clarification that there is no limitation period under the Limitation Act 1980 for specific performance, see *P & O Nedlloyd BV v Arab Metals Co, The UB Tiger* [2006] EWCA Civ 1717, [2007] 1 WLR 2288, and the commentary to s 26(3)(j) above. Similarly there appears to be no limitation period under the 1980 Act (whether directly or by analogy under s 36(1) of the 1980 Act) for injunctions, rescission (in equity), or rectification. Laches alone therefore applies. Where there is a limitation period (as, for example, for an account of profits) it would appear—although the authorities are not consistent—that the doctrine of laches can apply even where the statutory limitation period has not expired: see obiter dicta in *P & O Nedlloyd BV v Arab Metals Co, The UB Tiger* [2006] EWCA Civ 1717, [2007] 1 WLR 2288, at [55]–[63].

In contrast to the standard position under the Limitation Act 1980 of time running from the accrual of the cause of action, under the doctrine of laches the delay can only be unreasonable, and therefore only runs, from when the claimant discovered, or should reasonably have discovered, the reason for seeking the remedy: *Lindsay Petroleum Co v Hurd* (1874) LR 5 PC 221, PC (rescission for misrepresentation, treated as equitable rescission although the misrepresentation was fraudulent); *Erlanger v New Sombrero Phosphate Co* (1878) 3 App Cas 1218, HL (rescission for non-disclosure); *Alec Lobb Garages Ltd v Total Oil (GB) Ltd* [1985] 1 WLR 173, CA (rescission for exploitation of weakness). Cf *Leaf v International Galleries* [1950] 2 KB 86 (rescission for misrepresentation inducing a contract for the sale of goods where the reasoning that laches was a bar is problematic because the claimant only discovered the misrepresentation when he came to resell five years later). For judicial doubts as to whether *Leaf* remains good law—pointing out that it was decided prior to the Misrepresentation Act 1967 and the modern approach to acceptance barring rejection—see *Salt v Stratstone Specialist Ltd* [2015] EWCA Civ 745 at [32]–[35] and [48]. In respect of rescission for, for example, undue influence or exploitation of weakness—and assuming that one is seeking an equitable remedy so that laches applies—time will not run until the removal of the impairment: see, in the context of undue influence, *Allcard v Skinner* (1887) 36 Ch D 145, 187, CA.

30(8)

Although nothing in the Limitation Act 1980 explicitly allows the parties to set their own limitation periods and starting point, it is generally accepted that this is possible. For a general discussion, see *Limitation of Actions*, Law Commission Consultation Paper No 151 (1998) paras 9.7–9.11 and Report No 270 (2001) paras 3.170–3.175.

Example

By a term in a contract between A and B, it is agreed that any claim for breach is to be brought within 12 months of the breach. A is in breach. Although the normal limitation period would be 6 years from breach, this term is valid (subject to the general law on validity) so that a claim by B for damages for breach cannot be brought after 12 months.

As the Law Commission recognised, this contractual freedom is subject to the general law on the validity of the contract term (in particular, the controls under the Unfair Contract Terms Act 1977 and the Consumer Rights Act 2015). It would also be inappropriate, as the Law Commission again recognised, for there to be contractual modification of what, in this Restatement, are subsections 30(3) and (4).

31 Combining remedies

(1) Subject to subsections (2) and (3), a remedy for breach of contract may be combined with any other remedy, whether for breach of contract or not (for example, damages for breach of contract may be combined with termination or with specific performance or with a monetary restitutionary award for unjust enrichment).

(2) Remedies cannot be combined if the combination is inconsistent (for example, termination for breach and specific performance, or rescission for misrepresentation and damages for breach).

(3) Satisfaction of more than one monetary remedy is not permitted to the extent that it would produce double recovery.

31(1)

Section 3(2) has made clear that English law has accepted the principle of concurrent liability. The combining of remedies raises linked, but separate, issues. The basic principle, analogous to concurrent liability, is that remedies can be combined whether those remedies are for breach of contract or for other causes of action. So where a contract has been terminated by the claimant for the other's breach, it will be commonplace for the claimant to be awarded damages. Section 49 of the Senior Courts Act 1981 (and see also s 50 for equitable damages) expressly allows damages to be combined with specific performance: so, for example, in *Jaques v Millar* (1877) 6 Ch D 153 damages for the delayed performance were awarded along with an order of specific performance. Again, restitution of the purchase price paid for a (total) failure of consideration in the law of unjust enrichment may be combined with damages for breach of contract by the seller.

31(2)–(3)

The above principle that remedies can be combined is subject to two main restrictions: inconsistency and double recovery. As regards inconsistency, one cannot, for example, rescind a contract for misrepresentation at the same time as claiming damages for breach of that contract (because rescission wipes away the contract ab initio); nor can one terminate a contract for breach and have an order for specific performance of it (see *Johnson v Agnew* [1980] AC 367, 392, HL). As regards double recovery, even if consistent, one cannot have judgment satisfied for more than one monetary remedy where the combination would produce excessive recovery. The classic example of this in the law of obligations is that one cannot have satisfaction for both compensatory damages and an account of profits for an intellectual property tort. The same restriction applies, for example, where compensatory damages for breach of contract cover the price paid and there is also a claim in unjust enrichment for the price paid.

Where remedies cannot be combined, the law requires the claimant to make a choice, or election, between them. In the case of monetary remedies that election need not be made until judgment and, if the defendant fails to comply with the judgment, can be changed until satisfaction of the judgment (as established in the tort case of *United Australia Ltd v Barclays Bank Ltd* [1941] AC 1, 19, 21, 30, HL).

32 Change of circumstances constituting frustration

(1) Subject to the parties having expressly (see subsection (4)) or impliedly provided for the risk of this in the contract, a contract is frustrated where, after the making of the contract, there is such a change of circumstances that performance of the contract would be physically or legally impossible or would otherwise be rendered radically different from that which was promised.

(2) The mere fact that performance has been made more onerous or expensive does not constitute frustration.

(3) A contract is not frustrated where the party alleging a frustrating event is itself at fault for the occurrence of that event or chooses not to perform ('self-induced frustration').

(4) It is common for the parties to a written contract to deal with a change of circumstances outside their control, including what might otherwise be a frustrating event, by an express term (for example, what is commonly referred to as a 'force majeure' clause) which specifies the legal effects (such as termination, or suspension, of the contract and that money paid should be repaid) of there being a change of circumstances outside their control.

32(1)

The doctrine of frustration deals with a change in circumstances after the contract has been made. The kinds of event which amount to frustration may be regarded as rather narrow. The classic statement of the test for frustration, as reflected in s 32(1), is that of Lord Radcliffe in *Davis Contractors Ltd v Fareham Urban DC* [1956] AC 696, 729, HL. His Lordship said:

'[F]rustration occurs whenever the law recognises that without default of either party a contractual obligation has become incapable of being performed because the circumstances in which performance is called for would render it a thing radically different from that which was undertaken by the contract.'

Classic examples of frustration have been physical impossibility as in *Taylor v Caldwell* (1863) 3 B & S 826 (and s 7 of the Sale of Goods Act 1979); legal impossibility (that is, subsequent illegality) as in *Metropolitan Water Board v Dick Kerr and Co Ltd* [1918] AC 119, HL; and the cancellation of an event as in *Krell v Henry* [1903] 2 KB 740, CA. It is important to recognise, however, that in line with the test in s 32(1), the courts assess the impact of the change of circumstances on the particular contract in question. This explains why in other situations the destruction of the subject-matter (as in *Jackson v Union Marine Insurance Co Ltd* (1874) LR 10

CP 125) or subsequent illegality (as in *National Carriers Ltd v Panalpina (Northern) Ltd* [1981] AC 675, HL) or the cancellation of an event (as in *Herne Bay Steam Boat Company v Hutton* [1903] 2 KB 683, CA) have been held not to frustrate the contract.

Example 1

A enters into a contract with B for the use of B's hall for four concerts. Just before the first concert, the hall is burnt down by a third party. A sues B for damages for breach of contract in failing to provide the hall. Subject to there being a provision on this in the contract, the claim will fail because the contract is frustrated and terminated by reason of the fire which renders B's performance impossible. (This example is based on *Taylor v Caldwell*.)

As the opening words of this subsection make clear, frustration may be excluded by a provision in the contract which, expressly or impliedly, provides for what would otherwise be a frustrating event. In practice, this is extremely important and means that the law on frustration is rarely invoked and merely provides the default position. Given their importance and prevalence, 'force majeure' and similar express clauses are dealt with further in s 32(4).

Although there has been some doubt about this, it would appear that the better view is that the mere fact that an event has been foreseen does not exclude frustration: see *Ocean Tramp Tankers Corp v V/O Sovfracht, The Eugenia* [1964] 2 QB 226, CA. This is the better view in principle because if the parties have not expressly (or impliedly) provided for a foreseen event, the default position (that is, the doctrine of frustration) should apply.

Frustration in English law is an all-or-nothing doctrine so that it is incorrect to think of a contract as being partly frustrated. Having said that, much the same result may be achieved by a court construing a contract as partly excusing a party from performance because of a change of circumstances: see, for example, *Howell v Coupland* (1876) 1 QBD 258 (the destruction of most of a crop of potatoes excused the defendant from delivering the 200 tons promised but he was still bound to deliver the 80 tons that had not been destroyed); *Minnevitch v Café de Paris (Londres) Ltd* [1936] 1 All ER 884 (defendant café owner excused for not allowing—and hence not paying for—the claimant's cabaret performances on the day of King George V's death and the day after but not excused in respect of the four days after that).

32(2)

This makes clear that frustration is not a doctrine that allows a party to escape from a contract merely on the grounds that, as events have turned out, the bargain is a bad one for that party. The classic illustration is *Davis Contractors v Fareham UDC* [1956] AC 696, HL (see Example 2). Another example is that the failure of a seller's intended source of supply of goods does not generally frustrate a sale contract even though it may be very difficult and expensive to find an alternative supplier: see, for example, *Blackburn Bobbin Co v TW Allen & Sons* [1918] 2 KB 467, CA (outbreak of First World War cut off seller's normal supply of Finland birch timber); *CTI Group Inc v Transclear SA, The Mary Nour* [2008] EWCA Civ 856, [2008] 2 Lloyd's Rep 526 (no frustration of a contract for the sale of cement to the claimant buyers where the seller's suppliers had been pressurised, by the operation of a cartel, not to supply cement to the sellers). Viscount Simon in obiter dicta in *British Movietonews Ltd v London and District Cinemas Ltd* [1952] AC 166, 185, HL, said:

'The parties to an executory contract are often faced, in the course of carrying it out, with a turn of events which they did not at all anticipate—a wholly abnormal rise or fall in prices, a sudden depreciation of currency, an unexpected obstacle to execution, or the like. Yet this does not in itself affect the bargain they have made.'

Example 2

A contracts to build 78 houses for B. The fixed contract price, for completion within a year, is £15m. The cost of materials and labour significantly increases just before the work starts so that A knows that it cannot complete the contract other than at a huge loss. A submits that the contract is frustrated. That argument will fail. (This example is based on *Davis Contractors v Fareham UDC* although in that case the work had already been completed and the builder was alleging frustration in an attempt to recover more than the contract price by a claim in unjust enrichment.)

32(3)

This subsection deals with 'self-induced frustration', which occurs where the party alleging frustration is itself at fault for the event or chooses not to perform. Examples of self-induced frustration include *Maritime National Fish Ltd v Ocean Trawlers Ltd* [1935] AC 524, PC; *J Lauritzen AS v Wijsmuller BV, The Super Servant Two* [1990] 1 Lloyd's Rep 1, CA. The consequence of the frustration being self-induced is that the contract is not frustrated so that that party's failure to perform will constitute a breach of contract.

Example 3

A is booked by B to perform as the headline act at a music festival. The night before she is due to perform, A goes on a drug and alcohol binge and is in no fit state to perform at the festival. Her act is cancelled. B sues A for breach of contract. A cannot rely on the doctrine of frustration because her inability to perform is self-induced.

That 'self-induced frustration' is relevant only against the party alleging frustration is made clear by *Shepherd (FC) & Co Ltd v Jerrom* [1987] QB 301, CA: a contract of apprenticeship was held to be frustrated by a custodial sentence imposed on the apprentice and the apprentice could not rely on the frustration being self-induced by his own conduct (which, unusually, he wanted to rely on because it would have been beneficial to him in the context of establishing unfair dismissal).

32(4)

Many commercial contracts deal with subsequent events by express clauses (most obviously, 'force majeure' clauses but also, for example, 'material adverse change' clauses) in their contracts. These will typically specify the range of subsequent events, outside the parties' control, which may occur and their effect on the contract (including remedies), which can include an effect that the law would not otherwise prescribe (such as suspension of the contract). Such a clause ousts the operation of the doctrine of frustration and may also, of course, go beyond events that would otherwise frustrate the contract.

Inevitably, there may still be a question of interpretation as to whether an express clause covers an alleged frustrating event that has occurred and the courts have tended to take a strict approach in construing a clause that would oust the doctrine of frustration: see, for example, *Metropolitan Water Board v Dick Kerr and Co Ltd* [1918] AC 119, HL, where it was held that the clause in question did not cover the delay that had occurred so that the contract was frustrated.

In respect of subsequent illegality, it may be that a clause in the contract dealing with that risk is void or unenforceable as being illegal or contrary to public policy. So, for example, in *Ertel Bieber & Co v Rio Tinto Co Ltd* [1918] AC 260, HL, in which a contract between an English and Germany company was frustrated by the outbreak of the First World War, a force majeure clause in the contract, which allowed the contract to continue after the war, was held to be void as contrary to public policy as it involved trading with the enemy.

33 Effects of frustration

(1) Frustration terminates the contract automatically from the date of the frustration.

(2) Automatic termination means that the contract is terminated without any election by a party.

(3) Termination of the contract means that, subject to contrary agreement, the parties are discharged from their obligations under the contract which would arise after termination but not those which have arisen before.

(4) If a benefit has been obtained by one party from the other, under a contract that has been terminated for frustration, a right to restitution in respect of that benefit is governed by the law of unjust enrichment (which in this context is principally contained in the Law Reform (Frustrated Contracts) Act 1943).

33(1)–(3)

We have already seen that a repudiatory breach allows the innocent party to terminate the contract (see s 19). In contrast to breach, termination for frustration operates *automatically* without any choice or election by a party: see, for example, *J Lauritzen AS v Wijsmuller BV, The Super Servant Two* [1990] 1 Lloyd's Rep 1, CA. But the meaning of termination is the same as where a breach leads to termination. That is, termination does not wipe away the contract from the start. Rather it wipes away contractual obligations for the future but not for the past. This is subject to contrary agreement (so that, for example, an arbitration or jurisdiction clause will commonly apply after termination). Termination is commonly alternatively referred to as discharge (in the context of both breach and frustration).

33(4)

The restitution of benefits conferred under a contract that has been terminated for frustration is governed by the law of unjust enrichment the details of which lie outside the scope of this Restatement (see instead *A Restatement of the English Law of Unjust Enrichment* (2012)). Most of the law on this is contained in the Law Reform (Frustrated Contracts) Act 1943 although by s 2(5) of that Act the common law (of unjust enrichment) continues to apply to contracts for the carriage of goods by sea and voyage charterparties, contracts of insurance, and contracts for the sale of goods where the goods have perished. Note also that the parties can exclude by contract the liability in unjust enrichment that would otherwise arise (see, for example, s 2(3) of the 1943 Act).

PART 7
FACTORS RENDERING A CONTRACT DEFECTIVE

34 Void, voidable, unenforceable, rectifiable

(1) This Part makes provision about when a contract is—

    (a) void (as for mistake in limited circumstances);

    (b) voidable (as for, for example, misrepresentation or undue influence);

    (c) unenforceable (as for, for example, illegality);

    (d) rectifiable (as for mistake in limited circumstances).

(2) A void contract is invalid from the start and creates no contractual obligations but it may be that only one party can rely on the contract being void.

(3) A voidable contract is one that the party affected by the factor rendering the contract voidable (the 'claimant') can choose to rescind but is valid unless rescinded; and the effect of rescission is to invalidate the contract from the start.

(4) Rescission does not require an order of the court and is effected—

    (a) by the claimant informing the other contracting party that the contract is rescinded; or

    (b) where that is impossible, by the claimant making clear through any other act that the contract is rescinded.

(5) Rescission is barred where—

    (a) the claimant has affirmed the contract by unequivocally manifesting an intention to continue with it after knowing of the misrepresentation or non-disclosure or being free of the illegitimate threat, undue influence or weakness or incapacity;

    (b) a third party is a bona fide purchaser for value of property transferred under the contract without notice of the factor rendering the contract voidable;

    (c) restitution by the claimant to the other contracting party of benefits conferred on the claimant by the other contracting party is impossible; or

    (d) the claimant has delayed too long in seeking rescission so that, unless the rescission is at common law (as for, for example, fraudulent misrepresentation) rather than in equity (as for, for example, non-fraudulent misrepresentation or undue influence), the doctrine of laches applies (see section 30(7)).

(6) An unenforceable contract creates contractual obligations but cannot be enforced by one or, in some circumstances, either party.

(7) A rectifiable contract is a contract the written terms of which, because of a mistake by one or both parties, may in limited circumstances be amended by a court order for rectification (see section 35(6)).

(8) Rectification is barred where—

    (a) the party seeking rectification (the 'claimant') has affirmed the contract by continuing with it after knowing of the mistake;

    (b) a third party is a bona fide purchaser for value of property transferred under the contract without notice of the mistake; or

    (c) the claimant has delayed too long in seeking rectification so that the doctrine of laches applies (see section 30(7)).

(9) If a benefit has been obtained by one party from the other, under a contract that is defective in any of the ways set out in subsection (1), a right to restitution in respect of that benefit is governed by the law of unjust enrichment.

34(1)

Part 7 is concerned with the various factors that render a contract defective and which therefore, along with repudiatory breach and frustration (which have been dealt with in Parts 5 and 6), allow an escape from contractual liability. However, before looking at each of those factors in turn, this section examines the different types of defectiveness. So, depending on the factor in play, the contract may be void, voidable, unenforceable, or rectifiable.

34(2)

Although one tends to use the term 'void contract' where a purported contract has been made but is defective because of, for example, a common mistake as to the existence of the subject-matter, a void contract is equivalent to there being no contract.

A complicating twist is that, sometimes, only one of the parties can rely on the contract being void. This is most obviously so in respect of the types of unilateral mistake dealt with in s 35(4)(b) and (5).

Example 1

A enters into a contract with B. The contract is void for unilateral mistake as to identity induced by B's fraudulent misrepresentation (as to who B is) to A. As it transpires, the contract is a good one for A and a bad one for B. B cannot rely on the contract being void for A's mistake as to identity.

34(3)

Several factors render a contract voidable. This means that the contract is valid unless and until it is rescinded by the party who has the power to do so (for example, the misrepresentee). The effect of rescission is to invalidate (that is, to wipe away, to avoid, to set aside, or to unwind) the contract from the start. As made clear in *Johnson v Agnew* [1980] AC 367, HL, and *Photo Production Ltd v Securicor Transport Ltd* [1980] AC 827, HL, rescission is therefore different from termination (for breach or frustration).

The idea of partial rescission has not found judicial favour in England: *TSB Bank plc v Camfield* [1995] 1 WLR 430, CA; *De Molestina v Ponton* [2002] 1 Lloyd's Rep 271. Rather rescission is seen as an all-or-nothing remedy in the sense that the whole contract is regarded as being wiped away by rescission (albeit that restitution for unjust enrichment may follow). Note, however, that in the context of insurance contracts, there are statutory provisions in the Insurance Contracts Act 2015 (which is in force from 12 August 2016) and the Consumer Insurance (Disclosure and Representations) Act 2012 allowing a form of partial rescission for misrepresentation or, in non-consumer insurance contracts, non-disclosure.

Traditionally one could only rescind at common law in limited circumstances, for example where there was a fraudulent misrepresentation or duress. Rescission in equity went further and allowed rescission for, for example, innocent misrepresentation and undue influence. Although this is not entirely free from doubt, it would appear that the only significant remaining consequence of that historical distinction between common law and equitable rescission is that laches applies to equitable, but not common law, rescission (see s 30(7)). Certainly in principle, and if at all possible, any difference between common law and equitable rescission should be minimised.

34(4)

Rescission (whether at common law or, it is submitted, in equity) does not depend on a court order, although a claimant will often come to court in order to obtain consequential restitution. The leading case on how one rescinds is *Car and Universal Finance Co Ltd v Caldwell* [1965] 1 QB 525, CA. As made clear in the reasoning, communication is normally necessary; but, on the facts, where the fraudster to whom the misrepresentee had sold his car had disappeared, it was held that the contract had been validly rescinded by the misrepresentee informing the police and the Automobile Association. Although not entirely clear, it would appear that that exception to the need for communication is not confined to rescission for fraudulent misrepresentation.

34(5)

In addition to the standard four bars to rescission, see s 36(8) below for the discretion to award damages instead of rescission under s 2(2) of the Misrepresentation Act 1967.

34(5)(a)

We have already encountered the idea of affirmation in the context of termination for breach: see s 19(6). In the context of a voidable contract, affirmation applies where the party with the choice whether to rescind the contract unequivocally manifests an intention to stick with it (after knowing of the truth or being free from the effects of the threat, influence, or weakness). The idea behind affirmation is that a party cannot 'blow hot and cold' and, having made a choice, is bound by it. No (detrimental) reliance by the other party is required (cf promissory estoppel which is dealt with in s 12 above).

So, for example, a person who is induced by misrepresentation to buy goods cannot rescind if, after discovering the truth, she uses them (as in *United Shoe Machinery Co of Canada v Brunet* [1909] AC 330, PC). For a leading discussion of the requirements of affirmation, in which it was decided on the facts that there was no affirmation so that the claimant had validly rescinded the contract for fraudulent misrepresentation, see *Clough v London and North Western Rly Co* (1871) LR 7 Exch 26. For well-known decisions that affirmation barred rescission on the facts, in situations where the claimant had become free of the influence or threat, see *Allcard v Skinner* (1887) 36 Ch D 145, CA (undue influence) and *North Ocean Shipping Co Ltd v Hyundai Construction Co Ltd, The Atlantic Baron* [1979] QB 705 (duress). For an excellent discussion of affirmation in the context of rescission, see O'Sullivan, Elliott, and Zakrzewski, *The Law of Rescission* (2nd edn, 2014) ch 23.

34(5)(b)

It is clear that, where the claimant is rescinding a contract (for example, for misrepresentation or undue influence), the fact that the defendant is a bona fide purchaser without notice (which includes constructive notice) from a third party prevents the claimant revesting its proprietary rights in property that has subsequently been transferred to the defendant: *Cundy v Lindsay* (1878) 3 App Cas 459, 463–4; *Morley v Loughnan* [1893] 1 Ch 736. The conventional view is that bona fide purchase is a bar to rescission of the contract itself although some commentators have argued that it should not be: see Haecker, 'Rescission and Third Party Rights' [2006] RLR 21, esp at 36; O'Sullivan, Elliott, and Zakrzewski, *The Law of Rescission* (2nd edn, 2014) ch 20.

It is unclear whether other adverse effects on third parties of rescission may bar rescission (that is, other than where a transfer of property is in issue).

34(5)(c)

This bar to rescission has traditionally been expressed as applying where '*restitutio in integrum* is impossible'. The term 'counter-restitution' was used by the Court of Appeal in *Halpern v Halpern* [2007] EWCA Civ 291, [2008] QB 195 as the English equivalent of *restitutio in integrum* so that the bar can be expressed as being that 'counter-restitution is impossible'. The rationale of this bar is that, to be allowed rescission and consequent restitution, *the claimant* must be able to make restitution of what it has itself received from the defendant otherwise the law will produce the result that the claimant is itself left unjustly enriched at the defendant's expense. Therefore, if counter-restitution cannot be made—counter-restitution is impossible—the claimant should be denied rescission and restitution. The case law shows that the bar has been successfully invoked where the claimant has consumed, or disposed of, the benefit obtained: see, for example, *Vigers v Pike* (1842) 8 Cl & Fin 562, HL; *Clarke v Dickson* (1858) EB & E 148; *Ladywell Mining Co v Brookes* (1887) 35 Ch D 400, CA.

Example 2

A and B enter into a contract compromising an inheritance dispute. Under the agreement, A is to transfer substantial assets to B in return for B destroying certain documents (that might have assisted B in any proceedings against A). A now seeks to rescind the contract for duress by B. Applying the bar, A cannot rescind and have restitution from B because A cannot make counter-restitution of the benefit that A has derived from the destruction of the documents by B. (This example is based on the facts of *Halpern v Halpern* [2007] EWCA Civ 291, [2008] QB 195.)

However, the modern trend is for the courts to allow rescission provided counter-restitution can be achieved in a rough-and-ready way by a monetary award even if precise counter-restitution is impossible: see, for example, *Erlanger v New Sombrero Phosphate Co* (1878) 3 App Cas 1218, HL (non-disclosure); *O'Sullivan v Management Agency and Music Ltd* [1985] QB 428, CA (undue influence). Moreover, it can be strongly argued (and this argument was considered, but not ruled on, in *Halpern v Halpern*) that, in principle, the traditional bar focusing on the impossibility of counter-restitution is needlessly extreme because counter-restitution by a monetary equivalent, while sometimes raising difficult issues of assessment, is *never* impossible. If this argument were to be accepted, rescission would here not be barred as such but would rather be conditional on the claimant making counter-restitution.

It is worth adding that, where the rescission would involve consequential restitution (or counter-restitution), it would appear that change of position (see *A Restatement of the English Law of Unjust Enrichment* (2012) s 23) is a proportionate defence to that consequential restitution (or counter-restitution): see, for example, *Cheese v Thomas* [1994] 1 WLR 129 (helpfully analysed by Chen-Wishart, 'Loss Sharing, Undue Influence and Manifest Disadvantage' (1994) 110 LQR 173 at 178); *Royal Bank of Scotland plc v Etridge (No 2)* [2001] UKHL 44, [2002] AC 773, at [144].

34(5)(d)

We have already considered the operation of the doctrine of laches, including as a bar to equitable rescission, in s 30(7). Where the rescission is at common law (rescission at common law is available for, for example, fraudulent misrepresentation and duress) it would appear that there is no time bar as such although lapse of time may indicate affirmation which, as we have seen, is a bar (see O'Sullivan, Elliott, and Zakrzewski, *The Law of Rescission* (2nd edn, 2014) para 24.18; cf Cartwright, *Misrepresentation, Mistake and Non-Disclosure* (3rd edn, 2012) para 4.50).

34(6)

Although void and unenforceable contracts are often not distinguished, an unenforceable contract, in contrast to a void contract, may create contractual obligations albeit not ones that can be enforced in court by one or both parties. So, for example, money due under a contract may become time-barred. At that point, the contract has become unenforceable. But if the creditor is paid by the debtor, the debtor has no right to restitution of the money paid. This is because the money was owed under a contract. See *A Restatement of the English Law of Unjust Enrichment* (2012) s 3(6) and pp 32–5 (esp examples 5 and 9).

It used to be the case that contracts for the sale of land that were not evidenced in writing were unenforceable. The position was changed by the Law of Property (Miscellaneous Provisions) Act 1989 so that such contracts are void unless made in writing and signed. This leaves, as the main examples of unenforceable contracts in English law, a contract that is defective for incapacity or illegality/public policy or a contract where a limitation period has expired or, as set out in s 11(2)(b), a contract of guarantee that is not evidenced in writing and signed.

34(7)–(8)

Rectification of a contract, which is an equitable judicial remedy changing the written terms of a contract, is available only for mistake and only in certain circumstances: see s 35(6) below. It is subject to at least three of the same four bars as apply to rescission and which have been discussed immediately above. However, as rectification amends, rather than terminating or wiping away, the contract, it is hard to envisage circumstances in which the other bar ('counter-restitution is impossible') would have any role to play.

34(9)

Part of the law of unjust enrichment concerns benefits conferred under defective contracts. Where the contract is void, the unjust factor will most commonly be failure of consideration or mistake. As regards voidable contracts, there is a particularly close link between contract and unjust enrichment because, *where the contract has been executed*, the factor that renders the contract defective will also constitute the unjust factor that allows restitution consequent on the rescission. This explains why the discussion of rescission in contract books overlaps with that in books on unjust enrichment.

The details of the law of unjust enrichment that apply where a contract is defective (although it is not easy to envisage circumstances calling for restitution after *rectification* of a contract) lie outside the scope of this Restatement (see s 3 (1)) and are instead covered by *A Restatement of the English Law of Unjust Enrichment* (2012). For the reason just explained, however, there is an inevitable overlap in the discussion of rescission between this Restatement and that Restatement.

35 Mistake

(1) In this section, a mistake may include a mistake of law as well as a mistake of fact.

(2) Subject to the exceptions set out in subsections (3) to (6), a mistake made by both parties or by one party (whether or not known to the other) does not render the contract defective.

(3) A mistake in entering the contract renders the contract void if—

    (a) both parties make the same mistake so that, contrary to the parties' belief, performance of the contract is physically or legally impossible or the purpose of the contract cannot be achieved at the time the contract is made;

    (b) the parties have not expressly or impliedly provided in the contract for the risk of being so mistaken; and

    (c) the party who is alleging the mistake has not negligently induced the other party's mistake.

(4) A mistake in entering the contract renders the contract void (or, to put it another way, there is no acceptance of an offer and hence no contract) if—

    (a) the parties are at cross-purposes such that there is a central objective ambiguity as to what has been agreed; or

    (b) one party is mistaken and—

        (i) the other party knows, or ought reasonably to know, of that mistake;

        (ii) the mistake is as to the terms of the contract or as to the identity of the other party; and

        (iii) it is the mistaken party who is alleging that the contract is void.

(5) A signed contract is void under the doctrine of 'non est factum' if—

    (a) the document signed was mistakenly signed by the party who is alleging that it is void; and

    (b) that document is fundamentally different from what that party thought it to be; and

    (c) that party was not negligent in signing that document.

(6) The written terms of a contract may be rectified if—

    (a) those terms are inconsistent with the parties' outwardly manifested common intention that continued until the time the contract was made; or

    (b) one party was mistaken in entering into the contract and the other party knowing of that mistake unconscionably remained silent at the time the contract was made.

35

There are many different ways of analysing the role of mistake in English contract law (even putting to one side mistake induced by misrepresentation (see s 36) or non-disclosure (see s 42)). This makes it a particularly difficult topic. The view adopted in this Restatement is that English law does have a doctrine of common and unilateral mistake albeit that it is narrow. This is in contrast to the approach of some commentators who have sought to 'deconstruct' mistake so that it is seen as merely an application of the law on, for example, implied terms (as regards common mistake) or offer and acceptance (as regards unilateral mistake). The latter presents a particularly attractive alternative approach and, if that is the view preferred, the material covered here on unilateral mistake should instead be considered alongside s 7.

Leaving aside rectification (dealt with in s 35(6)), the doctrine of mistake is purely a common law doctrine so that, where it applies, the effect of the mistake is to render the contract void. A wider equitable doctrine of common mistake rendering the contract voidable not void (see *Solle v Butcher* [1950] 1 KB 671, CA) was rejected in *Great Peace Shipping Ltd v Tsavliris Salvage (International) Ltd, The Great Peace* [2002] EWCA Civ 1407, [2003] QB 679; and that rejection was applied to unilateral mistake in *Statoil ASA v Louis Dreyfus Energy Services LP, The Harriette N* [2008] EWHC 2257 (Comm), [2008] 2 Lloyd's Rep 685. Although the Supreme Court has not had the chance to consider *The Great Peace*, and while *Solle v Butcher* has its strong supporters, it seems highly unlikely that, after such a detailed review of the matter by the Court of Appeal, the equitable power to rescind for mistake will be restored. Having said that, *if* one considers that the present English law on common or unilateral mistake is too narrow, the obvious way forward would be to revisit equitable rescission.

35(1)

It now does not matter that the mistake is one of law rather than fact. The old law that the mistake had to be one of fact not law was departed from, as regards contract law, in *Brennan v Bolt Burden* [2004] EWCA Civ 1017, [2005] QB 303. This followed the decision in the law of unjust enrichment in *Kleinwort Benson Ltd v Lincoln City Council* [1999] 2 AC 349, HL, that restitution of payments can be granted for mistakes of law as well as fact.

35(2)

Assuming that there is a doctrine of unilateral mistake (where one party has made a mistake not shared by the other party) and common mistake (where both parties have made the same mistake), it is clear that the scope of each of those doctrines is narrow. One cannot generally escape from a contract by showing that a mistake was made in entering into it. It would otherwise be too easy for a party to escape from a bad bargain and the security of contracts would be undermined.

As regards unilateral mistake the general position was classically laid down in *Smith v Hughes* (1871) LR 6 QB 597. This established that a unilateral mistake, even if known about by the other party, does not invalidate a contract provided that, viewing their intentions objectively, there is agreement between the parties. That one of the parties is mistaken, or that the parties have different subjective intentions from each other, is in general irrelevant.

Example 1

A agrees to buy 100 bags of oats from B for £1,000. A wants old oats and thinks that the oats are old. B knows that the oats are in fact new oats but does not know that A is making a mistake. Nothing is said about the type of oats and there is no term to that effect. The contract for the sale of the oats is valid not void. (This example is based on *Smith v Hughes*.)

Example 2

A agrees to buy 100 bags of oats from B for £1,000. A wants old oats and thinks that the oats are old. B knows that the oats are in fact new oats and knows that A is making a mistake but B stays silent. Nothing is said about the type of oats and there is no term to that effect. The contract for the sale of the oats is valid not void. (This example is based on *Smith v Hughes*.)

Example 3

A agrees to buy a painting from B for £20,000. A thinks the painting is an original. B knows that A thinks the painting is an original and also knows that it is not. Nothing is said about the quality of the painting and there is no term to that effect. The contract is valid not void.

As regards common mistake the general position was classically laid down in *Bell v Lever Brothers Ltd* [1932] AC 161, HL (valid contract of severance between employer and employee even though both mistakenly thought that the underlying employment contract between them could only be terminated with compensation whereas it could have been terminated without compensation).

Example 4

A agrees to buy a painting from B for £50,000. It is not an original although both mistakenly think that it is. There is no representation, and no term, to that effect. The contract is valid not void.

35(3)(a)

This sets out the limited circumstances when, contrary to the general rule in s 35(2), a common mistake (sometimes referred to as 'mutual mistake') may make the contract void. It seeks to reflect the leading decisions in *Bell v Lever Brothers Ltd* [1932] AC 161, HL, and *Great Peace Shipping Ltd v Tsavliris Salvage (International) Ltd, The Great Peace* [2002] EWCA Civ 1407, [2003] QB 679. In neither of those cases was there held to be a common mistake of the type necessary to render the contract void but each recognised that a 'possibility' common mistake would do so.

For an example of a physical impossibility common mistake, see *Couturier v Hastie* (1856) 5 HLC 673 (at the time of the contract, the cargo of corn being sold no longer existed). See also s 6 of the Sale of Goods Act 1979: 'Where there is a contract for the sale of specific goods, and the goods without the knowledge of the seller have perished at the time when the contract is made, the contract is void.'

For an example of a legal impossibility common mistake, see *Cooper v Phibbs* (1867) LR 2 HL 149 (the claimant contracted to take a lease of a fishery from the defendant but, unknown to both parties, the defendant did not have any title to the fishery: as Lord Atkin explained in *Bell v Lever Bros*, this mistake would now be seen as rendering the contract void not, as was said in the case itself, voidable.) For another example, see *Associated Japanese Bank International Ltd v Credit du Nord SA* [1989] 1 WLR 255. Although the parties had there provided for the relevant risk in the contract, had they not done so Steyn J would have held the contract void for common mistake. There was legal impossibility (although that was not a term used) in the sense that the contract of guarantee had no possible application because it was guaranteeing obligations under the main contract that was itself void for common mistake as to the existence of the subject matter (the machines in question did not exist).

The idea of the contractual 'purpose' not being achievable (which one may regard as referring to impossibility in a wide sense) seeks to reflect the reasoning in *The Great Peace*. Lord Phillips MR, giving the judgment of the Court of Appeal and in speaking of the necessary impossibility, said, at [76], that common mistake counts if it is as to 'circumstances which must subsist if performance of the contractual adventure is to be possible'. See also *Griffith v Brymer* (1903) 19 TLR 434 (contract to hire a room to view the coronation of Edward VII held void because, unknown to the parties, at the time when the contract was made, the decision to operate on the King had already been taken so that the coronation could not go ahead).

35(3)(b)

The parties may displace the law on mistake by an express or implied term. As was said by Lord Phillips MR, giving the judgment of the Court of Appeal in *The Great Peace*, at [75]:

'Just as the doctrine of frustration only applies if the contract contains no provision that covers the situation, the same should be true of common mistake. If, on true construction of the contract, a party warrants that the subject matter of the contract exists, or that it will be possible to perform the contract, there will be no scope to hold the contract void on the ground of common mistake.'

The same point—that one must first decide whether the parties have allocated the risk of the common mistake thereby displacing any role for the doctrine of mistake—was emphasised by Steyn J in *Associated Japanese Bank International Ltd v Credit du Nord SA* [1989] 1 WLR 255 at 268: 'Logically, before one can turn to the rules as to mistake... one must first determine whether the contract itself, by express or implied condition precedent or otherwise, provides who bears the risk of the relevant mistake.' This is one explanation of the much-discussed Australian case of *McRae v Commonwealth Disposals Commission* (1951) 84 CLR 377, High Court of Australia, where a contract for the sale of a wrecked ship out on a reef was entered into where the ship did not exist. The seller was held to be in breach of contract and one of the grounds for this (and for the contract not being void despite the common mistake as to the existence of the subject matter) was that the seller had 'contracted that there was a tanker there' (see at 409).

In respect of initial illegality, it may be that a clause in the contract dealing with that risk is void or unenforceable as being illegal or contrary to public policy: see analogously the commentary on s 32(4) above.

35(3)(c)

The other explanation given for the *McRae* decision was that the seller was at fault in inducing the other party's mistake. This is reflected in the wording of s 35(3)(c).

There have been obiter dicta to the effect that, more generally, the fault of one or both parties may preclude successfully alleging common mistake. So, for example, in *The Great Peace* Lord Phillips MR, giving the judgment of the Court of Appeal, said at [76] that 'the non-existence of the state of affairs must not be attributable to the fault of either party'. But it is not clear what situations are here in mind beyond where the party alleging mistake has negligently induced the other's mistake. After all, many mistakes are negligently made; and if one has in mind a narrower category where a person is at fault for, for example, destroying the subject-matter of the contract prior to formation that person is in practice very unlikely to be mistaken as to the existence of that subject-matter.

This is a convenient point at which to stress that, although there are close similarities, common mistake differs from the doctrine of frustration (see Part 6) because the impossibility exists at the time the contract is made rather than subsequently. For a clear illustration of this, see the frustration case of *Amalgamated Investment & Property Co v John Walker & Sons Ltd* [1977] 1 WLR 164, CA (listing of a building being bought was made the day after the contract was made: it was held that the relevant doctrine to be applied was frustration, not common mistake, but that the contract was not frustrated because the listing did not make performance of the contract radically different). It also appears to be correct (see Peel, *Treitel on the Law of Contract* (14th edn, 2015) para 19-122) that the doctrine of frustration is wider than the doctrine of mistake in the sense that it can embrace events occurring after the contract is made that would render the performance radically different even though the performance is possible or the contractual purpose can be achieved. In other words, it may be expected that the law takes the view that parties should bear the risk of their mistakes more readily than they should bear the risk of subsequent events.

35(4)

This and the following subsection set out the limited circumstances in which a unilateral mistake (that is, a mistake of one party not shared by the other) makes a contract void. As has been said above (and this explains the words in brackets), some may prefer to interpret this area as dealing with the law on offer and acceptance so that this discussion is better placed alongside s 7.

35(4)(a)

The classic example of the law in this paragraph is said to be provided by *Raffles v Wichelhaus* (1864) 2 H & C 906 although there was no reasoning given by the judges in that case.

Example 5

B agreed to buy cotton from A to arrive 'ex *Peerless*' from Bombay. There were two ships named *Peerless* leaving Bombay, one in October and one in December. B meant the October ship but A meant the December ship. B's refusal to pay for the cotton delivered from the December ship was held not to be a breach of contract. One can say that there was objective ambiguity as to which

Peerless was being referred to (that is, the parties were at cross-purposes) so that the purported contract was void. (This example is based on *Raffles v Wichelhaus*.)

Another possible example is provided by *Scriven Brothers & Co v Hindley & Co* [1913] 3 KB 564 (contract held void where buyer at an auction thought it was buying a lot of hemp whereas the lot was in fact tow) although the reasoning appeared to treat the fault of the seller in inducing the mistake as also being relevant.

35(4)(b)

This paragraph applies where the unilateral mistake of one party was known about by the other or, as recognised in, for example, *OT Africa Line Ltd v Vickers plc* [1996] 1 Lloyd's Rep 700, 703, ought reasonably to have been known about by the other.

The leading case, establishing the general principle, is *Smith v Hughes* (1871) LR 6 QB 597. While laying down the objective approach that, in general, denies any escape from a contract for a mistake even if known about by the other party, it was accepted that a mistake as to the terms of the contract (that is, a mistake as to what the terms are), known about by the other party, does make the contract void. So, in contrast to the facts (see Examples 1 and 2 above), had the seller of the oats known that the buyer mistakenly thought that *it was a term of the contract that the oats were old* that would have rendered the contract void. This is also one explanation for the decision in *Hartog v Colin & Shields* [1939] 3 All ER 566 (contract void because, as the buyer knew, the seller mistakenly thought the contract was for the sale of 30,000 Argentinian hare skins 'per piece' rather than 'per pound').

Example 6

B advertises for sale on its website laser printers. By a mistake, a particular type of commercial printer is advertised for sale at £50 instead of £4,000. Before the mistake is corrected, A (along with hundreds of others) places an order for 300 printers. The orders are accepted by B's automated responses. A seeks to enforce the contract for 300 printers at £50. The contract is void because B's mistake as to the terms (on these facts, the price) is known about by A. (This example is based on the Singaporean case of *Chwee Kin Keong v Digilandmall. com Pte Ltd* [2005] 1 SLR 502.)

It is important to appreciate that an argument can be, and has been, made (see, for example, McLauchlan, 'The "Drastic" Remedy of Rectification for Unilateral

Mistake' (2008) 124 LQR 608, 614; *Chitty on Contracts* (32nd edn, 2015) paras 3-029–3-033) that the courts should not merely hold a contract void in the situation of a unilateral mistake as to the terms but should go further and should hold that there is a valid contract on the mistaken party's terms. This would mean, for example, that in *Hartog v Colin & Shields* there would be a valid contract for the sale of the skins 'per piece'. It is submitted, however, that it is a very significant and controversial step to regard there as being a contract on the mistaken party's terms rather than merely saying that the mistaken party can treat the contract as void. It is not clear what the basis for taking that step would be. It cannot be the application of objective offer and acceptance because objectively the contract is as the non-mistaken party alleges. Nor, absent additional unusual facts to the contrary, has the non-mistaken party led the other party reasonably to believe that it is agreeing to those terms (so that any form of 'estoppel' reasoning is, at least usually, inapplicable). For example, in *Hartog v Colin & Shields* the buyer did not lead the seller to believe anything but had rather simply 'snapped up' the mistaken offer; and surely it would be contrary to principle in Example 6 to say that there is a contract binding A to buy 300 printers at £4,000. It is true that, if the contract were written, it might exceptionally be possible to rectify it because of a party's unilateral mistake as to the terms known about by the other party (see s 35(6)(b)). But the precise basis for rectification for unilateral mistake is itself not entirely clear although it would appear to depend on the unconscionability of the non-mistaken party.

The main illustrations of the principle in s 35(4)(b) are where the mistake is not as to terms as such but is rather as to the identity of the person one is contracting with. A long line of cases establish that a mistake of identity, known to the other party, renders a contract void. However, the mistake has to be as to identity. This means that the mistake is as to whom one is contracting with where one has another named person in mind. A mistake as to the attributes (for example, creditworthiness) of the other party is not enough. *Cundy v Lindsay* (1878) 3 App Cas 459, HL, and *Shogun Finance Ltd v Hudson* [2003] UKHL 62, [2004] 1 AC 919, are usually regarded as relevant examples where there was held to be a mistake of identity rendering the contract void where the parties were contracting by correspondence rather than face to face. In contrast, where the parties are dealing face to face, the starting point (and, absent unusual facts, the end point) is that there is no mistake as to identity (the party is intending to contract with the person who is in front of him or her and not someone else): *Phillips v Brooks Ltd* [1919] 2 KB 243; *Lewis v Averay* [1972] 1 QB 198, CA.

Commonly in the cases raising mistake as to identity, the real dispute is between a seller of goods and an innocent third party buyer who has bought the goods from the original fraudulent buyer (who has misrepresented his identity and creditworthiness to the original seller). While the original contract of sale is voidable for misrepresentation, the original seller wishes to establish a mistake of identity because that renders the contract void (rather than voidable) so that no title can pass to the innocent third party. There would be no incentive to establish mistake as to identity if, like misrepresentation, that mistake rendered the contract voidable not void: and that a mistake of identity renders the contract voidable has sometimes been put forward as the better approach (see, for example, *Lewis v Averay* per Lord Denning MR; Lords Nicholls and Millett dissenting in *Shogun Finance Ltd v Hudson*; and this was also recommended by the Law Reform Committee, *Transfer of Title to Chattels* (1966, Cmnd 2598)). While that would have the advantage of removing the significance of the often fine line between identity and attributes (and between face to face dealings and dealings by correspondence) it would be a very bold step, given the recent rejection of this by the majority of the House of Lords in *Shogun Finance Ltd v Hudson*, for the Supreme Court now to reform the law in that way.

That it is the mistaken party alone who can allege that the contract is void is illustrated by Example 1 under s 34(2) above.

35(5)

The common law doctrine of *non est factum* ('it is not my deed') applies to mistakenly signed contracts. It applies to render a contract void at the instance of a party who has made a mistake in signing, whether or not the other party knows of that mistake. Not surprisingly, its requirements are strict. As laid down in *Saunders v Anglia Building Society (sub nom Gallie v Lee)* [1971] AC 1004, HL, the two essential restrictions (apart from mistaken signature) are those laid down in s 35(5) (b) and (c). In that case, the first of those two restrictions was held not to have been proved by the party seeking to establish *non est factum*.

35(6)

The clarification that there is now no scope for rescission of a contract for common or unilateral mistake (see the commentary at the start of this section) means that the sole equitable remedy for mistake is rectification of a written contract. As set out in s 34(7)–(8), rectification is an order of the court amending the written terms of a contract and is subject to the three bars of affirmation, bona fide purchaser, and laches.

Rectification is commonly sought as an alternative to a declaration that the correct interpretation of the contract means what the claimant says it means. The modern objective contextual approach to interpretation (s 14 above) may mean that there is less need to seek rectification than in the past when a more literal approach to interpretation was applied. However, an important practical difference remains that, in contrast to interpretation (see s 14(4)), the admissible evidence for rectification can include pre-contractual negotiations. Moreover, it may not be possible to cure by interpretation the omission (or inclusion) of a whole clause by mistake whereas that is straightforwardly the province of rectification: *Cherry Tree Investments Ltd v Landmain Ltd* [2012] EWCA Civ 736, [2013] Ch 305, at [132]–[138].

35(6)(a)

The essential requirement for rectification under s 35(6)(a) is that there is inconsistency between the written terms and the parties' outwardly manifested continuing common intention. It used to be thought that the continuing common intention needed to be in a binding contract so that rectification was an extremely narrow doctrine that was solely concerned with a mistake in the drawing up of the document that embodied the contract already made by the parties (hence the oft-cited dictum of James V-C in *Mackenzie v Coulson* (1869) LR 8 EQ 368 at 375 to the effect that courts do not rectify contracts but rather the instruments that purport to have been made in pursuance of contracts). However, it has been made clear subsequently—see, for example, *Jocelyn v Nissen* [1970] 2 QB 86, CA—that there is no need for there to be a prior contract: if that were the law, it would produce the unsatisfactory outcome that, for example, a prior agreement 'subject to contract' which was then inaccurately finalised in written form could not be rectified.

Having rightly moved away from the need for a prior contract, what is unfortunately far from clear is the precise nature of the required continuing common intention. In obiter dicta in *Chartbrook Ltd v Persimmon Homes Ltd* [2009] UKHL 38, [2009] 1 AC 1101, at [60], Lord Hoffmann (with whom the rest of the House of Lords agreed) thought that an objective approach (what a reasonable observer would have thought the intentions of the parties to be) should be applied to assessing the continuing common intention. On that approach, one is simply comparing the later written objective common intention with an earlier objective common intention and rectification is permitted where those two versions clash. Indeed, applying that approach, the language of a 'common mistake' may be thought somewhat misleading because all that is required is that the two objective versions clash; and certainly on the facts of *Chartbrook Ltd v Persimmon Homes Ltd* rectification was granted even though the parties did not make the same mistake (and unilateral mistake, as in s 35(6)(b), was not in issue).

An alternative view is that one should not lose sight of the root idea that rectification is a remedy for mistake and mistake is a subjective concept about the actual intentions of the parties. On this view, one is looking for a common mistake in the sense that there is a clash between the later written terms and the earlier subjective common intention (albeit that that earlier subjective common intention must be outwardly manifested). Indeed one can argue that Lord Hoffmann's objective approach is contradicted by the earlier reasoning of the majority (Hobhouse and Glidewell LJJ, Hoffmann LJ dissenting) in *Britoil plc v Hunt Overseas Oil Inc* [1994] CLC 561, at 573–4, CA. Certainly the courts have subsequently found it far from straightforward to apply Lord Hoffmann's objective approach to the continuing common intention: see, for example, *Daventry DC v Daventry and District Housing Ltd* [2011] EWCA Civ 1153, [2012] 1 WLR 1333.

The Restatement seeks to leave open this difficult question of which of those two different approaches (the objective or subjective) to the continuing common intention is to be preferred. (For the purposes of s 6(1), the possible departure from the usual objective approach to ascertaining the intentions of the parties may be said to be because this is required by the context, namely that one is here looking for a common mistake). For a careful consideration of the two approaches, ultimately favouring the objective approach, see Calnan, *Principles of Contractual Interpretation* (2013) paras 9.07–9.51. For preference for the subjective approach, see the reasoning of Leggatt J in *Tartsinis v Navona Management Co* [2015] EWHC (Comm) 57 at [83]–[99]; *Snell's Equity* (33rd edn, 2015) para 16-015.

In some cases, it makes no difference whether one takes an objective or subjective approach, but in other cases it will be crucial. To illustrate this, one can consider a number of examples based on the facts, and then variations of the facts, in the leading case of *Rose (Frederick E) (London) v Pim (William H) Junior & Co* [1953] 2 QB 450, CA.

Example 7

B is asked by C to supply 'feveroles'. A (seller) tells B (buyer), innocently but mistakenly, that feveroles are ordinary horsebeans. In fact feveroles are top quality horsebeans. B therefore buys 'horsebeans' from A and supplies them to C (that is, there is an oral agreement between B and A for the sale of ordinary horsebeans and the written contract refers to horsebeans). C claims damages from B for supplying ordinary horsebeans and not feveroles. B seeks rectification of the contract with A so that the word horsebeans is replaced by feveroles. B seeks this so that B can then claim damages from A to cover the damages B has to pay C. Rectification will be refused. Although B and A have made a common mistake in entering into the written contract (both believe that feveroles and ordinary horsebeans are the same), there is no inconsistency between the written contract and either the parties' objective common intention or their subjective common intention. (These were the facts, and that was the decision, in *Rose v Pim*.)

In the following variations, assume in Examples 8–10 that the parties can prove an outwardly manifested subjective common intention to buy/sell ordinary horsebeans.

Example 8

A (seller) and B (buyer) have a written contract for the sale of feveroles. Both mistakenly believe that feveroles and ordinary horsebeans are the same and their objective oral agreement was for ordinary horsebeans. A now seeks rectification so that ordinary horsebeans replaces feveroles. The parties have made a common mistake and there is inconsistency between the objective common intention and the written contract. There is also inconsistency between the subjective common intention (for ordinary horsebeans) and the written contract. Rectification should be granted.

Example 9

A (seller) and B (buyer) have a written contract for the sale of ordinary horsebeans. Both mistakenly believe that feveroles and ordinary horsebeans are the same. While it is clear from what the parties have said to each other during negotiations that they each have in mind ordinary horsebeans, they have used the word feveroles so that their objective oral agreement was for feveroles. B now seeks to rectify the contract so that feveroles replace ordinary horsebeans. The parties have made a common mistake and there is inconsistency between the objective oral agreement and the written contract. Lord Hoffmann's objective reasoning would indicate that there should be rectification. But the written contract is consistent with the subjective common intention (for ordinary horsebeans) so that, applying the subjective approach, there should be no rectification.

Example 10

A (seller) and B (buyer) have a written contract for the sale of feveroles. Both mistakenly believe that feveroles and ordinary horsebeans are the same. While it is clear from what the parties have said to each other during negotiations that they each have in mind ordinary horsebeans, they have used the word 'feveroles' so that their objective oral agreement was for feveroles. A now seeks rectification of the contract so that ordinary horsebeans replace feveroles. The parties have made a common mistake but there is no inconsistency between the objective oral agreement and the written contract. Lord Hoffmann's objective reasoning indicates that there should be no rectification. However, there is inconsistency between the written contract and the subjective common intention (for ordinary horsebeans). Applying the subjective approach, there should be rectification.

Example 11

A (seller) and B (buyer) have a written contract for the sale of ordinary horsebeans. A mistakenly believes that ordinary horsebeans and feveroles are the same. B knows that feveroles are top quality horsebeans. Their objective oral agreement was for feveroles. B seeks rectification so that feveroles replace ordinary horsebeans. There is inconsistency between the objective oral agreement and the written contract. Lord Hoffmann's objective reasoning indicates that there should be rectification. But there is no subjective common intention (A thinks selling ordinary horsebeans, B thinks buying feveroles) and there is no common mistake and the final written contract is exactly as A subjectively intended. Applying the subjective approach, there should be no rectification.

35(6)(b)

Rectification under s 35(6)(a) was traditionally all that was permitted, but it has more recently been accepted that so-called 'unilateral mistake' rectification is also possible. Hence the inclusion of s 35(6)(b). Leading cases include *Roberts & Co Ltd v Leicestershire CC* [1961] Ch 555; *Thomas Bates & Son Ltd v Wyndham's (Lingerie) Ltd* [1981] 1 WLR 505, CA; *Commission for the New Towns v Cooper (GB) Ltd* [1995] Ch 259, CA. It would appear that in the standard case here, the objection is not that the written contract inaccurately reflects a prior common intention. Rather the written contract often accurately reflects the fact that, in the prior negotiations, one party was mistaken and that mistake was known about by the other. What then is the precise basis for this type of rectification? This is not entirely clear. The Restatement uses the language of the courts in referring to the 'unconscionability' of the non-mistaken party as the crucial concept although one might alternatively talk of 'bad faith'. As made clear in the *Commission for the New Towns* case, knowledge of the other's mistake can include 'shut-eye' or 'Nelsonian' knowledge.

Example 12

A submits a building tender to B. This includes a time estimate for the work of 78 weeks. This would lead to completion on 30 September 2013. As B wants to spread the payment out, it does not actually want completion until 30 September 2014. B puts that date in a memorandum to A and that is the date inserted into the written contract even though B knows that A is assuming that the completion date is 30 September 2013. A is entitled to rectification of the contract so that the date for completion is amended to 30 September 2013. (This example is based on *Roberts & Co Ltd v Leicestershire CC*.)

36 Misrepresentation

(1) A contract is voidable where a party to the contract ('the claimant') entered into it in reliance on a misrepresentation, whether fraudulent, negligent or innocent, by the other contracting party ('the defendant') or, in certain circumstances set out in section 39, by a third party.

(2) A misrepresentation is a false representation, by words or conduct, of present fact or law.

(3) A statement of intention contains a representation as to the present state of mind of the person making it.

(4) A statement of opinion contains a representation that the person making the statement holds that opinion; and in certain circumstances (as where the person making the statement may be expected to have special knowledge in relation to it) a statement of opinion contains a representation that the person making the statement has reasonable grounds for holding that opinion.

(5) To prove reliance it must be shown that the claimant would not have entered into the contract (whether at all or on the same terms) but for the misrepresentation unless—

    (a) the misrepresentation was fraudulent, in which case the misrepresentation need merely have been a reason for entering into the contract or present in the claimant's mind at the time the contract was entered into; or

    (b) the misrepresentation and another factor rendering the contract voidable (for example, duress) were each independently sufficient to induce the claimant to enter into the contract.

(6) A claimant who has relied on a misrepresentation in entering into a contract has a right to damages from the person by whom the misrepresentation was made (the 'misrepresentor')—

    (a) for the tort of deceit where the misrepresentation was fraudulent;

    (b) for the tort of negligence where the misrepresentation was negligent and there was a duty of care owed by the misrepresentor to the claimant;

    (c) under section 2(1) of the Misrepresentation Act 1967 (except where disapplied in relation to a misrepresentation to a consumer by section 2(4) of that Act) provided that—

        (i) the misrepresentor was a party to the contract, and

        (ii) the misrepresentor fails to prove that it had reasonable grounds to believe and did believe up to the time the contract was made that the representation was true.

(7) A claimant may both rescind a contract for misrepresentation and be awarded damages for the tort of deceit or negligence or under section 2(1) of the

Misrepresentation Act 1967; but satisfaction of more than one monetary remedy is not permitted to the extent that it would produce double recovery.

(8) A claimant may be awarded damages instead of rescission for a non-fraudulent misrepresentation under section 2(2) of the Misrepresentation Act 1967 (except where disapplied in relation to a misrepresentation to a consumer by section 2(4) of that Act) but only where it is just to do so.

36(1)

This makes clear that a misrepresentation that has induced a contract (that is, that has been relied on in entering into a contract) renders the contract voidable. It has been explained in s 34 above that a voidable contract is one that can be rescinded at the choice of the claimant. Section 34 has also explained what the effect of rescission is, how the rescission may be brought about, and what the bars to rescission are.

It is clear that one can rescind a contract for a non-fraudulent (as well as a fraudulent) misrepresentation, as shown, for example, by *Redgrave v Hurd* (1881) 20 Ch D 1, CA; and indeed the misrepresentation can be purely innocent (that is, not even negligence need be proved).

A fraudulent misrepresentation is one that is dishonestly made: that is, the person making the representation knows that it is false or is reckless as to whether it is true or false (*Derry v Peek* (1889) 14 App Cas 337, HL, is the leading case on this definition albeit that that case concerned a claim for damages for the tort of deceit not rescission of a contract). A negligent misrepresentation, in contrast to a purely innocent misrepresentation, is one which a reasonable person exercising reasonable care would avoid making. With the possible exception of awarding damages in lieu of rescission under s 2(2) of the Misrepresentation Act 1967 (see s 36(8)), nothing appears to turn, as regards rescission (contrast damages), on whether the misrepresentation is negligent or innocent.

36(2)

Section 36(2) defines what a misrepresentation is. Normally there is a false statement by words but there can be a misrepresentation by conduct: see, for example, Lord Campbell in *Walters v Morgan* (1861) 3 De GF & J 718 at 724, who clarified that 'a nod or a wink, or a shake of the head, or a smile' may suffice. A misrepresentation may now be one of law as well as fact: *Pankhania v Hackney BC* [2002] EWHC 2441 (Ch). Silence in itself is not a misrepresentation but a half-truth can be (*Dimmock v Hallett* (1866) LR 2 Ch App 21) as can be a failure to correct an earlier representation which has been falsified by a subsequent change of circumstances during the negotiations (*With v O'Flanagan* [1936] Ch 575, CA; *Spice Girls Ltd v Aprilla World Service BV* [2002] EWCA Civ 15, [2002] EMLR 27).

Example 1

A is considering buying a flat from B. B deliberately covers up patches of dry rot in the flat before showing A round the flat. Thinking that the flat is in good condition and does not suffer from dry rot, A buys the flat. A can rescind the contract for fraudulent misrepresentation, where B's deliberate concealment constitutes a misrepresentation by conduct that the flat does not suffer from dry rot. (This example is based on *Gordon v Selico Ltd* (1986) 18 HLR 219, CA.)

Example 2

A, a vendor of land, informs B, a prospective purchaser of the land, that two farms on the land are fully let. That is correct but a half–truth and misleading because the tenants have given notice to quit. Assuming reliance, B is entitled to rescind the contract of sale for misrepresentation. (This example is based on *Dimmock v Hallett.*)

Example 3

A, a vendor of a business, represents to B, a prospective purchaser, that the annual turnover is £100,000. That is correct. Five months later, when the contract is entered into, the turnover of the business has dwindled to £1,000 per month. A does not inform B of that change of circumstance. Assuming reliance, B is entitled to rescind the contract for misrepresentation. Although A's statement was initially not a misrepresentation, it has become so prior to the making of the contract. (This example is based on *With v O'Flanagan.*)

36(3)

A statement of intention contains a representation of (present) fact, namely the present state of mind of the person making it. Hence a dishonest statement of intention in a company's prospectus was held to be a fraudulent misrepresentation of fact as to the maker's present state of mind in *Edgington v Fitzmaurice* (1885) 29 Ch D 459, CA.

36(4)

Within a statement of opinion is a representation of (present) fact that the person making the statement holds that opinion and, in some circumstances, has reasonable grounds for holding that opinion. A dishonest statement of opinion is therefore a fraudulent misrepresentation. Not every carelessly made statement of opinion contains a misrepresentation. But there will be a negligent misrepresentation where the person expressing the opinion could be expected to have particular knowledge in respect of that opinion. For example, there was held to be a misrepresentation in *Smith v Land and House Property Corp* (1884) 28 Ch D 7, CA, in which the landlord making the statement would have been expected to know, from the past record of rent payments, that the tenant was not 'a most desirable tenant'. In contrast, in *Bisset v Wilkinson* [1927] AC 177, PC, an opinion was expressed by the vendor that land being sold for a sheep farm 'would carry two thousand sheep'. This was held not to be a misrepresentation because the vendor could not have been expected to know the capacity of the farm (as the purchaser knew, neither the vendor nor anyone else had carried out sheep farming on the land in question).

Example 4

A sells his land to B telling B that he thinks the land may be 'ripe for development'. After buying the land, B cannot obtain planning permission for developing it. Even assuming reliance by B, A's statement (absent dishonesty or this being in a context where A could be expected to have particular knowledge) would be regarded as a statement of opinion and not a misrepresentation of fact so that B could not rescind the contract for misrepresentation.

36(5)

For the misrepresentation to render the contract voidable, it must have been relied on by the claimant in entering into the contract. The law on the test for reliance is surprisingly opaque but it would appear that, subject to exceptions, it is for the claimant to establish the 'but for' test (which is the standard test of causation in the civil law): *JEB Fasteners Ltd v Marks Bloom & Co* [1983] 1 All ER 583, CA. The most important exception is where the misrepresentation is fraudulent, for in that context it is sufficient that the misrepresentation was a reason or 'present to his mind' or 'influenced' the claimant, even if the claimant would have entered into the contract had there been no misrepresentation: *Edgington v Fitzmaurice* (1885) 29 Ch D 459, CA (where the claim was for damages for the tort of deceit). Indeed it may be that, in a fraudulent misrepresentation case, the burden of proof in respect of that less stringent test lies on the defendant: see, for example, *Barton v County Natwest Bank Ltd* [1999] Lloyd's Rep Banking 408, CA.

In principle (as reflected in s 36(5)(b)), it must also be correct that, where there is more than one factor that is sufficient to render the contract defective (including misrepresentation by more than one person), the 'but for' test is inappropriate (because it would produce the result that neither factor was causative).

The formulation of the 'but for' test in s 36(5) refers to the claimant not having entered into the contract but for the misrepresentation. This primarily covers where the claimant would not have entered into the contract at all but, as made clear by the words in brackets—'whether at all or on the same terms'—it is wide enough to cover situations where the claimant would not have entered into the contract on the same terms. That the latter is included was clarified in *Raiffeisen Zentralbank Osterreich AG v Royal Bank of Scotland plc* [2010] EWHC 1392 (Comm), [2011] 1 Lloyd's Rep 123, at [171]–[172], per Christopher Clarke J.

The role of 'materiality' is confused and confusing. In general, it would seem that materiality is not a separate requirement: that is, the best interpretation is that materiality has no role to play independent of establishing reliance. Hence it is not mentioned in the Restatement. However, it should be noted that, on some inter-pretations, materiality is a separate requirement laying down that the claimant must show that it was reasonable to rely on the misrepresentation. Alternatively, materi-ality has sometimes been thought relevant in shifting the burden of proof in establishing reliance: that is, if it would have been reasonable for the claimant to rely on the misrepresentation, it is for the defendant to disprove reliance (see, for example, *Dadourian Group International Inc v Simms* [2009] EWCA Civ 169, [2009] 1 Lloyd's Rep 601, at [99]–[101]).

Insurance contracts have traditionally been an exception to there being no separate requirement of materiality. Perhaps because of the link to non-disclosure (see s 42(2)), it has traditionally been thought that the misrepresentation must be material (as well as being relied on): see, for example, s 20 of the Marine Insurance Act 1906 (which codified the common law in that area). Similarly (when it comes into force on 12 August 2016) the Insurance Act 2015, which repeals s 20 of the 1906 Act, covers both misrepresentation and non-disclosure under a 'duty of fair presentation' owed by an insured and has requirements of both materiality and reliance; and by s 7(3) 'a circumstance or representation is material if it would influence the judgment of a prudent insurer in determining whether to take the risk and, if so, on what terms'. In contrast, in consumer insurance contracts, where the focus is on misrepresentation rather than non-disclosure, the Consumer Insurance (Disclosure and Representations) Act 2012 has a requirement of reliance (s 4) but not materiality. Note also that both those recent insurance statutes lay down a specific regime of remedies for an insurer for pre-contractual negligent or fraudulent misrepresentations by an insured which, in some respects, differs from the common law (for example, in allowing a court to grant partial rescission).

If the claimant has relied on a misrepresentation, it is no bar to rescission that the claimant had a reasonable opportunity to check the truth but failed to do so: *Redgrave v Hurd* (1881) 20 Ch D 1, CA. (Nor, absent very special circumstances, will this constitute contributory negligence so as to reduce, under the Law Reform (Contributory Negligence) Act 1945, damages in tort for negligent misrepresenta-tion at common law or under s 2(1) of the Misrepresentation Act 1967: *Gran Gelato Ltd v Richcliff (Group) Ltd* [1992] Ch 560, 574.)

36(6)

Although the details of liability in tort lie outside the scope of this Restatement (s 3 (1)), it would be misleading to consider rescission for misrepresentation without making clear that the claimant may alternatively or additionally have a claim for damages for the misrepresentation either for the tort of deceit (as in *Derry v Peek* (1889) 14 App Cas 337, HL) or for the tort of negligence in respect of a negligent misrepresentation (as in *Hedley Byrne & Co Ltd v Heller & Partners Ltd* [1964] AC 465, HL; *Esso Petroleum Co Ltd v Mardon* [1976] QB 801, CA) or under section 2(1) of the Misrepresentation Act 1967. By s 2(1) of the 1967 Act:

'Where a person has entered into a contract after a misrepresentation has been made to him by another party thereto and as a result thereof he has suffered loss, then, if the person making the misrepresentation would be liable to damages in respect thereof had the misrepresentation been made fraudulently, that person shall be so liable notwithstanding that the misrepresentation was not made fraudulently, unless he proves that he had reasonable ground to believe and did believe up to the time the contract was made that the facts represented were true.'

Possible advantages of establishing the tort of deceit (as opposed to the tort of negligent misrepresentation or liability under s 2(1)) are that there is a more generous ('directness' rather than 'reasonable foreseeability') remoteness rule (*Doyle v Olby (Ironmongers) Ltd* [1969] 2 QB 158, CA; *Smith New Court Ltd v Scrimgeour Vickers (Asset Management) Ltd* [1997] AC 254, HL); and contributory negligence does not apply to reduce damages for the tort of deceit. However, the 'fiction of fraud' wording in s 2(1) was controversially (and, with respect, incorrectly) interpreted in *Royscot Trust Ltd v Rogerson* [1991] 2 QB 297, CA, to mean that the wider remoteness test also applies under s 2(1) of the 1967 Act. As regards a negligent misrepresentation inducing a contract between the parties, the claimant is better off proceeding under s 2(1) than at common law because there is no need to establish a duty of care under the Act and the burden of proving negligence is reversed.

The measure of (compensatory) damages under the tort of deceit or for a negligent misrepresentation at common law or under s 2(1) of the Misrepresentation Act 1967 is the reliance measure, which contrasts with the expectation measure for breach of contract (see s 20(2) above). The aim is therefore to put the claimant into as good a position as if no representation had been made: see, for example, *Doyle v Olby (Ironmongers) Ltd* [1969] 2 QB 158, CA.

The torts of deceit and negligent misrepresentation are more wide-ranging than s 2(1) because (outside the context of this Restatement) they extend to all misrepresentations and are not confined to misrepresentations inducing a contract between the parties.

The words in brackets in s 36(6)(c) reflect the fact that the scope of s 2(1) of the 1967 Act has been significantly narrowed by the Consumer Protection (Amendment) Regulations 2014 (SI 2014/870). So as to avoid duplication, s 2 (4) of the 1967 Act (inserted by reg 5 of the 2014 Regulations) removes any entitlement to damages under s 2(1) where a consumer has a right to redress under Part 4A of the Consumer Protection from Unfair Trading Regulations 2008 (SI 2008/1277) (see s 40 of the Restatement) in respect of the conduct constituting the misrepresentation. This seems ill-conceived not only because of the complexity added but also because, with the sole exception of s 2 of the 1967 Act, the existing law is left in place by the 2014 Regulations, even where overlapping with the consumer's rights under the 2008 Regulations (and indeed reg 27L explicitly deals with the avoidance of double recovery). It should be noted, in particular, that the consumer's right to damages for the common law tort of negligence in respect of negligent misrepresentation has not been removed.

36(7)

There is no inconsistency between both, on the one hand, rescinding a contract for misrepresentation and, on the other hand, being awarded damages for tortious misrepresentation or under s 2(1) of the 1967 Act. They are consistent because, in contrast to damages for breach of contract (which would be inconsistent with rescinding the contract), the basis of the damages in tort or under s 2(1) is not that there has been a valid contract that has been broken. However, a combination of monetary remedies must not produce double recovery (see analogously s 31(3) of the Restatement) as it might do where there is restitution consequent on the rescission plus damages.

36(8)

Section 2(2) of the 1967 Act reads:

'Where a person has entered into a contract after a misrepresentation has been made to him otherwise than fraudulently, and he would be entitled, by reason of the misrepresentation, to rescind the contract, then, if it is claimed, in any proceedings arising out of the contract, that the contract ought to be or has been rescinded the court or arbitrator may declare the contract subsisting and award damages in lieu of rescission, if of opinion that it would be equitable to do so, having regard to the nature of the misrepresentation and the loss that would be caused by it if the contract were upheld, as well as to the loss that rescission would cause the other party.'

It would appear that the purpose of this peculiar provision is not to add to the misrepresentee's remedies but to give the courts discretion to cut back the remedy of rescission where the misrepresentation has been, for example, trivial or wholly innocent and rescission would cause undue hardship to the misrepresentor. It follows that the discretion does not arise if rescission would be barred by one of the four bars set out in s 34(5) above: *Government of Zanzibar v British Aerospace (Lancaster House) Ltd* [2000] 1 WLR 2333; *Salt v Stratstone Specialist Ltd* [2015] EWCA Civ 745. Where the discretion to award damages under s 2(2) of the 1967 Act is exercised, the measure of damages should certainly not be greater than tortious (reliance) damages although it might be less (cf *William Sindall plc v Cambridgeshire CC* [1994] 1 WLR 1016, CA, criticised by Beale, 'Damages in Lieu of Rescission for Misrepresentation' (1995) 111 LQR 60).

The words in brackets reflect the fact that the scope of s 2(2) of the 1967 Act has been significantly narrowed by the Consumer Protection (Amendment) Regulations 2014. As in relation to s 2(1) of the 1967 Act, s 2(4) of the 1967 Act (inserted by reg 5 of the 2014 Regulations) removes any entitlement to damages under s 2(2) where a consumer has a right to redress under Part 4A of the Consumer Protection from Unfair Trading Regulations 2008 (see s 40 of the Restatement) in respect of the conduct constituting the misrepresentation. This can be criticised as an ill-conceived reform for the reasons outlined above in respect of s 2(1) of the 1967 Act (see the commentary on s 36(6)).

It may be helpful to point out at the end of this commentary on misrepresentation that the legislative control of clauses excluding liability or remedies for misrepresentation has been dealt with in Part 4 of the Restatement. On the exclusion of liability for fraud, see also s 44(5).

37 Duress
(1) A contract is voidable where a party to the contract ('the claimant') was induced to enter into it by an illegitimate threat ('duress') of the other contracting party or, in certain circumstances set out in section 39, of a third party.
(2) The illegitimate threat may be express or implied.
(3) For this purpose a threat—
    (a) is illegitimate if the conduct threatened is unlawful (as in the case of a threat to commit a crime or a tort or a breach of contract);
    (b) may in some circumstances be illegitimate even though the conduct threatened is lawful (as in the case of a threat to prosecute, or expose the truth about, the claimant or a member of the claimant's family).
(4) But if the illegitimate threat is a threat to break a contract (and possibly in respect of some other types of threat), the contract is voidable only if the claimant had no reasonable alternative to giving in to the threat.

(5) For the purposes of subsection (1)—

    (a) the standard test of causation is the 'but for' test by which it must be shown that the claimant would not have entered into the contract (whether at all or on the same terms) but for the illegitimate threat, but

    (b) there are exceptions to the 'but for' test where—

        (i) the threat was to the person in which case the threat need merely have been a reason for entering into the contract or present in the claimant's mind at the time the contract was entered into;

        (ii) duress and another factor rendering the contract voidable (for example, misrepresentation) were each independently sufficient to induce the claimant to enter into the contract.

37(1)

That there are two essential elements of duress—(i) an illegitimate threat (ii) causing the claimant to enter into the contract—was established in the two leading cases: *Universe Tankships Inc of Monrovia v International Transport Workers' Federation, The Universe Sentinel* [1983] 1 AC 366, HL; *Dimskal Shipping Co SA v International Transport Workers' Federation, The Evia Luck (No 2)* [1992] 2 AC 152, HL. Essentially the same law applies where no contract has been entered into but the claimant has paid money under duress. This explains why these provisions on duress in this Restatement are very similar to those on duress in *A Restatement of the English Law of Unjust Enrichment* (2012). It also explains why some of the cases referred to in the commentary involve non-contractual payments.

It has been explained in s 34 above that a voidable contract is one that can be rescinded at the choice of the claimant. Section 34 has also explained what the effect of rescission is, how the rescission may be brought about, and what the bars to rescission are.

37(2)

The perhaps obvious point that the threat may be express or implied was made clear by Lord Goff in the unjust enrichment case of *Woolwich Equitable Building Society v IRC* [1993] AC 70, 165: 'In cases of compulsion, a threat which constitutes the compulsion may be expressed or implied'. This is supported by other cases: see, for example, *B & S Contracts and Design Ltd v Victor Green Publications Ltd* [1984] ICR 419, 424, CA ('veiled threat'); and *The Alev* [1989] 1 Lloyd's Rep 138, 142, 145.

37(3)(a)

What is meant by an illegitimate threat? The main traditional category was duress of the person, where the illegitimate threat was of violence to the claimant or the claimant's family, as in *Barton v Armstrong* [1976] AC 104, PC. Traditionally duress of goods did not make a contract voidable (*Skeate v Beale* (1841) 11 Ad & El 983) but this was rejected in the modern cases accepting economic duress such as *The Siboen and The Sibotre* [1976] 1 Lloyd's Rep 293. In cases on duress of the person (or of goods) the conduct that is threatened is a tort (for example, trespass to the person). The same can be said of the two leading cases on economic duress, *The Universe Sentinel* and *The Evia Luck (No 2)*, in which the threatened tort was to induce another to break a contract by the unlawful 'blacking' of a ship. Most of the cases on economic duress have involved the threat to break a contract, which is, again, a civil wrong. It would seem, therefore, that all threats to commit a crime or civil wrong (whether a tort or equitable wrong or breach of contract) should be treated as illegitimate.

37(3)(b)

The very language chosen by the courts of the threat needing to be illegitimate (rather than unlawful) suggests that there can be 'lawful act' duress. This is borne out by the case law. A long-established area, although traditionally thought of as within the equitable doctrine of undue influence rather than the common law doctrine of duress (an historical difference that, in this area, we can cut through so as to unite all examples of illegitimate threats: see the commentary to s 38(1)–(2)), has comprised illegitimate threats by, for example, threatening to prosecute or expose the truth about the claimant or a relative of the claimant: see, for example, *Williams v Bayley* (1866) LR 1 HL 200; *Mutual Finance Ltd v John Wetton and Sons Ltd* [1937] 2 KB 389. Again, although rare, it has been accepted that economic duress can extend to threatened lawful acts: *CTN Cash and Carry Ltd v Gallaher Ltd* [1994] 4 All ER 714, CA; *Alf Vaughan & Co Ltd v Royscot Trust plc* [1999] 1 All ER (Comm) 856; *R v A-G for England and Wales* [2003] UKPC 22; *Progress Bulk Carriers Ltd v Tube City IMS LLC* [2012] EWHC 273 (Comm), [2012] 1 Lloyd's Rep 501.

37(4)

The most debated category of duress is the one that has featured in most of the recent cases, namely economic duress by threatened breach of contract. See, for example, *The Siboen and The Sibotre* [1976] 1 Lloyd's Rep 293; *North Ocean Shipping Co Ltd v Hyundai Construction Co Ltd* [1979] QB 705; *Pao On v Lau Yiu Long* [1980] AC 614, PC; *B & S Contracts and Design Ltd v Victor Green Publications Ltd* [1984] ICR 419, CA; *Atlas Express Ltd v Kafco Ltd* [1989] QB 833; *Huyton SA v Peter Cremer GmbH & Co* [1999] 1 Lloyd's Rep 620; *DSND Subsea Ltd v Petroleum Geo-Services ASA* [2000] BLR 530; *Adam Opel GmbH v Mitras Automotive (UK) Ltd* [2007] EWHC 3481 (QB); *Kolmar Group AG v Traxpo Enterprises Pvt Ltd* [2010] EWHC 113 (Comm), [2010] 2 Lloyd's Rep 653.

It remains unclear precisely when a threat to break a contract will constitute duress. No single approach can reconcile all the cases. The approach adopted in the Restatement is to say that every threatened breach of contract is illegitimate and that the ambit of economic duress is controlled by causation and by insisting in this context on the additional requirement that the claimant had no reasonable alternative other than giving in to the threat.

That there is that additional element for economic duress, in the context of a threatened breach of contract, appears to have been accepted in a number of cases: see especially Dyson J in *DSND Subsea Ltd v Petroleum Geo-Services ASA* [2000] BLR 530 at [131]. In contrast, it appears to have been rejected in other contexts: *Astley v Reynolds* (1731) 2 Stra 915 (restitution of money paid under duress of goods). Although the Restatement accepts that third requirement at least in relation to a threatened breach of contract (and, in principle, it is hard to see any reason why it should not extend to other types of economic duress, such as a threatened economic tort), it is unlikely that it will be of much practical significance because normally there is no reasonable alternative (given the cost and delay involved in taking legal action). Certainly, there appears to be no reported case in which rescission for duress was denied because, despite causation being satisfied, the claimant was held to have had a reasonable alternative which was not taken.

The effect of treating every threatened breach of contract as illegitimate is that one has a wide doctrine of economic duress which tends to protect the original contract made. It is very important to recognise that, if genuine renegotiations are not to be curbed, the courts will need to be astute to ensure that a party's genuine warnings as to the difficulties it has in performing are not too readily construed as constituting threats to breach. Under the old law the original contract was protected in a blunt way by the rule that performing, or a promise to perform, one's pre-existing contractual duty was not good consideration for a payment of extra money. That was departed from in *Williams v Roffey Bros and Nicholls (Contractors) Ltd* [1991] 1 QB 1, CA, (see s 8(5)) in favour of an approach that relies on economic duress to draw the line between renegotiations that one wishes to protect and those that should not be upheld.

An alternative approach to that adopted in the Restatement, which does have some attractions, would be to reject the idea that every threatened breach of contract is illegitimate and to develop a narrower test for when a threatened breach of contract is illegitimate. One possible such test (see Birks, *An Introduction to the Law of Restitution* (1989) 183) would be whether the threat to break the contract was made in bad faith as being concerned to exploit the claimant's weak position rather than to solve genuine problems in performing of the party making the threat. For support for bad faith as a relevant factor in assessing the illegitimacy of a threatened breach of contract, see Dyson J in *DSND Subsea Ltd v Petroleum Geo-Services ASA* [2000] BLR 530 at [131]. However, in general, the English cases do not appear to have embraced that approach and reliance on 'bad faith' may be thought alien to traditional English contract law.

Example

B is bound by contract to supply strawberries during June and July to A's restaurant at 80p per pound. At the time that that price was agreed, B anticipated buying in the strawberries at 50p per pound. Severe weather has since meant that there has been a failure of many strawberry crops so that B cannot buy in the strawberries for less than £6 per pound. B tells A in May that it will be unable to deliver unless A enters into a new contract to pay £6 per pound and agrees to waive any right to damages. A very reluctantly does so as it cannot find an alternative supplier. But, in August, A seeks rescission of the new contract and restitution of £5.20 for each pound of strawberries bought from B. A's claim should probably succeed. There has been economic duress because B threatened a breach of contract which caused A to enter into the new contract and A had no reasonable alternative. The original contract is therefore protected by the doctrine of economic duress (as indeed it would have been had A, instead of giving in to the threat, sought damages for breach by B). It is irrelevant (applying the approach accepted in the Restatement) that B was not acting in bad faith concerned to exploit A's weakness.

37(5)

To constitute duress, the illegitimate threat must have caused the claimant to enter into the contract. It would appear that the normal causation test is the 'but for' test: *Huyton SA v Peter Cremer GmbH* [1999] 1 Lloyd's Rep 620, 636; *Kolmar Group AG v Traxpo Enterprises Pvt Ltd* [2010] EWHC 113 (Comm), [2010] 2 Lloyd's Rep 653 at [92]; and see, analogously, the commentary to s 36(5) on misrepresentation. But exceptions to this are where there is more than one factor rendering the contract voidable (see the commentary to s 36(5)(b)) or where physical duress is in issue, in which case the less stringent 'a reason' or 'present in the claimant's mind' test applies (*Barton v Armstrong* [1976] AC 104, PC, which also indicated that the burden of proof was on the defendant).

Although the language of the claimant's will being overborne has sometimes been used (for example, by Lord Scarman in *Pao On v Lau Yiu Long* [1980] AC 614, 635, PC) that approach was thought to be unhelpful by Lord Diplock in *The Universe Sentinel* [1983] 1 AC 366, 384, and by Lord Goff in *The Evia Luck (No 2)* [1992] 2 AC 152, HL.

38 Undue influence

(1) A contract is voidable if it was entered into while a party to the contract ('the claimant') was under the undue influence of the other contracting party ('the defendant') or, in certain circumstances set out in section 39, of a third party.

(2) A claimant is under the undue influence of another person if, because of the relationship between them, the claimant's judgement is not free and independent of that person.

(3) There is a rebuttable presumption of undue influence if—

    (a) the claimant was in a relationship of influence with the defendant or the third party at the time the contract was entered into; and

    (b) the contract was disadvantageous to the claimant in the sense that it was not readily explicable by reference to the motives on which people ordinarily act.

(4) A relationship of influence—

    (a) is to be treated as existing in certain relationships (for example, parent and young child, solicitor and client, doctor and patient, and spiritual adviser and follower), but

    (b) otherwise must be proved on the facts.

(5) It is for the defendant to rebut the presumption mentioned in subsection (3) by proving that the claimant exercised free and independent judgement; and an obvious way for the defendant to try to prove this is by showing that the claimant obtained the fully informed and competent independent advice of a qualified person, such as a solicitor or other legal adviser.

38(1)–(2)

The (equitable) doctrine of undue influence in the past embraced illegitimate threats that fell outside the then narrow (common law) doctrine of duress. As recognised by many commentators and by some judges (see Lord Nicholls in *Royal Bank of Scotland v Etridge (No 2)* [2001] UKHL 44, [2002] 2 AC 773 at [8]), in the light of the acceptance of economic duress it is rational, in order to avoid an overlap of undue influence and duress, to cut through the equitable/common law divide and to treat all cases on illegitimate threats as examples solely of duress. So if one takes out examples of duress, undue influence is concerned with where, as a result of the relationship between them, one party has undue influence over the other so that the claimant does not exercise a full and free judgement, independent of the other person, in relation to the contract.

It has been explained in s 34 above that a voidable contract is one that can be rescinded at the choice of the claimant. Section 34 has also explained what the effect of rescission is, how the rescission may be brought about, and what the bars to rescission are. Essentially the same law applies where no contract has been entered into but the claimant has made a gift (or otherwise paid money) under undue influence. This explains why these provisions are very similar to those on undue influence in *A Restatement of the English Law of Unjust Enrichment* (2012). It also explains why some of the cases referred to in the commentary involve gifts not contracts.

In contrast to mistake and duress, it would appear that it is not a requirement for undue influence that 'but for' causation is satisfied (see *UCB Corporate Services Ltd v Williams* [2002] EWCA Civ 555, [2003] 1 P & CR 12) and indeed it would be odd to insist even on the influence being 'present' in the claimant's mind or 'a reason' given the likelihood that the claimant is precisely unaware of the influence. It is sufficient that, at the time of, and in relation to, the contract, the claimant was under undue influence, and it does not matter that the claimant would have acted in the same way even if not under undue influence.

Ever since *Allcard v Skinner* (1887) 36 Ch D 145, CA, undue influence has been divided into two categories: actual and presumed. In *Royal Bank of Scotland v Etridge (No 2)* [2001] UKHL 44, [2002] 2 AC 773, the House of Lords clarified, or redefined, the difference between the categories. Undue influence is a single concept. It does not have two different forms. The presumption of undue influence is an evidential (not a legal) presumption. It follows that the correct analysis of the categories is that they refer to two different ways of *proving* undue influence. As the Restatement shows, one can manage without the two categories, although many courts subsequent to *Etridge* have continued to use them. Presumed undue influence refers to where the person alleging undue influence relies on an evidential presumption. Actual undue influence refers to where the person alleging undue influence relies on direct proof (of there being no free and independent judgement exercised because of the relationship) and does not raise an evidential presumption. Not surprisingly, cases in which a person has sought to establish undue influence (as distinct from duress) by direct proof, rather than by relying on an evidential presumption, are very rare. In other words, one is almost always concerned with presumed, rather than actual, undue influence.

Nevertheless, undue influence by direct proof ('actual undue influence') tends to arise where the claimant can point to threats or pressure which, in the context of the relationship between the parties, unacceptably undermines the claimant's independent judgement. While normally such threats would not be illegitimate (and are, therefore, arguably not examples of duress) they may be viewed as actual undue influence because of the relational context. These include, for example, threats by children to stop caring for their father (*Langton v Langton* [1995] 2 FLR 890), threats by a long-time landlady not to allow her elderly lodger back home (*Killick v Pountney* [2000] WTLR 451), and threats by a nephew to sue his elderly aunt (*Drew v Daniel* [2005] EWCA Civ 507, [2005] 2 P & CR DG14). Another example of actual undue influence might be where the claimant can establish by evidence that she does whatever her partner tells her to do and, in line with this, the evidence is that she simply signed the contract as she was told to do.

38(3)

As *Etridge* made clear, there are two requirements for establishing the evidential rebuttable presumption of undue influence. First, as reflected in s 38(3)(a), a relationship of influence. Secondly, as reflected in s 38(3)(b), that the contract is disadvantageous to the claimant in the sense of being 'not readily explicable by reference to the motives on which people ordinarily act'. These words seek to reflect the words used by Lindley LJ in *Allcard v Skinner* at 185 ('not to be reasonably accounted for on the ground of friendship, relationship, charity or other ordinary motives on which ordinary men act') which Lord Nicholls in *Etridge* said were more accurate, in this context, than the phrase 'manifestly disadvantageous'.

38(4)(a)

The relationship of influence is most easily made out by showing that the parties were within certain well-established categories of relationship which, by their very nature, involve influence by one over the other. These are relationships in which there is a legal rule (sometimes judicially referred to, in confusing and inappropriate language, as an 'irrebuttable legal presumption') that the relationship is one of influence (but note that this is not a legal rule that there is *undue* influence). Examples of such relationships include doctor over patient (*Mitchell v Homfray* (1881) 8 QBD 587, CA), spiritual adviser over follower (*Allcard v Skinner* (1887) 36 Ch D 145, CA), solicitor over client (*Wright v Carter* [1903] 1 Ch 27, CA), or parent over young child (*Lancashire Loans Ltd v Black* [1934] 1 KB 380, CA). Although there has been some doubt over this, it also appears that trustee and beneficiary is such a relationship (*Plowright v Lambert* (1885) 52 LT 646; *Tito v Waddell (No 2)* [1977] Ch 106, 241). However, a husband and wife relationship is not a relationship of this type (that is, it is not automatically a relationship of influence): *Barclays Bank plc v O'Brien* [1994] 1 AC 180, HL; *Royal Bank of Scotland v Etridge (No 2)* [2001] UKHL 44, [2002] 2 AC 773.

Example 1

A, after spending two years as a 'novice' at a convent run by B, the Mother Superior, joins the convent as a nun. On so doing, she enters into a contract by deed with B to give all her inherited wealth, worth some £750,000, to B for the sisterhood. A obtains no independent advice. A is entitled to rescind the contract for undue influence. Applying s 38(3) and (4), there is a rebuttable presumption of undue influence by B over A constituted by, first, the relationship of influence as between a spiritual adviser and follower (s 38 (4)(a)) and, secondly, the transaction being disadvantageous to A in the sense of not being readily explicable on ordinary motives (s 38(3)(b)). On the face of it, B will not be able to rebut that presumption (under s 38(5)) because A has not obtained any independent advice. (This example is based on *Allcard v Skinner* albeit that that famous case involved a gift not a contract.)

Although it is clear that there is the legal rule set out in s 38(4)(a), one may doubt its validity. In some, admittedly rare, situations it seems odd to say that the relationship is one of influence (for example, where a Supreme Court judge is advised by his solicitor). The Restatement reflects the present and long-established law, but to regard the fixed relationship as setting up a rebuttable factual presumption of influence would probably be preferable to regarding it as a legal rule.

38(4)(b)

As an alternative to the fixed categories, the claimant may be able to establish that, on the facts, there was a relationship in which he or she was under the defendant's influence: *Tate v Williamson* (1866) 2 Ch App 55, CA. In important modern cases a factual relationship of influence has been established between a husband and a wife (*Royal Bank of Scotland v Etridge (No 2)*), between a housekeeper and her elderly charge (*Re Craig* [1971] Ch 95), between a bank and its elderly customer (*Lloyds Bank Ltd v Bundy* [1975] QB 326, CA), between a manager and his pop singer 'employer' (*O'Sullivan v Management Agency and Music Ltd* [1985] QB 428, CA), between a farm manager and an elderly farm owner (*Goldsworthy v Brickell* [1987] Ch 378, CA), and between an employer and a junior employee (*Crédit Lyonnais Bank Nederland v Burch* [1997] 1 All ER 144, CA).

Example 2

A, an elderly retired businessman, has become increasingly reliant on his son, B, for advice and assistance. He has absolute trust in B and is also concerned not to upset B lest B should stop visiting him. B's own business is in difficulty and he needs a large sum of money to save it. He suggests to A that A should transfer shares (worth some £75,000) to B for a nominal consideration. A points out to B that this might leave him short of the assets to pay for the homecare that he needs. B expresses deep upset that A does not trust him to be doing the right thing and, following an argument between them, A reluctantly signs the contract for the sale of the shares. Assuming no bar, it is likely that A can rescind the contract for undue influence. There appears to be a rebuttable presumption of undue influence by B over A constituted by, first, a relationship of influence built up on the facts (s 38(4)(b)) and, secondly, the transaction being disadvantageous to A in the sense of not being readily explicable on ordinary motives. On the face of it, B will not be able to rebut that presumption (under s 38(5)) because A has not obtained any independent advice.

38(5)

If the two requirements for the evidential rebuttable presumption of undue influence in s 38(3) are established by the claimant, the evidential onus of proof switches to the defendant to rebut the presumption by proving that the claimant exercised free and independent judgement. Although neither necessary nor conclusive, the primary method of rebuttal is to show that the claimant obtained the fully informed and competent independent advice of a qualified person, most obviously a solicitor: *Inche Noriah v Shaik Allie Bin Omar* [1929] AC 127, PC; *Royal Bank of Scotland v Etridge (No 2)*.

39 Misrepresentation, illegitimate threat or undue influence by a third party
(1) The misrepresentation or illegitimate threat or undue influence may be that of a third party but, if so, the contract is voidable by the party to the contract ('the claimant') only if—
  (a) the third party was acting as the agent of the other contracting party ('the defendant');
  (b) the defendant had actual notice of the misrepresentation or illegitimate threat or undue influence; or
  (c) the defendant is deemed to have had notice of the misrepresentation or illegitimate threat or undue influence under subsections (2) to (4).
(2) Unless subsection (3) applies, the defendant is deemed to have had notice of a misrepresentation, illegitimate threat or undue influence of a third party if—
  (a) the defendant is a financial institution with whom the claimant entered into a contract of suretyship guaranteeing the repayment of a loan made by the defendant other than a loan, including a joint loan, to the claimant; and
  (b) the claimant has a non-commercial relationship with the third party, known about by the defendant, and entered into the contract because the misrepresentation or illegitimate threat was made by the third party or while under the undue influence of the third party.
(3) The defendant is not deemed to have had notice of a misrepresentation or illegitimate threat or undue influence of a third party if, before the contract was entered into, it—

      (a) informed the claimant, by direct communication, that it required written confirmation from the claimant's adviser that the adviser had fully explained to the claimant the nature and practical implications of the contract;

      (b) forwarded to the claimant's adviser details of the financial circumstances regarding the loan application to it;

      (c) informed the claimant's adviser of any facts which had led the defendant to believe or suspect that there had been a misrepresentation, illegitimate threat, or undue influence by the third party; and

      (d) received confirmation from the claimant's adviser that the adviser had provided the claimant with fully informed and competent advice.

(4) In subsection (3) 'adviser' means a solicitor or other legal adviser.

39(1)

The standard situation in mind here is where a contract of suretyship, between a wife and a bank under which the wife guarantees the debts of her husband or his company, has been induced by the undue influence of the third party husband; and the same law applies to misrepresentation (or, presumably, duress) by the third party husband: see *Barclays Bank plc v O'Brien* [1994] 1 AC 180, HL, which concerned misrepresentation by the husband to the wife. It was in *O'Brien* that it was first established that, unless the third party was acting as the defendant's agent (which will be very rare), the relevant concept establishing the liability of the defendant is notice, which at least sometimes can include constructive as well as actual notice. Although the use of constructive notice in this context was approved, and elaborated on, in *Royal Bank of Scotland v Etridge (No 2)* [2001] UKHL 44, [2002] 2 AC 773, it seems an odd and misleading choice of label. This is not least because a bank which reasonably believes, or ought reasonably to believe, that there may have been undue influence is regarded as not having constructive notice provided it has taken the steps laid down in the *Etridge* case. But those steps constitute a code of reasonable conduct for a bank that have nothing to do with notice (that is, with finding out more about the facts). The Restatement has therefore avoided the language of 'constructive notice' by referring instead to 'deemed notice', which at least has the merit of making clear that the reference to notice is here fictional.

    What remains unclear is whether *Etridge* is best interpreted as confining deemed, as opposed to actual, notice to non-commercial guarantees only. On the one hand, it can be argued that there is no good reason why those contracts alone should trigger the concept of deemed, rather than actual, notice (and note, in particular, that guarantees, whether commercial or non-commercial, are binding contracts under which the consideration for the surety's promise is the lender's payment to the borrower). On the other hand, one might say (and this is the interpretation favoured in O'Sullivan, Elliott, and Zakrzewski, *The Law of Rescission* (2nd edn, 2014) ch 9) that the application of deemed notice was being specially fashioned for, and confined to, non-commercial guarantees which were in issue in *O'Brien* and *Etridge*. At this stage in the development of the law, the Restatement adopts the latter view so that the general requirement is that there is actual notice. Subsections (2)–(4) set out what was laid down as regards deemed notice in *Etridge*.

Example

C induces A to enter into a contract for the purchase of goods from B by a misrepresentation as to the quality of the goods. A can rescind the contract with B, and recover the purchase price paid, if B has actual notice of C's misrepresentation to A.

The application of even actual notice in three-party misrepresentation cases appears to produce an unresolved conflict with the rules on non-induced mistake (see s 35(2) above and the leading case of *Smith v Hughes* (1871) LR 6 QB 597) where knowledge of the other party's mistake is in general irrelevant in deciding whether the contract is valid despite the mistake: see Cartwright, *Misrepresentation, Mistake and Non-Disclosure* (3rd edn, 2011) paras 4.72–4.78.

It is worth pointing out that the requirement of notice (or agency) does not apply to where a third party, by misrepresentation or undue influence or duress, induces A to make a gift to B, and A seeks restitution of the gift from B. A is straightforwardly entitled to restitution from B (that is, B's restitutionary liability is, as usual in the law of unjust enrichment, strict): *Bridgeman v Green* (1757) Wilm 58; and see the commentary to s 12(7) in *A Restatement of the English Law of Unjust Enrichment* (2012).

39(2)–(4)

The concept of deemed (or, in its preferred terminology, 'constructive') notice was accepted by the House of Lords (in *Barclays Bank v O'Brien* [1994] 1 AC 180, HL and *Royal Bank of Scotland v Etridge (No 2)* [2001] UKHL 44, [2002] 2 AC 773) at least as regards non-commercial guarantees. In line with that, s 39(2) summarises when the concept of deemed notice is applicable. That it does not apply where the surety (let us assume, a wife) is guaranteeing a joint loan to herself and her husband (unless the bank is aware that the loan is being made solely for the husband's purposes) was made clear in *CIBC Mortgages plc v Pitt* [1994] 1 AC 200, HL, and *Etridge* at [48].

In *Etridge*, the House of Lords clarified the steps a bank needs to take in order to avoid being fixed with deemed notice. Section 39(3) sets out those steps.

40 Legislative consumer protection against misleading or aggressive commercial practices

(1) Under Part 4A of the Consumer Protection from Unfair Trading Regulations 2008, a consumer has a legislative right to redress in respect of a contract with a trader for, for example, the sale or supply of a product by the trader, where—

    (a) there has been a commercial practice by the trader that is a misleading action or aggressive; and

    (b) that commercial practice was a significant factor in the consumer's decision to enter into the contract.

(2) A commercial practice is a misleading action if—

    (a) it contains false information or is likely to deceive the average consumer as to the existence or nature of the product or its main characteristics or the price or the rights of the parties; and

    (b) it is likely to cause the average consumer to take a transactional decision that would not otherwise have been taken.

(3) A commercial practice is aggressive if—

    (a) through the use of harassment, coercion, or undue influence, it is likely significantly to impair the average consumer's freedom of choice or conduct in relation to the product; and

    (b) it is likely to cause the average consumer to take a transactional decision that would not otherwise have been taken.

(4) The legislative right to redress includes the right to rescind the contract, the right to a discount, and the right to damages.

40

This section has been inserted to reflect the legislative reforms made by the Consumer Protection (Amendment) Regulations 2014 (SI 2014/870). The purpose of the Regulations is to give a consumer direct civil rights of redress in relation to the unfair commercial practices that were made criminal by (what are now called) the Consumer Protection from Unfair Trading Regulations 2008 (SI 2008/1277), which implemented the EU Directive on Unfair Commercial Practices (2005/29/EC). The legislative rights sit alongside, and do not remove, the judge-made doctrines of misrepresentation, duress, and undue influence. A consumer in a contract with a trader may well therefore rely on both the common law and the Regulations although in some respects (for example, the entitlement to damages for undue influence) the Regulations appear to go beyond the common law. The Regulations have been poorly drafted and in several respects seem more complex than necessary. What is set out in the Restatement may be said to cover their core elements but one will need to refer to the Regulations if one wishes to know the details. As has been said in relation to the legislative control of exemption clauses and unfair terms, this section of the Restatement should be read as a guide to, and not as a substitute for, reading the legislation. See also *Chitty on Contracts* (32nd edn, 2015) paras 38-145–38-191.

The meanings of 'consumer', and 'trader', and 'average consumer' have been set out in s 6 of the Restatement. Those meanings are the ones set out in the Consumer Rights Act 2015. To all intents and purposes they are the same as the meanings in reg 2 of the 2008 Regulations.

40(1)

The Consumer Protection (Amendment) Regulations 2014 have principally amended the Consumer Protection from Unfair Trading Regulations 2008 (originally called merely the Unfair Trading Regulations 2008) by inserting a new Part 4A (comprising regs 27A–L) into those Regulations.

As laid down in reg 27A, the relevant contracts covered are those for the sale or supply of a 'product' (defined by reg 2 to include, for example, goods, digital content, or a service, subject to certain exclusions such as, by reason of reg 27D, some financial services) by a trader to a consumer and the sale of goods by a consumer to a trader.

The relevant commercial practices, as laid down in reg 27B, are a misleading action (as defined in reg 5) and an aggressive commercial practice (as defined in reg 7). Reflecting the common law's reluctance to require disclosure, a commercial practice that is a misleading omission (as defined in reg 6) rather than a misleading action does not give rise to a civil action.

The necessary causal link—that the commercial practice was a significant factor in the consumer's decision to enter into the contract—is laid down in reg 27A(6).

40(2)

This correlates to reg 5 of the 2008 Regulations.

40(3)

This correlates to reg 7 of the 2008 Regulations. Reg 7(3)(b) defines 'undue influence' as meaning 'exploiting a position of power in relation to the consumer so as to apply pressure…in a way which significantly limits the consumer's ability to make an informed decision'. This does not neatly tie in with the meaning of undue influence at common law as set out in s 38 of the Restatement: for example, it may conceivably include 'exploitation of weakness' as dealt with in s 41 of the Restatement.

40(4)

The principal rights to redress are the right to unwind (reg 27E–G)—which is equivalent to the right to rescission—the right to a discount (reg 27I) (which is roughly equivalent to a right to restitution and counter-restitution), and the right to damages (reg 27J). The damages, which are analogous to compensatory damages for a tort, are expressly stated to cover non-pecuniary loss as well as pecuniary loss.

41   Exploitation of weakness

(1) A contract is voidable if one party to the contract ('the claimant') entered into it as the result of a weakness of the claimant having been exploited by the other contracting party ('the defendant').

(2) The weakness may be—

(a) a mental weakness (such as inexperience, confusion because of old age, or emotional strain); or

(b) in exceptional cases, a difficult position that the claimant is in.

(3) The claimant's weakness has been exploited by the defendant if—

(a) the terms of the contract were clearly disadvantageous to the claimant, and

(b) the defendant knew of the claimant's weakness and that the terms of the contract were clearly disadvantageous to the claimant,

unless the claimant obtained, and was able to act on, the fully informed and competent independent advice of a qualified person, such as a solicitor or other legal adviser.

41(1)

'Exploitation of weakness' is the term that has been chosen as the best description of the principle underpinning both the equitable jurisdiction to set aside 'unconscionable bargains' and the common law jurisdiction to set aside extortionate salvage agreements.

It has been explained in s 34 above that a voidable contract is one that can be rescinded at the choice of the claimant. Section 34 has also explained what the effect of rescission is, how the rescission may be brought about, and what the bars to rescission are.

Note that, in contrast to misrepresentation and duress, there is no 'but for' causation or 'presence in the mind' requirement: analogously to undue influence (see s 38) and incapacity (see s 43), it is sufficient that, at the time of entering into the contract, the claimant had the mental weakness, or was in the difficult position, that the defendant has exploited.

Although traditionally confined to contracts, there is no reason why 'exploitation of weakness' should not extend to gifts or other non-contractual transactions (and this derives support from *Louth v Diprose* (1992) 175 CLR 621, High Court of Australia); and this explains why these provisions are very similar to those on exploitation of weakness in *A Restatement of the English Law of Unjust Enrichment* (2012).

41(2)

The types of weakness in past cases can be divided into mental weakness (s 41(2)
(a)) and circumstantial weakness (s 41(2)(b)). Examples of the former are: inexperience (as in the 'expectant heir' cases such as *Earl of Aylesford v Morris* (1873) 8
Ch App 484, CA, and the 'poor and ignorant' cases such as *Evans v Llewellin* (1787)
1 Cox Eq Cas 333, *Fry v Lane* (1888) 40 Ch D 312, and *Creswell v Potter* [1978] 1
WLR 255n); infirmity by reason of old age (as in *Boustany v Pigott* (1995) 69 P &
CR 298, PC); and emotional strain (see obiter dicta in *Backhouse v Backhouse*
[1978] 1 WLR 243, 251). These forms of mental weakness fall short of incapacity, to
which different rules apply (see s 43); in particular, for exploitation of weakness, as
opposed to incapacity, substantive unfairness is required.

A main example of circumstantial weakness is where a person requires salvage as
in the extortionate salvage agreement cases of *The Medina* (1876) 1 PD 272 (affd
(1876) 2 PD 5, CA) and *The Port Caledonia and Anna* [1903] P 184. While these
were Admiralty cases, that is not a rational reason for ignoring them. Although not
established on the facts, the reasoning in *Alec Lobb Garages Ltd v Total Oil (GB) Ltd*
[1985] 1 WLR 173, CA, may also be interpreted as recognising that, in an exceptional case, exploitation of another's financial weakness may be a ground for
rescinding a contract. However, the precise ambit of this principle is vague, and
more decided cases are needed in order to put 'flesh' on what constitutes an
'exceptional' case. That the case must be 'exceptional' is shown by the following
routine example where the contract could not be rescinded for exploitation
of weakness.

Example 1

A (a company) contracts to sell some of its assets at very low prices to B, in
order to pay off urgent debts and to avoid going into liquidation. Even if B was
acting in bad faith in the relevant sense (see s 41(3)(b)), the contract would not
be voidable for exploitation of weakness.

41(3)

It is not the weakness per se that is unacceptable but rather the exploitation of that
weakness. The exploitation has three elements.

First, substantive unfairness (s 41(3)(a)). The need for the terms to be clearly
disadvantageous to the claimant has been expressed in various ways. See, for
example, 'a considerable undervalue' in *Fry v Lane* (1888) 40 Ch D 312, 322, per
Kay J; and 'manifestly disadvantageous' in *Portman Building Soc v Dusangh* [2000]
2 All ER (Comm) 221, 228, CA (per Simon Brown LJ).

Secondly, bad faith (that is, reprehensible conduct) (s 41(3)(b)). The Restatement
has incorporated this idea by requiring that the exploiting party had a blameworthy

state of mind in that he or she knew of the claimant's weakness and of the substantive unfairness. Although it is not absolutely clear that this is a requirement, the better view is that it is. Reasoning supporting such a requirement includes that in *O'Rorke v Bolingbroke* (1877) 2 App Cas 814, HL; *Alec Lobb Garages Ltd v Total Oil (GB) Ltd* [1985] 1 WLR 173, CA; *Portman Building Soc v Dusangh* [2000] 2 All ER (Comm) 221, CA.

Thirdly, no independent advice ('unless the claimant obtained, and was able to act on, the fully informed and competent independent advice of a qualified person'). The importance of independent advice was mentioned in *Fry v Lane* (1888) 40 Ch D 312, 322 and is consistent with the reasoning and decisions in all the relevant cases. According to the reasoning in several cases, and by analogy to undue influence, it is best to see the evidential burden of proving this to be on the defendant.

Example 2

An elderly man, A, who is often confused but has mental capacity, unexpect-edly sells his car to his neighbour, B, for five per cent of its market value. B realises that A is confused and also knows that A's family members would not approve of the sale. A may be entitled to rescind the contract for exploit-ation of weakness. But note that without a civil wrong, such as the tort of deceit, A will not be entitled to compensation for any consequential loss (for example, taxi fares that he has to incur because he no longer has a car).

Assuming that the second of the three elements is indeed required, it marks a significant difference between exploitation of weakness, on the one hand, and misrepresentation, duress, and undue influence on the other. Misrepresentation, duress, and undue influence do not *require* a blameworthy state of mind (although this will often be present): that is, one does not need dishonesty (or even negli-gence). This leads naturally on to the fact that a contract can be rescinded even though the misrepresentation, duress, or undue influence has been exerted by a third party. In contrast, once one insists on a blameworthy state of mind (bad faith) for exploitation, it would make no sense to regard there as being a separate issue regarding rescission for exploitation of weakness by a third party. Assume, for example, that A has entered into a contract with B following C's exploitation of A's mental weakness. To require the other contracting party (B) to have knowledge of C's exploitation would inevitably mean that B itself has exploited A's weakness. There is nothing to be gained by seeing this as a separate third party issue. Put another way, rescission in this context can be regarded as always requiring exploit-ation of the weakness by the other contracting party.

It is worth adding at the end of this section that ss 140A–140C of the Consumer Credit Act 1974 may be regarded as analogous to the common law's protection against exploitation of weakness in the context of the claimant's need for credit. Those provisions provide a wide range of remedies for the undoing of credit agreements (for example, loans with an extortionate rate of interest) where the relationship between the creditor and the debtor is unfair to the debtor. Note, however, that the analogy is a loose one in the sense that, for example, the legislative protection is not necessarily restricted to where the creditor's conduct was reprehensible.

42   Non-disclosure
(1) The general rule is that a contract is not voidable merely because one party to the contract ('the defendant') did not disclose to the other contracting party ('the claimant') an important matter of fact or law relevant to the contract.
(2) There are legislative provisions (for example, in respect of insurance contracts where the insured is not a consumer) which require the disclosure of information by one contracting party to the other.
(3) Other exceptions to the general rule in subsection (1) include—
   (a) that a contract is voidable for non-disclosure of a material circumstance if the defendant was in a fiduciary relationship with the claimant; and
   (b) that a contract of suretyship guaranteeing the payment of a debt to the defendant is voidable for non-disclosure of an unusual feature of that debt and, therefore, of the contract of suretyship.
(4) A contract is voidable under subsection (3) only if the defendant's non-disclosure induced the claimant to enter into the contract in the sense that the claimant would not have entered into the contract (whether at all or on the same terms) had it known about the matter of fact or law that was not disclosed.

42(1)

That there is no general 'duty' of disclosure ties in with the narrow doctrine of mistake in English law (see s 35) and with the fact that, in general, silence does not constitute a misrepresentation (see commentary to s 36(2)). At a deeper level it is consistent with the reluctance of English law to recognise a general duty to negotiate in good faith. So in general, as shown in the leading case of *Smith v Hughes* (1871) LR 6 QB 597, a contract is valid even though one of the parties knows that the other party is making an important mistake about the contract and does not inform them of the true facts. See Examples 1–3 in the commentary to s 35. As was said by Lord Atkin in *Bell v Lever Bros Ltd* [1932] AC 161, 227: 'Ordinarily the failure to disclose a material fact which might influence the mind of a prudent contractor does not give the right to avoid the contract.'

42(2)

Traditionally the main exception to there being no requirement of disclosure was in a contract of insurance; and this exception was explained by saying that a contract of insurance was a contract *uberrimae fidei* ('of utmost good faith'). The exception was developed at common law and was then codified in the Marine Insurance Act 1906.

However, the law on disclosure in insurance contracts has been transformed by recent legislation. Under the Consumer (Disclosure and Representations) Act 2012 there is no longer any requirement of disclosure by a consumer in a consumer insurance contract (although the Act makes clear that a failure to correct earlier details can amount to a misrepresentation). As regards non-consumer insurance contracts, the Insurance Act 2015 (which comes into force on 12 August 2016 but does not require any amendment to the deliberately very general words used in this subsection of the Restatement) replaces the codified common law of disclosure by what is termed a 'duty of fair presenta-tion'. The Act then goes on to provide some further details as to what it is that the insured is required to disclose to the insurer (including, for example, whose knowledge within the insured's organisation counts for these purposes) in order to satisfy that duty of fair presentation. While it may be doubted how far the 2015 Act changes the law in substance, it certainly changes the terminology that has traditionally been used (so that, for example, it becomes unhelpful to talk of a contract of insurance being a contract of utmost good faith). The Act also changes aspects of the remedy of rescission (and conse-quent restitution) for non-disclosure: for example, what is in effect partial rescission is provided for and, if the non-disclosure has been deliberate or reckless, the insurer may avoid the contract without making restitution of the premiums paid.

Other important legislative provisions imposing a requirement of disclosure include: the Financial Services and Markets Act 2000, s 80, requiring disclosure in relation to company prospectuses; and the Consumer Contracts (Information, Cancellation and Additional Charges) Regulations 2013 (SI 2013/3134), which require certain information to be given to consumers depending on the type of contract in question (for example, whether an 'on-premises contract' or a 'distance contract').

42(3)

As we have just explained, the law on disclosure in insurance contracts was traditionally the main 'common law' exception to there being no requirement of non-disclosure. In this subsection, we are concerned with what will remain common law exceptions after the Insurance Act 2015 comes into force.

One clear example is that there is a requirement of disclosure in respect of a contract where there is a fiduciary relationship between the parties (s 42(3)(a)). The rationale for this is that these are contracts under which one party is expected to act in the interests of the other rather than in self-interest. Some relationships are automatically fiduciary, such as that between principal and agent or solicitor and client; others can be built from the facts (see analogously the law on undue influence: s 38(4)). A leading example of rescission for non-disclosure by a fiduciary is *Erlanger v New Sombrero Phosphate Co* (1878) 3 App Cas 1218, HL.

Example

B, the promoter of a company, A, buys an island for himself. A few days later, B sells the island to A for mining for double the price B had paid and without disclosing that B has recently bought the island for half the price. A can rescind the contract (that is, the contract is voidable) for the non-disclosure by B who, as the promoter of A, is in a fiduciary relationship with A. (This example is based on *Erlanger v New Sombrero Phosphate Co.*)

The facts (or it could be matters of law) that must be disclosed are those that are 'material'. In the leading case of *Pan Atlantic Insurance Co Ltd v Pine Top Insurance Co Ltd* [1995] 1 AC 501, HL—which applies analogously to where the parties are in a fiduciary relationship—a reinsured, in negotiating a reinsurance contract, disclosed some of the losses it had incurred under the insurance policy in previous years but not all the losses. It was held that, in respect of an insured's requirement of disclosure, the test of materiality was whether the facts in question would have had an effect on the mind of the prudent insurer in weighing up the risk. It is not necessary, in order to establish materiality, to show that the facts would have had a decisive influence on the insurer albeit that, in addition to materiality, there is the separate requirement that the non-disclosure induced the contract (see s 42(4)). One might argue that, as inducement has to be established, 'materiality' is an unnecessary initial requirement. But in the context of non-disclosure (contrast misrepresentation) materiality does serve a useful role in guiding a person as to the scope of the information that should be disclosed.

Although not mentioned as an example in the Restatement, not least because there are few modern reported cases on this, another traditionally accepted example of a contract requiring disclosure of a material circumstance (and often classified as a contract of utmost good faith) is a compromise of a dispute over property between members of a family: *Gordon v Gordon* (1821) 3 Swan 400; cf *Wales v Wadham* [1977] 1 WLR 199. Another example is where parties are negotiating a partnership agreement: *Bell v Lever Bros Ltd* [1932] AC 161, 227; *Conlon v Simms* [2006] EWCA Civ 1749, [2008] 1 WLR 484, at [127].

As regards s 42(3)(b), there is a requirement of disclosure, albeit limited, in the context of negotiations for a contract of suretyship. A creditor must disclose to a surety any unusual feature of the debt under the principal contract between the creditor and the debtor: *Levett v Barclays Bank plc* [1995] 1 WLR 1260; *Royal Bank of Scotland v Etridge (No 2)* [2001] UKHL 44, [2002] 2 AC 773 at [81], [114], [185]–[188]; *North Shore Ventures Ltd v Anstead Holdings Ltd* [2011] EWCA Civ 230, [2012] Ch 31.

Where a common law exception applies, non-disclosure renders the contract voidable. It has been explained in s 34 that a voidable contract is one that can be rescinded at the choice of the claimant. Section 34 has also explained what the effect of rescission is, how the rescission may be brought about, and what the bars to rescission are.

In general, non-disclosure is not a civil wrong that triggers the remedy of damages (and even if dishonest, there can be no liability in the tort of deceit without a separate misrepresentation) so that the only remedy for non-disclosure is rescission of the contract (and consequent restitution): *Banque Financière de la Cité SA v Westgate Insurance Co Ltd, sub nom Banque Keyser Ullmann SA v Skandia (UK) Insurance Co Ltd* [1990] 1 QB 665, CA; affirmed [1991] 2 AC 249, HL. (Cf *Conlon v Simms* [2006] EWCA Civ 1749, [2008] 1 WLR 484, in which it was controversially and, with respect, incorrectly accepted that there can be liability in the tort of deceit on the reasoning that, where there is a requirement of disclosure, there is an implied representation that there is nothing relevant to disclose.) It follows from this that, strictly speaking, it is incorrect to talk in this context of a 'duty' of disclosure and better to talk of a requirement of disclosure.

However, non-disclosure by a fiduciary constitutes the civil wrong of breach of fiduciary duty, which triggers the remedies of equitable compensation and an account of profits. These can be awarded in addition to rescission of the contract subject to not producing double recovery (see analogously s 36(7)).

42(4)

As has been mentioned under the previous subsection, it was established in *Pan Atlantic Insurance Co Ltd v Pine Top Insurance Co Ltd* that, in an insurance contract, the non-disclosure must have had a causative effect by inducing the contract; and that approach appears to be applicable by analogy to the other situations where, at common law, disclosure is required. Although not spelt out what the relevant test for inducement is, it would seem that, by analogy to the 'but for' test for misrepresentation, the relevant test is whether the claimant would have entered into the contract (whether at all or on the same terms) had it known about the circumstance that was not disclosed.

43   Incapacity

(1) Subject to subsection (2), a contract with an individual who is under 18 (a 'minor') is unenforceable against the minor unless the minor ratifies the contract after becoming 18.

(2) A contract with a minor—

    (a) is voidable, and can be rescinded by the minor before, or within a reasonable time after, becoming 18 if the contract is—

        (i)   a contract for the acquisition of an interest in land;

        (ii) a contract for the acquisition of shares in a company;

        (iii) a partnership agreement; or

        (iv) a marriage settlement;

    (b) is valid and enforceable by and against the minor if it is a contract for necessaries or a beneficial contract of service or an analogous contract.

(3) Subject to subsection (5), a contract is voidable where an individual enters into it while lacking mental capacity or while incapacitated by intoxication provided the other party to the contract knew of that lack of mental capacity or intoxication.

(4) For the purpose of subsection (3), an individual lacks mental capacity if at the time of entering into the contract he or she is unable to make the decision for himself or herself to enter into the contract because of an impairment of, or a disturbance in the functioning of, the mind or brain.

(5) There is a special rule applicable to a contract of compromise made by an individual while lacking mental capacity according to which the contract is voidable if, at the time of entering into it, he or she did not have a litigation friend (that is, an individual permitted to act in court proceedings on behalf of an individual who lacks capacity).

(6) By reason of section 39 of the Companies Act 2006, a contract with a non-charitable company is not void or otherwise defective on the ground that the company is acting outside the powers in its constitution.

(7) A contract made with a public authority acting outside its powers is void.

43

The law on contracts made by those who lack capacity depends on the incapacity in question. There are three types of human incapacity: infancy (s 43(1)–(2)), mental incapacity, and intoxication (s 43(3)–(5)). Institutional incapacity is now in practice confined to a public authority acting outside its powers (s 43(7)).

43(1)–(2)

Since the repeal of the Infants' Relief Act 1874 by the Minors' Contracts Act 1987, the law on contracts where one of the parties is under the age of majority (18) is almost entirely common law (although s 2 of the Minors' Contracts Act 1987 clarifies that contracts of guarantee are enforceable by the minor; and s 4 of that Act confers on the courts a rather obscure discretion to require the minor to give restitution of property, or property representing it, acquired under a contract that is defective for infancy).

It is helpful to distinguish three categories of contracts with a minor. Under the first two categories (s 43(1) and s 43(2)(a)) the contracts are defective. In the other category (s 43(2)(b)), the contracts are valid and enforceable by and against the minor. In none of the three categories is it relevant whether the adult knew or not that the other party was under 18. Rationalising these three categories is far from easy. In general terms, they respond to the perceived need for minors to be protected against themselves and against advantage being taken of their inexperience. On the other hand, it is recognised that it would be highly inconvenient and detrimental to minors if they could not enter into, for example, beneficial and necessary contracts.

The first category (covering contracts which are outside the other two categories and can be regarded as setting out the general position) comprises contracts that are unenforceable against the minor unless ratified by the minor on reaching adulthood (s 43(1)). For an example of such a contract see *Pearce v Brain* [1929] 2 KB 310 (purchase of a car). Ratification means that the minor makes clear, expressly or impliedly, that she considers herself bound by the contract (see, for example, *Rowe v Hopwood* (1868–9) LR 4 QB 1). The idea of a contract being unenforceable against one party unless ratified appears to be unique to the law on minors' contracts.

Example 1

A, who is 17, contracts to buy a painting for £20,000 from B (an adult). The painting is worth £15,000. When A refuses to take delivery of the painting, B sues A for breach of contract seeking damages of £5,000. The claim will fail. This is because the contract is unenforceable against A, who is a minor (unless A ratifies the contract after becoming 18).

The second category (s 43(2)(a)) covers contracts that are voidable (that is, that can be rescinded or, as it is sometimes misleadingly said, 'repudiated') by the minor before becoming 18 or within a reasonable time thereafter, namely contracts for an interest in land or shares in a company (as in *Steinberg v Scala (Leeds) Ltd* [1923] 2 Ch 452, CA) or partnership agreements or a marriage settlement (as in *Edwards v Carter* [1893] AC 360, HL). These contracts share the common feature of having potentially beneficial long-term effects for minors.

The meaning of rescission and how one rescinds have been dealt with in s 34(3)–(4) above. It would appear that the usual bars to rescission apply (see s 34(5)) although it should be noted that delay applies (separately, it would seem, from affirmation) even though the 'rescission' in question (often referred to as 'repudiation') is at common law not in equity: that is, the minor loses the power to rescind once a reasonable time has elapsed after becoming 18 (see, for example, *Edwards v Carter* [1893] AC 360, HL, where a delay of five years since becoming an adult barred rescission).

The third category comprises contracts that are valid and enforceable, by and against the minor, most obviously contracts for necessaries or beneficial contracts of service (s 43(2)(b)). 'Necessaries' tends to be given a wide meaning. As is said in *Anson's Law of Contract* (eds Beatson, Burrows, and Cartwright, 29th edn, 2010) at 234: 'It has always been held that a minor may be liable for the supply, not merely of the necessaries of life, but of things suitable to his or her station in life and particular circumstances at the time.' A contract was held to be valid as a beneficial contract of service with a minor in *Clements v London and North Western Railway Co* [1894] 2 QB 482, CA. For a contrasting case, where the contract of service was held to be overall more onerous than beneficial and therefore unenforceable against the minor, see *De Francesco v Barnum* (1890) 45 Ch D 430. A beneficial publishing contract was held to be analogous to a contract of service and valid and enforceable against the minor in *Chaplin v Leslie Frewin (Publishers) Ltd* [1966] Ch 71, CA.

Example 2

A, already a well-known author at the age of 16, enters into a lucrative contract with B to write a book to be published by B. A completes the book but then, in breach of contract, refuses to allow B to publish it and instead sends it to another publishing house. B is entitled to damages for breach of contract from A because, although A was a minor, the contract is analogous to a beneficial contract of service and is therefore valid and enforceable by and against A.

Although this is not reflected in the Restatement, because it has never been directly in issue in the decided cases and is highly unlikely to arise in practice, it would appear to be the case that a very young child may not be bound by even a contract for necessaries: that is, as a minimum threshold, a child must be of an age where he or she is capable of understanding the nature of the transaction. For obiter dicta of Scott LJ on this, see *R v Oldham MBC* [1993] 1 FLR 645 at 661–2 (decision affd [1993] AC 509, HL).

The tangled law on the restitution of benefits conferred under the two categories of contract that are defective for infancy is dealt with in *A Restatement of the English Law of Unjust Enrichment* (2012) s 14 and the relevant commentary and will not be repeated here: see generally s 3(1) above. A minor's obligation to pay a reasonable price for necessary goods sold and delivered to him, imposed by s 3(2) of the Sale of Goods Act 1979, is probably best interpreted as restitution for unjust enrichment rather than as a contractual liability because that provision appears to be inapplicable to executory contracts. (That provision also applies to incapacity by reason of drunkenness; and see, analogously, as regards mental incapacity, s 7 of the Mental Capacity Act 2005, which also covers necessary services supplied.)

43(3)–(4)

The meaning of mental incapacity is given in s 2(1) of the Mental Capacity Act 2005: 'a person lacks capacity in relation to a matter if at the material time he is unable to make a decision for himself in relation to the matter because of an impairment of, or a disturbance in the functioning of, the mind or brain.' Presumably the equivalent inability to make a decision for himself is required if intoxication (whether by drink or drug-taking) is involved so that one is talking about extreme intoxication and not someone who has merely had a few drinks. Assuming that the person is not under the control of the Court of Protection and therefore retains control of his or her own affairs, a contract is only voidable if the other party knew of the mental incapacity (or intoxication): *Imperial Loan Co v Stone* [1892] 1 QB 599, CA; *Hart v O'Connor* [1985] AC 1000, PC; *Irwani v Irwani* [2000] 1 Lloyd's Rep 412, at 425, CA.

In obiter dicta in *Dunhill v Burgin* [2014] UKSC 18, [2014] 1 WLR 933, at [25], Lady Hale (with whom the other Justices agreed) said that it was now generally accepted that the rule in *Imperial Loan Co v Stone* extended to where the other party ought to have known of the mental incapacity. However, with respect, caution may here be needed so as not to water down what has traditionally been a clear and certain test to one of mere negligence (which would seem insufficient).

43(5)

This is the special rule established in *Dunhill v Burgin* [2014] UKSC 18, [2014] 1 WLR 933. It cuts across s 43(3) because, without a litigation friend (that is, someone—whether, for example, a relative or lawyer—who is permitted to act in court proceedings on behalf of a person who lacks capacity: see Civil Procedure Rules Part 21), the contract of compromise can be set aside even though the other contracting party did not know (and could not reasonably have known) that the person lacked mental capacity. (Note that although that special rule no doubt also applies to where a minor enters into a contract of compromise (as pointed out by Lady Hale in *Dunhill v Burgin* at [29]), the normal rules in s 43(1) and (2) will protect the minor in any event.)

43(6)

It used to be the law that a contract was ultra vires and void if made by a company outside the objects in the company's memorandum. This doctrine has since been abolished (for non-charitable companies). By s 39(1) of the Companies Act 2006, '[t]he validity of an act done by a company shall not be called into question on the ground of lack of capacity by reason of anything in the company's constitution.'

43(7)

In practice, the legislative reform of the law on the capacity of companies set out in the previous subsection means that institutional incapacity is now largely confined to public authorities that are acting outside their statutory powers in making the contract in question.

Although there have been suggestions in the past that an ultra vires contract is merely unenforceable against the public authority, it was assumed in a series of recent high-profile cases, concerning restitution of money paid under interest-rate swap transactions, that such contracts are void: see, for example, *Westdeutsche Landesbank Girozentrale v Islington London BC* [1996] AC 669, HL; *Kleinwort Benson Ltd v Lincoln City Council* [1999] 2 AC 349, HL.

Even in the context of public authorities, the practical importance of the ultra vires doctrine for contracts has been reduced, as regards local authorities, by two statutes: the Local Government (Contracts) Act 1997 and the Localism Act 2011. Neither removes the rule that a contract made by a local authority ultra vires is void. However, the 1997 Act allows a local authority to certify that a contract is intra vires, subject to judicial review; and on such an application for judicial review, a court can decide that the contract should be treated as intra vires having regard 'to the likely consequences for the financial provision of the local authority, and for the provision of services to the public, of a decision that the contract should not have effect' (s 5(3)(b)). Section 1 of the 2011 Act confers on local authorities the general power to do anything which an individual of full capacity may do. Limits are then placed on that general power by ss 2–4 of the Act.

44 Illegality and public policy
(1) If the formation, purpose or performance of a contract involves conduct that is illegal (such as a crime) or contrary to public policy (such as a restraint of trade), the contract is unenforceable by one or either party if to deny enforcement is an appropriate response to that conduct.
(2) There are legislative provisions which—
 (a) prohibit a contract so that it is unenforceable by either party;
 (b) lay down that a contract or contract term is unenforceable by one or either party (or void).

(3) A contract that would otherwise be unenforceable as mentioned in subsection (1) or (2) may be severed so that the objectionable part of the contract is disregarded and the rest of the contract is enforceable; but severance is possible only if—

    (a) the objectionable part of the contract does not form the main consideration under the contract;

    (b) the objectionable part of the contract can be separated from the rest of the contract without rewriting; and

    (c) severance would not entirely alter the nature of the agreement.

(4) If a contract is unenforceable by one or either party as mentioned in subsections (1) and (2), a contract that is linked to such a contract may be unenforceable by one or either party for the same reasons.

(5) A term excluding liability for a person's own fraudulent misrepresentation is contrary to public policy and void.

(6) Where there are proceedings before a court relating to a contract involving conduct that appears to be illegal or contrary to public policy, the court must consider whether the contract or term is unenforceable or void even if not raised by the parties unless the court considers that it has insufficient legal and factual material to do so.

44(1)

(i) The uncertainty of the present law

Leaving aside the law on what one can loosely label 'statutory illegality'—which is set out in subsection (2) and appears to be relatively settled—the law on the effect of illegality in contract (which one may loosely refer to as the 'common law of illegality') is in a state of flux. This has made it a particularly difficult area to restate.

Traditionally, two Latin maxims have often been referred to without greatly illuminating the legal position: *ex turpi causa non oritur actio* ('no action arises from a disgraceful cause') and *in pari delicto potior est conditio defendentis* ('where both parties are equally in the wrong the position of the defendant is the stronger'). As previously understood, illegality in the law of contract—as developed from those Latin maxims—was governed by a series of rules which tended to distinguish, for example, between illegality in formation and illegality in performance. Unfortunately, commentators and courts have found it very difficult to state those rules with confidence and precision. Hence the textbook treatments not only differ from each other but are characterised by long-winded attempts to explain the law. Sharp propositions when offered by the courts or the books have to be qualified by reference to cases or hypothetical examples that do not fit those rules; and convincing justifications of those rules have proved elusive. More recently, therefore, and in line with a similar trend in respect of illegality as a defence in tort, some courts have favoured greater flexibility culminating in a 'range of factors' approach aimed at achieving a proportionate response to contractual illegality in preference to the traditional rule-based approach. The leading case in contract adopting this approach is *ParkingEye Ltd v Somerfield Stores Ltd* [2012] EWCA Civ 1338, [2013] QB 840. This approach has drawn heavily on the work of the Law Commission, which initially favoured introducing a structured discretion by statute (on the grounds that this approach could not be reached by standard judicial decision-making) but ultimately concluded that a similar approach was largely attainable by the courts so that legislation was largely unnecessary.

The conflict of approach to illegality as a defence has resurfaced in no fewer than three recent cases in the Supreme Court. Although none dealt with illegality in contract as such, they are of great importance generally to the illegality defence.

In *Hounga v Allen* [2014] UKSC 47, [2014] 1 WLR 2889, the fact that the claimant was an illegal immigrant was held not to be a defence to her claim for the statutory tort of unlawful racial discrimination. The majority's judgment given by Lord Wilson (with whom Lady Hale and Lord Kerr agreed) openly saw the issue as turning on a consideration of various public policy factors with a focus on preserving the integrity of the legal system, which in turn involved examining whether the claimant had profited from the wrongdoing and deterrence. It should be stressed that there was no dispute in this case about enforcement of the contract. The claimant accepted that illegality was a defence to any claim that she might have had for breach of the contract of employment (or unfair dismissal). This is probably best explained by reference to s 42(2) of the Restatement: the contract of employment was impliedly prohibited by the relevant legislation and could not therefore be enforced.

However, a very different approach (but see the valiant attempt by Sales LJ in *R (Best) v Chief Land Registrar* [2015] EWCA Civ 17, [2015] 2 P & CR 1, to reconcile the two) was favoured by the majority of the Supreme Court only three months later in *Les Laboratoires Servier v Apotex Inc* [2014] UKSC 55, [2015] AC 430, a decision in which *Hounga v Allen* was not even mentioned by the majority. The claim was for damages under a cross-undertaking in damages given by Servier who had been granted an injunction against Apotex to restrain infringement of a patent. It transpired that Servier should not have been granted that injunction because it had no valid patent in this jurisdiction. The question was whether Apotex's illegality, by acting in breach of Servier's valid Canadian patent, constituted a defence to Apotex's claim for damages under the cross-undertaking. In the Court of Appeal in that case ([2012] EWCA Civ 593, esp at [66], [73], and [75]) Etherton LJ had applied the approach of seeking to reach a proportionate response to the illegality taking into account various factors (and his approach in this case was heavily relied on by the Court of Appeal in *ParkingEye v Somerfield*). The Supreme Court unanimously upheld the decision of the Court of Appeal that the illegality should not be a defence. However, it did so on the narrow ground that the commission of a tort (here the infringement of a patent) was not in itself the sort of illegal conduct that counted for the purposes of the defence (which, in Lord Sumption's words, at [25], must be criminal or quasi-criminal). One can readily agree with the decision, which was plainly correct. More controversially, the majority of the Supreme Court (with the exception of Lord Toulson at [62]) criticised the Court of Appeal's general approach to illegality.

In the third case, *Jetivia SA v Bilta (UK) Ltd* [2015] UKSC 23, [2015] 2 WLR 1168, claims were brought by a company against its directors and others seeking compensation for, inter alia, breach of fiduciary duty, the tort of unlawful means conspiracy, and dishonest assistance in respect of a VAT fraud. The question at issue was whether the company's claims were met by the illegality defence: ie did the illegal conduct of the directors mean that the company itself was acting illegally so as to trigger the illegality defence to the company's claims? The seven-man Supreme Court unanimously decided that the illegality defence was inapplicable in this situation because the illegal conduct of the directors could not be attributed to the company (and, per Lords Toulson and Hodge, to deny the claim would defeat the policy behind the rules of law in question). While recognising the apparent inconsistency of approach to illegality between *Hounga v Allen* and *Les Laboratoires*—and while Lords Toulson and Hodge on the one hand and Lord Sumption on the other indicated their preference for a flexible 'balancing' approach and a rule-based approach respectively—their Lordships expressed the view that this was not an appropriate case for considering the general approach to the illegality defence. They expressed the hope that the court would have an opportunity in the near future to address that central and important question. In the words of Lord Neuberger (giving the joint judgment of himself, Lord Clarke, and Lord Carnwath) at [15]:

'[W]hile the proper approach to the defence of illegality needs to be addressed by this court . . . as soon as appropriately possible, this is not the case in which it should be decided. We have had no real argument on the topic: this case is concerned with attribution, and that is the issue on which the arguments have correctly focussed. Further, in this case, as in the two recent Supreme Court decisions of *Les Laboratoires* and *Hounga*, the outcome is the same irrespective of the correct approach to the illegality defence.'

For similar sentiments, see Lord Mance at [34] and Lords Toulson and Hodge at [174].

It is clear, therefore, that the law on illegality in contract is at a crossroads. The uncertainty in the courts is mirrored by uncertainty amongst practitioners and academics. In general terms, there is a split between those who consider that the law can be stated in one or more rules; and those who consider that the factors in play are so variable that a more flexible approach is preferable and, as shown in the context of contract by *ParkingEye Ltd v Somerfield Stores Ltd* [2012] EWCA Civ 1338, [2013] QB 840, is attainable by the courts without legislation.

Given this degree of uncertainty, the Restatement in s 44(1) sets out a high-level principle, which both 'camps' can agree with, that can then be 'fleshed out' by either a 'rule-based' approach or a 'range of factors' approach. This commentary will now set out both of those approaches while making clear that the view of the author is that, at least at this stage in the development of the law, the latter approach is to be preferred.

(ii) A rule-based approach

Applying a traditional rule-based approach, how might one restate the law? In other words, in the language of the high-level principle, what are the rules ensuring that to deny enforcement is an appropriate response to the illegal conduct?

One formulation, which on one interpretation may be said to be supported in recent years by *Tinsley v Milligan* [1994] 1 AC 340, HL, and *Les Laboratoires Servier v Apotex Inc* [2014] UKSC 55, [2015] AC 430, is to focus entirely (or at least primarily) on whether the claimant is relying on the illegality in order to establish its cause of action. This focus explains why according to some (see, for example, Nicholas Strauss QC in *Watts v Watts* [2014] EWHC 3056 (Ch) at [126]) the reliance rule has become the modern interpretation of the Latin maxim *ex turpi causa non oritur actio*. A formulation of this single reliance master rule might therefore be:

If the formation, purpose or performance of a contract involves conduct that is illegal (such as a crime) or contrary to public policy (such as a restraint of trade), a party cannot enforce the contract if it has to rely on that conduct to establish its claim.

Applying this approach, it might be said, for example, that in *Hounga v Allen* the reason why illegality was not a defence to the claim for unlawful racial discrimination was that the claimant did not need to rely on her own performance of illegal work (as an 'illegal immigrant') in order to show that she had been the victim of racial discrimination in being dismissed. In contrast, illegality would have been a defence had she been seeking wages under her contract of employment because then she would have had to rely on her own performance of illegal work to make out the claim.

An alternative rule-based formulation sees the reliance rule as only one of a number of rules and as being essentially confined, as was the issue in *Tinsley v Milligan*, to the creation of proprietary rights by consent, including by a contract (although the facts of that case involved an underlying non-contractual domestic agreement). On this alternative formulation, the leading cases to consider alongside *Tinsley v Milligan* are, for example, *Anderson Ltd v Daniel* [1924] 1 KB 138, CA,

Archbolds (Freightage) Ltd v Spanglett Ltd [1961] 1 QB 374, CA, and *Ashmore Benson Peace & Co Ltd v AV Dawson Ltd* [1973] 1 WLR 828, CA, in each of which there was extensive consideration of the appropriate rules for illegality in contract. See also *Chitty on Contracts* (32nd edn, 2015) paras 16-011, 16-016–16-020. Leaving aside statutory illegality (see s 44(2) of the Restatement) these cases may be said to support the following rules. Rule 1 refers to 'illegality in formation' (that is, the contract is illegal as made), whereas rule 2 is referring to 'illegality in performance'.

Rule 1

A contract which has as its purpose, or is intended to be performed in a manner that involves, conduct that is illegal (such as a crime) or contrary to public policy (such as a restraint of trade) is unenforceable—

　　(a) by either party if both parties knew of that purpose or intention; or

　　(b) by one party if only that party knew of that purpose or intention.

Rule 2

If rule 1 is inapplicable because it is only the performance of a contract that involves conduct that is illegal or contrary to public policy, the contract is unenforceable by the party who performed in that objectionable way but is enforceable by the other party unless that party knew of, and participated in, that objectionable performance.

To these two rules, one could then add the reliance rule, derived from *Bowmakers Ltd v Barnet Instruments Ltd* [1945] KB 65, CA, and applied in *Tinsley v Milligan* [1994] 1 AC 340, HL, as a third rule concerned with the creation of proprietary rights by contract. So one might state this third rule as follows:

Rule 3

Proprietary rights created by a contract that involves conduct that is illegal or contrary to public policy will not be recognised unless the claimant can establish the proprietary rights without reliance on that conduct.

(iii) Criticisms of those rules/a rule-based approach

One only has to state the above rules to see immediate difficulties with them. What follows are six criticisms of those rules and, more generally, of a 'rule-based' approach to illegality.

1. The central problem with the reliance rule (whether formulated as a master rule or as rule 3 above) is that it can produce different decisions depending on the procedural technicality, which has nothing to do with the policies in question, of whether the claimant needs to plead the illegality or not. Fortuitously this produced the desired result on the facts of *Tinsley v Milligan*. However, even though the illegality involved would be identical, a different result would have been reached on those facts if the parties had been father and daughter.

Example 1

C and D (same-sex partners) both provide the money for the purchase of a house. Under an agreement between them, the house is registered solely in C's name so that D can make false benefit claims to the Department of Social Security. C and D fall out and C moves out. C brings a claim for possession of the house as hers alone. D counterclaims that she is jointly entitled under a presumed resulting trust. (These were the facts in *Tinsley v Milligan*.)

Example 2

The facts are the same as in Example 1 except that, instead of being partners, D is the father of C so that there is no presumed resulting trust but rather a presumption of advancement.

Applying a reliance rule, D's counterclaim succeeds in Example 1 because, as there is a presumed resulting trust, D does not have to rely on the illegal scheme. In contrast, in Example 2, the counterclaim fails because D has to rely on the illegal scheme to rebut the presumption of advancement.

McHugh J in the High Court of Australia in *Nelson v Nelson* (1995) 184 CLR 538 was particularly clear and forthright in his criticisms of *Tinsley v Milligan*. Having said that the reliance rule would produce results that were 'essentially random', he went on at 609:

'The [reliance] rule has no regard to the legal and equitable rights of the parties, the merits of the case, the effect of the transaction in undermining the policy of the relevant legislation or the question whether the sanctions imposed by the legislation sufficiently protect the purpose of the legislation. Regard is had only to the procedural issue; and it is that issue and not the policy of the legislation or the merits of the parties which determines the outcome. Basing the grant of legal remedies on an essentially procedural criterion which has nothing to do with the equitable positions of the parties or the policy of the legislation is unsatisfactory, particularly when implementing a doctrine that is founded on public policy.'

Supporters of a reliance rule may seek to defend it by arguing that it is not a technical rule of pleading but rather a substantive rule. What matters is whether in substance one has to rely on the illegal conduct to make out one's claim. But it is hard to understand what the rule would then mean or how precisely it would be applied. In trying to make it more palatable and less technical, the certainty of the rule (which, one might say, is its only merit) would be lost.

2. Turning to rule 1 above, the leading case exposing some of the difficulties with that rule is *ParkingEye v Somerfield*. The illegality in that case went to the contract as formed: that is, the claimant intended from the outset to perform the contract (operating supermarket car parks for the defendant) by sending out to customers

letters that contained some deliberate inaccuracies. The question was whether that illegality was a defence to what would otherwise have been a contractual entitlement to damages of £350,000 for the defendant's repudiatory breach of contract. In rejecting the validity of rule 1, the Court of Appeal pointed out that that rule was flawed in not allowing for any differentiation between trivial and serious illegality or between peripheral and central illegality. At [32], Jacob LJ cited with approval para 3.31 of *The Illegality Defence*, Law Commission (second) Consultation Paper No 189 (2009):

'[I]t clearly cannot be in every case that a contract is unlawfully performed, even where this was the original intention, that the offending party loses his or her remedies. Such a proposition would result in the widespread forfeiture of contractual remedies as a result of minor and incidental transgressions.'

And as the Law Commission had earlier said at para 7.30 of *Illegal Transactions: the Effect of Illegality on Contracts and Trusts*, Consultation Paper No 154 (1999):

'A major criticism of the present rules ... is that they take little account of the seriousness of the illegality that is involved. So, for example, it would appear that there is no difference in the rules applied where a party enters into a contract intending to commit murder in its performance, and where a party enters into a contract in the knowledge that he or she will have to commit a parking offence in order to perform it.'

Jacob LJ also thought, at [33], that there was 'something distinctly odd about the supposed "intention from the outset" rule'. This was because if the intention had only been formed after execution of the main contract, rule 2 and not rule 1 would apply (and that would then require consideration of 'participation' by the party seeking enforcement).

3. As with the main criticism of rule 1, the reference to performance that involves illegal conduct in rule 2 above fails to reflect the important fact that the varieties of illegal performance can vary hugely from trivial infractions of a statutory offence to serious criminal illegality. If rule 2 were accurate, it would mean, for example, that a party who performs a contract of carriage by speeding on the motorway for 100 metres would be unable to sue for the agreed contract price on delivery of the goods. No doubt for this sort of reason, several important cases appear to contradict rule 2. So, for example, in *St John Shipping Corp v Joseph Rank Ltd* [1957] 1 QB 267 a shipping company performed a contract of carriage by overloading the ship thereby committing a statutory offence. The master was fined and prosecuted for that offence. The company's claim for the agreed price was successful despite that illegal performance. Similarly, in *Shaw v Groom* [1970] 2 QB 504, CA, a landlord committed an offence by failing to provide his tenant with a proper rent-book but that did not preclude him from recovering the rent. It should be added that the

idea of 'participation' in rule 2 is unclear. In *Ashmore Benson Peace & Co Ltd v AV Dawson Ltd* [1973] 1 WLR 828, CA, the claimant's goods were loaded onto a lorry that was not licensed to carry goods of that weight. It was held that the contract could not be enforced by the claimant (his goods had been damaged when the lorry toppled over during the journey) because the claimant had seen the goods being loaded and that that amounted to 'participation' in the illegal performance. It is hard to see why standing by, doing nothing, amounts to participation.

4. More generally, while a purported advantage of the rule-based approach (as opposed to a more flexible approach) is its certainty, there are cases that do not fit those rules. In truth, the courts have often sought ways round the above rules because they do not like the results reached by applying them. This led the Law Commission to argue that the problems of the traditional approach were not merely that it produced undesirable results but also that the law was uncertain. The implication is that the flexible approach would not only produce more acceptable results but would in practice be no less certain than the rule-based approach.

5. It is sometimes suggested, as if a defence of the rule-based approach, that the fact that it produces undesirable outcomes is irrelevant because, as made clear as long ago as 1775 by Lord Mansfield in *Holman v Johnson* (1775) 1 Cowp 341, 343, the illegality defence operates as a rule of policy and is not designed to achieve justice between the parties. Certainly it is correct that the illegality defence is not designed to achieve justice as between the parties: if it were, there should be no illegality defence and the parties' normal rights and remedies would apply. However, that does not mean that any result, however arbitrary, is acceptable: one should surely be striving for the most desirable policy outcome and it may be that that is best achieved by taking into account a range of factors rather than applying a fixed rule.

6. It may be argued that, if there are deficiencies in the traditional rules, the way forward is to refine those rules so as to remove those deficiencies rather than departing from the rules altogether. However, it is a daunting task to try to redraw the rules, so as to cater for exceptions, and it is not one that any judge or commentator has successfully accomplished. There is a simple reason for this. Unless one is to take the extreme view that illegality should (almost) never be a defence or should (almost) always be a defence, the relative importance of the factors that rationally ought to be in play vary greatly from case to case. In particular, the seriousness of the illegality can vary hugely, but other obvious variables are the intentions of the parties, the centrality of the illegality to the contract or its performance, the effect of denying the defence, and the sanctions that the law already imposes. Similarly it is difficult to assess other than on a case by case basis how far the purpose behind a particular illegality will or will

not be served by allowing the defence or how far it is desirable to use the illegality defence in contract as a deterrent. In other words, to reach the best result in terms of policy the judges need to have the flexibility to consider and weigh a range of factors in the light of the particular facts of the case before them.

This is not to suggest that the central aspects of the previous rules are irrelevant, but rather that those aspects should be flexibly weighed up against others rather than being straitjacketed into fixed rules. Several judgments over the years have indicated the need for a more flexible approach (see, for example, *Hardy v Motor Insurers Bureau* [1964] 2 QB 745, CA, in which Diplock LJ said at 768, 'The court has to weigh the gravity of the anti-social act and the extent to which it will be encouraged by enforcing the right sought to be asserted against the social harm which will be caused if the right is not enforced'); and, drawing on developments in tort law (see, for example, *Saunders v Edwards* [1987] 1 WLR 1116, CA), this led the courts in the early 1990s (see esp *Howard v Shirlstar Ltd* [1990] 1 WLR 1292, CA) to accept, in contract as well as tort, the discretionary test of whether in all the circumstances it would be an affront to the public conscience to afford the claimant the relief sought. That 'shocking the public conscience' test was rightly rejected, not least for being far too vague, by the House of Lords in *Tinsley v Milligan*, but unfortunately the majority of their Lordships approved instead the rigid reliance rule considered above. In due course, this led to the work of the Law Commission which, as we have seen, favoured a more flexible approach. That was subsequently judicially accepted and applied in the context of contract in *ParkingEye v Somerfield*.

(iv) A 'range of factors' approach

Applying a flexible 'range of factors' approach, a possible formulation would read as follows:

If the formation, purpose, or performance of a contract involves conduct that is illegal (such as a crime) or contrary to public policy (such as a restraint of trade), the contract is unenforceable by one or either party if to deny enforcement would be an appropriate response to that conduct, taking into account where relevant—

(a) how seriously illegal or contrary to public policy the conduct was;

(b) whether the party seeking enforcement knew of, or intended, the conduct;

(c) how central to the contract or its performance the conduct was;

(d) how serious a sanction the denial of enforcement is for the party seeking enforcement;

(e) whether denying enforcement will further the purpose of the rule which the conduct has infringed;

    (f) *whether denying enforcement will act as a deterrent to conduct that is illegal or contrary to public policy;*

    (g) *whether denying enforcement will ensure that the party seeking enforcement does not profit from the conduct;*

    (h) *whether denying enforcement will avoid inconsistency in the law thereby maintaining the integrity of the legal system.*

This formulation sets out all the factors that a consideration of past decisions indicates might be taken into account in deciding whether the denial of enforcement of the contract is an appropriate response to the illegal conduct or conduct that is contrary to public policy. Those factors were largely spelt out in, and have therefore been taken from the judgments in, *ParkingEye v Somerfield* (especially the judgment of Toulson LJ). These also include the factors specifically spelt out by the Law Commission in its two consultation papers. It is not clear that all the factors (for example, the first four) can be accurately described as 'policy factors' except in the loose sense that they are together seeking the best answer to a policy question. Many past cases, including those applying a rule-based approach, have had one or more of these factors in mind. In other words, one might say that this approach is best viewed as bringing to the surface what has often, albeit covertly, underpinned this area of the law.

It is not being suggested that all those factors will be in play in every case. Rather the approach would require the courts to consider the relevance of those factors to the particular facts; and to spell out those factors that are considered important and decisive in arriving at the conclusion that to deny enforcement would, or would not, be an appropriate response to the conduct.

A word should be said about the last of these factors, (h). This was stressed as being of primary importance by the Supreme Court in *Hounga v Allen* following the emphasis given to it by the Supreme Court of Canada in the tort case of *Hall v Hebert* [1993] 2 SCR 159 at 176. It is the same idea as not 'stultifying the law', which was the language used by Lord Radcliffe in *Boissevain v Weil* [1950] AC 327, HL. However, this idea leaves open what one means by consistency and could justify almost any approach to the defence of illegality. Some would say that there is inconsistency in only a very narrow range of cases as, for example, where the criminal law has imposed one sanction (imprisonment or payment of a fine) and then an award of damages would contradict that (by giving the claimant damages for having been in prison, or having paid that fine, consequent on a negligently inflicted injury causing the claimant to commit the crime for which he has been imprisoned or fined). Others would say that the very approach of weighing up several different factors so as to achieve an appropriate response is designed to ensure that there is no inconsistency in the law. So while this factor has been included in the list, it is not clear that it operates on the same level as the other factors.

Note that although the formulation of the 'range of factors' approach includes conduct that is contrary to public policy alongside illegality, the assessment of at least some of the factors may be applied at an earlier stage in relation to contracts contrary to public policy than in relation to contracts affected by illegality. In other words, by deciding that a contract is contrary to public policy (for example, that it is an unreasonable restraint of trade) it has usually already been decided, as a matter of policy, that it cannot be enforced by one or both parties so that no further consideration of the factors set out above is required at the enforcement stage.

(v) The application of the different approaches to some examples

Talking about the effect of illegality and public policy in the abstract may be less illuminating than considering examples. What therefore follows is an examination of how the master reliance rule, the three rules formulated above, and the 'range of factors' approach would be applied to some examples.

Example 3

D contracts with C for C to murder D's wife/steal a car for D/ensure that D is given a knighthood/print libellous stories about D's enemy/spread rumours about D's enemy. C carries these out but D refuses to pay.

It will be assumed that the last two contracts involve conduct that is classed as illegal or contrary to public policy.

Applying the master reliance rule, it would appear that, as C would have to rely on the conduct that is illegal or contrary to public policy in order to make out its claim in all these variations, the contracts will be unenforceable by C.

Applying the three rules, all these variations will fall within rule 1. Applying that, the contracts will be unenforceable by C.

Applying the range of factors approach, there may be a difference in answer as between the first three and the last two variations because of the seriousness of the illegality involved. It will also be relevant in looking at the last two to consider, for example, the sums involved and the deterrent effect.

Example 4

C enters into a contract of carriage with D to carry D's goods for a price. The goods are illegal drugs/illegal weapons. C performs the contract but D refuses to pay. (a) C knew what the goods were; (b) C did not know what the goods were.

Applying the master reliance rule, it would appear that C's claim will succeed both in (a) and (b). C does not need to rely on the illegal conduct to establish its claim to the price: it merely has to show that the carriage contract has been performed.

Applying the three rules, both variations would fall within rule 1. C will therefore fail in (a) (applying rule 1(a)) but will succeed in (b) (applying rule 1(b)).

Applying the range of factors approach, the claim will fail in (a) because of the seriousness of the illegality and the knowledge of C, but is likely to succeed in (b) because of C's lack of knowledge.

Example 5

C enters into a contract of carriage with D to carry D's goods for a price which is only to be paid if the goods reach Liverpool on time. C complies with this but only (a) by speeding for a small section of the motorway or (b) using a vehicle that is not roadworthy and is uninsured.

Applying the master reliance rule, C will succeed. C does not need to rely on the illegal conduct to establish its claim to the price: it merely has to show that the carriage contract has been performed.

Applying the three rules, both variations fall within rule 2. C will fail (applying rule 2).

Applying the range of factors approach, C's claim is likely to succeed in relation to (a) because of the triviality of the illegality but will probably fail in relation to (b) although this may also depend, for example, on the other sanctions being imposed and whether there is a need for deterrence.

Example 6

C enters into a contract of carriage with D to carry D's goods by lorry from France to England. Unknown to D, C also uses the lorry to transport illegal immigrants to England. C carries the goods but D refuses to pay.

Applying the master reliance rule, C will succeed. C does not need to rely on the illegal conduct to establish its claim to the price: it merely has to show that the carriage contract has been performed.

Applying the three rules, this falls within rule 2. It is not entirely clear what the answer to this would be applying that rule, but the probable answer is that C's claim will fail (as the performance of the contract involves conduct that is illegal).

On the range of factors approach, C will be likely to fail because of the seriousness of the illegality and C's knowledge/intention and the need for deterrence (although one will also need to take into account that the illegal conduct is not central to the contract).

Example 7

C and D (daughter and father) both provide the money for the purchase of a house (worth £300,000). Under an agreement between them, the house is registered solely in C's name so that D can make false benefit claims (of £10,000 in total) to the Department of Social Security. C and D fall out and C moves out. C brings a claim for possession of the house as hers alone. D counterclaims that he is jointly entitled under a resulting trust.

Applying the master reliance rule, D's counterclaim will fail because D has to rely on the illegal scheme to rebut the presumption of advancement.

Applying the three rules, this falls within rule 3 and again therefore D's counterclaim will fail because D has to rely on the illegal scheme to rebut the presumption of advancement.

Applying the range of factors approach, D's counterclaim will probably succeed because the illegality involved is relatively trivial in relation to the level of sanction if one denies enforcement; and there are more effective ways of furthering the purpose of the rule against social security fraud than denying enforcement.

(vi) General points

It should be noted that, whether applying a range of factors or a rule-based approach, it seems unhelpful to try to define what constitutes an illegal contract or a contract contrary to public policy. It is more straightforward to focus instead on the idea of a contract involving *conduct* that is illegal or contrary to public policy.

'Conduct that is illegal' includes most obviously a crime (including a statutory offence). So this covers, for example, a contract to commit a murder or a contract performed by overloading a ship and thereby committing a statutory offence (as in *St John Shipping Corp v Joseph Rank Ltd* [1957] 1 QB 267). Until *Les Laboratoires Servier v Apotex Inc* [2014] UKSC 55, [2015] AC 430, it has also been regarded as including conduct (irrespective of dishonesty) that constitutes a civil wrong (other than the mere breach of the contract in question) such as a tort or statutory wrong (for example, *Clay v Yates* (1856) 1 H & N 73: contract to publish a libel). But it was laid down in *Les Laboratoires* that the sort of conduct that counts as 'turpitude' for the purposes of this area of the law is confined to criminal and, what Lord Sumption termed, 'quasi-criminal' conduct. According to his Lordship, at [25], 'quasi-criminal' conduct covers 'a limited category of acts which, while not necessarily criminal ... engage the public interest in the same way'. As examples he referred to cases of dishonesty and corruption, prostitution, and competition law. This is conduct that has more traditionally been labelled as being 'contrary to public policy' but also includes civil wrongs where dishonesty is an essential element. On the facts of the case itself, one was concerned merely with a tort (infringement of patent) which was not based on dishonesty. The conduct in question did not therefore constitute 'turpitude' or, in the more traditional language, that conduct was not illegal or contrary to public policy.

'Conduct that is…contrary to public policy' in this context has traditionally covered, for example, contracts involving sexual immorality (*Pearce v Brooks* (1866) LR 1 Exch 213: hire of a carriage to be used for prostitution); or interference with the administration of justice (*Kearley v Thomson* (1890) 24 QBD 742, CA: contract not to oppose discharge of a bankrupt); or the doing of a criminal act in a friendly foreign country (*Foster v Driscoll* [1929] 1 KB 470, CA: contract to smuggle whisky into the US during prohibition); or, most important in practice, a restraint of trade (see, for example, *Esso Petroleum Co Ltd v Harper's Garage (Stourport) Ltd* [1968] AC 269, HL). For 'contracts contrary to public policy' and 'contracts in restraint of trade', see *Chitty on Contracts* (32nd edn, 2015) paras 16-019–16-141; Peel, *Treitel on the Law of Contract* (14th edn, 2015) paras 11-032–11-109.

The courts recognise that public policy may change over time (see, for example, *Evanturel v Evanturel* (1874) LR 6 PC 1, 29; *Bowman v Secular Society Ltd* [1917] AC 406, HL; cf *Coral Leisure Group Ltd v Barnett* [1981] ICR 503, 507, EAT) so that contracts that in the past were regarded as contrary to public policy are no longer problematic: for example, contracts involving cohabitation between unmarried partners, including same-sex partners. Indeed one may have some doubts whether in the context of sexual immorality there should be any continued role for public policy that goes beyond illegality. Take the following three examples.

Example 8

A is a van rental firm. It rents out a van to B even though A's agent knows that B uses the van to have sex with prostitutes some of whom are under the age of 16. B fails to pay for the hire of the van.

Example 9

A is a sex-dating agency. B enters into a contract with A whereby, in return for a fee, A sets up 'sex-dates' for B. B fails to pay A the agreed price.

Example 10

B enters into a contract with A under which A is to be paid for taking part in an orgy. B fails to pay A the agreed price.

One might argue that, unless illegal conduct (that is, a crime) is involved, these contracts should be straightforwardly enforceable without any reference to 'public policy'.

The Restatement focuses on the unenforceability of the contract by one or either party. At common law (cf s 44(2)(b)), this seems more accurate than describing the effect of illegality or public policy as rendering the contract void. So, for example, it is well-accepted that title to property can pass under an 'illegal contract': *Singh v Ali* [1960] AC 167, PC; *Bowmakers Ltd v Barnet Instruments Ltd* [1945] KB 65, CA; *Belvoir Finance Co Ltd v Stapleton* [1971] 1 QB 210, CA.

The traditional law on the restitution of benefits conferred under 'illegal contracts' is complex. It has been fully explained (including the law which encourages the claimant to abandon an illegal purpose by giving a right to restitution by withdrawal during the *locus poenitentiae* ('opportunity for repentance')) in *A Restatement of the English Law of Unjust Enrichment* (2012) pp 107–10, 136–41. It will not be repeated here except to note that the view there taken, prior to the Supreme Court in *Les Laboratoires Servier v Apotex Inc* [2014] UKSC 55, [2015] AC 430, was that a 'range of factors' approach was within the interpretative reach of the courts.

44(2)

If a legislative provision has expressly or impliedly dealt with the effect on a contract of the objectionable conduct in question, then the courts must apply that. This has often been referred to as 'statutory illegality' to distinguish it from the 'common law illegality' dealt with in s 44(1). But where the courts are deciding, as a matter of statutory interpretation, whether a contract has been prohibited by implication, it would appear that they take into account in construing the purpose of the statute at least some of the factors set out in the range of factors approach or which underpin the rules set out above. In this sense there is, as one would expect, some convergence between the question of statutory interpretation and the approach to 'common law illegality'.

As regards s 44(2)(a), one of the best-known examples of prohibition of a contract by a legislative provision is *Re Mahmoud and Ispahani* [1921] 2 KB 716, CA. Here a wartime order, made by delegated legislation, prohibited the purchase or sale of linseed oil without a licence from the Food Controller. The claimant (who had a licence) contracted to sell linseed oil to the defendant, who did not have a licence, although the claimant was told by the defendant that he had. The defendant refused to accept the oil but the claimant's action for damages for non-acceptance failed because the contract was prohibited by the legislation and was therefore unenforceable by either party. A modern example is the Human Tissue Act 2004, s 32. This prohibits commercial dealings in human parts or material for transplantation other than by someone who has been authorised by the Human Tissue Authority.

This is probably the best explanation for the assumption in *Hounga v Allen* [2014] UKSC 47, [2014] 1 WLR 2889, that an illegal immigrant will not be able to enforce a contract of employment (including by bringing proceedings for unfair dismissal). The Immigration Act 1971 s 24 makes it a criminal offence to enter the UK without an appropriate visa (or, without reasonable excuse, to contravene a condition as to work). It would seem that, by necessary implication, a contract of employment entered into by such a person is prohibited and cannot be enforced by either party.

In contrast it was decided in *St John Shipping Corp v Joseph Rank Ltd* [1957] 1 QB 267 that the statute that prohibited the overloading of a ship did not also prohibit contracts of carriage.

Turning to s 44(2)(b), legislation may of course lay down that a contract or a contract term is unenforceable by one or either party (or void). We have already seen examples of this in earlier sections of the Restatement: for example, in relation to formal requirements for a contract (s 11(2)) and in relation to the legislative control of exemption clauses and unfair terms (see Part 4). Other examples are best included here as aspects of the law on illegality or public policy. So, for example, the Marine Insurance Act 1906, s 4(1), lays down that 'every contract of marine insurance by way of gaming or wagering is void' (a provision that remains in force despite the Gambling Act 2005, which has reformed the law on gaming and wagering contracts generally); and the Equality Act 2010, s 142 (1), provides that 'a term of a contract is unenforceable against a person in so far as it constitutes, promotes or provides for treatment of that or another person that is of a description prohibited by this Act'.

Also of great practical importance are ss 26–30 of the Financial Services and Markets Act 2000, which deal with unauthorised investment business, investment business transacted through unauthorised intermediaries, and investment business resulting from unlawful financial promotion. The provisions lay down that the relevant contract is 'unenforceable against [the customer]' but there is a discretion to enforce the contract if a court is satisfied that it is 'just and equitable in the circumstances of the case'. There are also provisions dealing with the restitutionary consequences and with the award of compensation.

44(3)

It is usually said that the power to sever is initially dependent on public policy so that, for example, severance will not be permitted if the agreement involves serious moral turpitude, such as the deliberate commission of a serious criminal offence: see, for example, *Bennett v Bennett* [1952] 1 KB 249, 253–4. It is to be noted that, if a 'range of factors' approach were taken under s 44(1), this reference to public policy would follow on naturally: that is, severance would be appropriate in a situation where the non-enforcement of only part of the contract would be an appropriate response to the conduct taking into account the factors set out.

The three prerequisites in s 44(3) seek to ensure that, as a practical matter, severance is fair and feasible. Severance is not appropriate where it would remove the main consideration as shown by *Bennett v Bennett* [1952] 1 KB 249, CA (cf *Goodinson v Goodinson* [1954] 2 QB 118, CA); severance is only permissible where, applying the 'blue pencil' test, one can simply strike out the offending words without rewriting (*Goldsoll v Goldman* [1915] 1 Ch 292, CA); and severance must not entirely alter the nature of the agreement (*Attwood v Lamont* [1920] 3 KB 571, CA, in which Lord Sterndale MR, at 580, said that severance was inappropriate because it would 'alter entirely the scope and intention of the agreement').

Example 11

A entered into a contract with his wife B. Under the contract, A promised to pay B an annuity in return for B promising (i) not to apply to the Court for maintenance, (ii) to maintain the children herself, and (iii) to indemnify A against any legal expenses arising out of the contract. A failed to pay and was sued by B. The objectionable part of the contract (that requiring B not to apply for maintenance thereby ousting the jurisdiction of the courts) could not be severed from the rest because it was the main consideration provided by B under the contract. (These were the facts, and that was the decision, in *Bennett v Bennett*.)

Example 12

A contracted with his wife B to pay her a weekly sum in return for her promise (i) to indemnify him against any debts incurred by her using his account, (ii) not to pledge A's credit, and (iii) not to divorce him. B sued A for not paying the agreed weekly sum. The objectionable part of the contract (the promise not to divorce him) could be severed from the rest because it was not the main consideration provided by B. (These were the facts, and that was the decision, in *Goodinson v Goodinson*.)

Example 13

A sold his imitation jeweller's business to B and covenanted that for a period of two years he would 'not carry on the business of a vendor or dealer in real or imitation jewellery in the United Kingdom or any other country in the world'. Shortly afterwards, A joined a rival firm of jewellers in the same street. B sought an injunction to restrain the breach of contract. Although the restrictive covenant was unenforceable as it stood, the objectionable parts could be 'blue pencilled' (by deleting the words 'real or' and 'or any other country in the world') and the injunction was granted. (These were the facts, and that was the decision, in *Goldsoll v Goldman*.)

Example 14

A owned a clothing department store selling off-the-peg and made-to-measure clothes and hats for men, women, and children. B was a tailor, employed by A. B covenanted that, after termination of his employment, he would not be concerned in the trade or business of a tailor, dressmaker, general draper, milliner, hatter, haberdasher, gentlemen's, ladies', or children's outfitter within ten miles of A's place of business in Kidderminster. The restrictive covenant was unenforceable because it was contrary to public policy as an unreasonable restraint of trade; and it could not be severed, so as to leave the covenant as applying only to work as a tailor, because the contract was to protect A's whole business and not merely a part of it so that severance would alter entirely the nature of the agreement. (These were the facts, and that was the decision, in *Attwood v Lamont*.)

It is noteworthy that it is through the common law doctrine of severance that a particular term may be isolated as void or unenforceable for illegality or public policy while leaving the rest of the contract intact. Similarly, as we have seen (see commentary to s 44(2)(b)), a statute may explicitly target a particular contract term only (so that, depending on how central a term, the rest of the contract may be left intact).

44(4)

If one contract will not be enforced by reason of illegality or public policy, the same may apply to a second contract that is linked to that first contract. In other words, the second contract may be tainted by the illegality: see, for example, *Fisher v Bridges* (1854) 3 El & Bl 643; *Spector v Ageda* [1973] Ch 30.

Example 15

A enters into a contract with B to sell B illegal drugs for £30,000. B pays £25,000 but fails to pay the remaining £5,000. B makes a contract by deed with A to pay A the remaining £5,000. The contract by deed is 'tainted' by the illegality and is therefore as unenforceable as the main contract.

44(5)

It was made clear in *HIH Casualty General Insurance Ltd v Chase Manhattan Bank* [2003] UKHL 6, [2003] 2 Lloyd's Rep 61, at [16], [24], [76], [121]–[122], that, *as a matter of public policy*, one cannot exclude liability for one's own fraudulent misrepresentation. In contrast, it would appear to be the case that public policy does not extend to preventing a principal excluding its liability for an agent's fraudulent misrepresentation although, as a matter of interpretation, such a clause will need to be clearly expressed if it is to apply.

Three further points are noteworthy. First, although this rule of public policy applies only to a particular term rather than a whole contract, it plainly sits neatly alongside the law on contracts tainted by conduct that is contrary to public policy. Secondly, the question of whether, as a matter of public policy, one can exclude liability for other forms of conduct, somewhat analogous to fraud, such as duress or undue influence, appears not to have been decided or judicially discussed. The analogy may not be as straightforward as it may at first sight seem because dishonesty is necessarily required for fraud but not for duress or undue influence. Thirdly, this rule of public policy is of limited practical importance because, in any event, there is legislative control of exemption clauses including clauses excluding liability for misrepresentation (ss 16–17).

44(6)

Illegality and public policy can be, and indeed should be, raised by a court of its own motion and do not need to be pleaded: see *Chitty on Contracts* (32nd edn, 2015) para 16-222. This is because illegality and public policy involve matters that go beyond the interests of the parties involved. See also s 17(10).

45 Privity of contract

(1) A contract can be enforced only by, or against, a party to the contract (the 'privity of contract' rule).

(2) The rule in subsection (1) is subject to exceptions to, or circumventions of, that rule (see sections 47 to 50).

(3) For the purposes of this Part—

'the promisor' means the party to the contract against whom the contract is enforceable; and

'the promisee' means the party to the contract by whom the contract is enforceable.

45(1)–(2)

The privity of contract rule or doctrine—which, along with the doctrine of consideration, has traditionally been a distinctive feature of the law of contract in common law systems—lays down that a contract can only be enforced by, and is only enforceable against, a party to that contract. (For discussion of the meaning of parties, see the commentary on s 4 above.)

Example 1

A contracts with B to pay £1,000 to C. If A fails to pay C, C cannot enforce A's promise even though C is the intended beneficiary of the contract because C is not a party to the contract.

Example 2

A contracts with B that C shall pay B £500. C is not bound by that contract to pay B because C is not a party to it.

As regards the benefit side of the privity doctrine—that a third party cannot enforce a contract—classic authorities establishing, or applying, the doctrine include *Tweddle v Atkinson* (1861) 1 B & S 393, *Dunlop Pneumatic Tyre Co Ltd v Selfridge* [1915] AC 847, HL (although in both those cases the rule was expressed in terms of 'consideration not moving from the claimant'), *Scruttons Ltd v Midland Silicones Ltd* [1962] AC 446, HL, and *Beswick v Beswick* [1968] AC 58, HL. This rule against enforcement by a third party has long been a matter of controversy—if the parties have contracted for C to have a legal right of enforcement, why should the law deprive C of that right?—and a wide range of exceptions to, or ways of avoiding, the rule have been developed. These are set out in ss 47–50. The most wide-ranging exception—albeit one which does not go as far as completely abolishing the privity rule on its benefit side—is laid down in the Contracts (Rights of Third Parties) Act 1999.

In contrast, the burden side of the privity doctrine—the rule that a contract cannot be enforced against a third party—is at root uncontroversial (it justifiably protects the autonomy of the third party). Note, however, that s 48(a) (agency), s 48(d) (covenants concerning land), and s 48(g) (bailment) may be regarded as exceptions to, or ways of avoiding, it. See also the commentary to s 48(h) on the Carriage of Goods by Sea Act 1992, s 3.

45(3)

For shorthand purposes in this Part, it is convenient to refer to 'the promisor' and 'the promisee' as here defined.

46 Enforcement by the promisee

(1) A promisee's damages for breach of a contract made for the benefit of a third party are normally concerned to compensate the loss of the promisee, not the loss of the third party, so that those damages will often be nominal.

(2) A promisee may be granted specific performance requiring the promisor to perform for the benefit of the third party where a court is satisfied that the damages for the promisee, in particular nominal damages, would be inadequate to produce a just result.

(3) A prohibitory injunction may be granted to a promisee to enforce a negative contractual promise in favour of a third party.

(4) As an exception to subsection (1) a promisee can recover a third party's loss on a contract for the benefit of a third party relating to property (whether goods or land) where—

(a) the parties contemplated that the loss in respect of that property would be suffered by the third party; and

(b) the third party does not itself have a right against the promisor to recover the third party's loss.

46

The privity of contract doctrine prevents a third party enforcing a contract. It plainly does not prevent the contracting party (the promisee) enforcing the contract even though the contract is one for the benefit of a third party. The question arising is, what remedies can the promisee obtain in this situation? The answer is that, in essence, one is merely applying to this situation the standard law on remedies set out in Part 5. However, it is important to spell out some particular features.

46(1)

Applying the standard approach (s 20), the aim of compensatory damages for breach of contract is to put *the claimant* into as good a position as if the contract had been performed. As it was the third party who was to benefit from the performance of the contract, it follows that the damages for the claimant promisee will often be nominal.

That the promisee is recovering for its own loss and not the loss of the third party was made clear in, for example, *Beswick v Beswick* [1968] AC 58, HL, and *Woodar Investment Development Ltd v Wimpey Construction UK Ltd* [1980] 1 WLR 277, HL. That the damages will often be nominal was accepted (Lord Pearce dissenting on this point) in *Beswick v Beswick* (and indeed was part of the basis for their Lordships' decision that specific performance should instead be ordered).

However, it should not be thought that, even adhering to the standard rule under which the promisee is recovering for its own loss, damages will necessarily be nominal. For example, the promisee may have been using the contract to pay off a debt to the third party which will still be outstanding; or the promisee may be entitled to a cost of cure measure of damages (s 20(4)(b))—that is, what it will now cost the promisee to confer the benefit on the third party—which may be substantial. (Cf Lord Griffiths's 'broad ground' in *Linden Gardens Trust Ltd v Lenesta Sludge Disposals Ltd* [1994] 1 AC 85, HL.)

Example 1

B owes C £10,000. In order to pay off that debt, B enters into a contract with A under which, in return for work by B, A agrees to pay C £10,000. B carries out the work but A fails to pay C the £10,000. In an action by B against A, B's loss is £10,000 because that is the value of the debt owed by B to C that would have been discharged had A paid C.

46(2)

The classic illustration of this principle is *Beswick v Beswick* [1968] AC 58, HL, where specific performance was ordered because nominal damages for the promisee would have been inadequate to produce justice. The bar to specific performance of damages (or the award of an agreed sum) being adequate (see s 26(2)) was therefore interpreted as taking into account the injustice that the privity doctrine might otherwise cause in a contract for the benefit of a third party.

Example 2

B enters into a contract with A whereby, in return for transferring B's business to A, A will pay C (B's wife) £5 a week for the rest of C's life after B's death. B dies but A fails to pay C as promised. B's personal representative (stepping into B's shoes and equated with B for these purposes) brings an action against

A. B's compensatory damages will be nominal but B may be granted an order of specific performance requiring A to pay C as promised. (This example is based on *Beswick v Beswick*.)

46(3)

A prohibitory injunction, in contrast to specific performance, is a readily available remedy to enforce a negative contractual promise: see s 27(2). A promisee, in a contract for a third party's benefit, may therefore readily obtain an injunction preventing the breach of a negative promise by the promisor. A useful illustration is *Snelling v John G Snelling Ltd* [1973] 1 QB 87. (Cf *Gore v Van der Lann* [1967] 2 QB 31, CA.)

Example 3

A contracts with B not to sue C. In breach of contract, A threatens to sue C. B will readily be granted an injunction ordering A not to pursue an action against C. (This example is based on *Snelling v Snelling*.)

46(4)

We have seen in relation to s 46(1) that the general rule is that the claimant can recover damages for its own loss and not the loss of the third party. Dissatisfaction with that rule has led to the development of the exception here set out. Often referred to as the '*Albazero* exception', after the leading case, it has been extended from its initial application to contracts for the carriage of goods (in *The Albazero* [1977] AC 774, HL) to building contracts (in *Darlington BC v Wiltshier Northern Ltd* [1995] 1 WLR 68, CA; *Alfred McAlpine Construction Ltd v Panatown Ltd* [2001] 1 AC 518, HL). The proviso—that the exception does not apply where the third party can itself sue—was laid down in the last of those cases. The rationale for that proviso is that there is no need to allow the promisee to recover the third party's loss where the third party itself has the right to sue. Given the subsequent enactment of the Contracts (Rights of Third Parties) Act 1999 it may be that this proviso will commonly knock out this exception.

47 Enforcement by a third party under the Contracts (Rights of Third Parties) Act 1999

(1) Under the Contracts (Rights of Third Parties) Act 1999 ('the 1999 Act') an expressly identified third party may enforce a term of the contract if—

    (a) the contract expressly provides that the third party may; or

    (b) the term purports to confer a benefit on the third party unless on a proper construction of the contract the parties did not intend the term to be enforceable by the third party.

(2) The requirement of express identification in subsection (1) means that the third party must be expressly identified in the contract by name, as a member of a class, or as answering a particular description but need not be in existence when the contract is entered into.

(3) A third party's right to enforce a term of a contract in subsection (1) means that, subject to the terms of the contract, there shall be available to the third party any remedy that would have been available to the third party in an action for breach of contract had the third party been a party to the contract.

(4) Subject to an express term to the contrary, where a third party has a right under subsection (1), the parties may not extinguish or alter that right without the consent of the third party if—

    (a) the third party has communicated its assent to the term to the promisor, or

    (b) the third party has relied on that term and the promisor is aware of that reliance or could reasonably have foreseen it.

(5) Subject to an express term to the contrary, where a third party brings proceedings to enforce a right under subsection (1), the promisor may rely on any defence that would have been available to the promisor had the proceedings been brought by the promisee.

(6) Subject to the promisor not being made doubly liable for the same loss, the right of the third party under subsection (1) does not affect any right of the promisee to enforce the contract.

(7) A third party who has a right under subsection (1) to enforce a written arbitration agreement, or has a right under subsection (1) to enforce a term that, by reason of a written arbitration agreement, is conditional on resolving any dispute by arbitration, is to be treated as a party to the contract for the purposes of the Arbitration Act 1996.

(8) Some types of contract are excluded from the 1999 Act, including—

    (a) a contract on a bill of exchange, promissory note or other negotiable instrument;

    (b) in general, a contract for the carriage of goods.

47

The most wide-ranging exception to the benefit side of the privity doctrine is the Contracts (Rights of Third Parties) Act 1999. This section of the Restatement seeks to set out the main scheme of the 1999 Act although it does not attempt to capture every detail. For those details, one must read the Act itself. This section should be read as a guide to, and not as a substitute for, reading the legislation.

47(1)–(2)

These correlate to s 1 of the 1999 Act. They lay down the two tests of enforceability which tell us when it is that a third party has the right to enforce a term of the contract. The 1999 Act focuses on third parties enforcing 'a term of the contract' rather than the whole contract (although this is not to deny that a third party may be given the right to enforce every term).

Each of the two tests requires that the third party is expressly identified (as defined in s 47(2)). The first test is where the third party is expressly given a right to enforce the contract. The second test deals with where the third party is impliedly given a right to enforce the contract: the implication arises where the term purports to confer a benefit on the expressly identified third party but this may be rebutted where the proper construction of the contract is that the parties did not intend the third party to have that right. For application of the second test see, for example, *Nisshin Shipping Co Ltd v Cleaves & Co Ltd* [2003] EWHC 2602 (Comm), [2004] 1 Lloyd's Rep 38; *Laemthong International Lines Company Ltd v Artis, The Laemthong Glory (No 2)* [2005] EWCA Civ 519, [2005] 1 Lloyd's Rep 688.

It will be obvious from the two tests that it is, of course, open to the contracting parties to make clear that third parties have no rights under the 1999 Act by including a term such as: 'A person who is not a party to this contract shall have no rights under the Contracts (Rights of Third Parties) Act 1999 to enforce any of its terms.'

It should be stressed that the 1999 Act (see s 1(6) of the Act) applies to the third party enforcing not only positive rights (for example, a term requiring payment to the third party) but also negative rights (for example, a clause excluding the liability of the third party); and that in that context 'enforcement' should be construed as availing oneself of the exclusion or limitation.

47(3)

This correlates to s 1(5) of the 1999 Act. It makes clear the third party is entitled to, for example, damages, the award of an agreed sum, specific performance, and injunctions as if it had been a party to the contract. The rules set out above in ss 20–31 of the Restatement therefore apply by analogy to the third party's action.

47(4)

This correlates to s 2 of the 1999 Act. It lays down the point at which the contracting parties can no longer take away the right of the third party by consensually varying or rescinding the contract. However, it sets up a default position only, which may be overridden by an express term of the contract.

47(5)

This correlates to s 3 of the 1999 Act. It lays down that defences that would have been available to the promisor in an action by the promisee are also available in an action by the third party. Again this is a default position only, which may be overridden by an express term of the contract. Note that, although s 3 of the 1999 Act refers to 'defence or set-off', the word 'defence' is sufficiently wide to include a set-off (whether operating as a total or partial defence).

47(6)

This correlates to s 4 of the 1999 Act. It makes clear that the right of the third party under the Act is additional to, and does not replace, the right of the promisee; nor is the right of the promisee transferred to the third party. This is subject to the proviso that the promisor is not made doubly liable for the same loss (for example, the promisor should not be held liable to pay substantial damages to both the promisee and the third party for the same loss).

47(7)

This correlates to the complex provision of the 1999 Act on arbitration agreements (s 8). What that provision essentially seeks to ensure is that the rules in the Arbitration Act 1996 are applicable where a third party under the 1999 Act has either a right to enforce an arbitration agreement or a right to enforce a (substantive) term conditional on going to arbitration. See for consideration of s 8, *Nisshin Shipping Co Ltd v Cleaves & Co Ltd* [2003] EWHC 2602 (Comm), [2004] 1 Lloyd's Rep 38; *AES Ust-Kamenogvok Hydropower Plant v Ust-K* [2010] EWHC 772 (Comm), [2010] 2 Lloyds' Rep 493, at [26]–[32] (affirmed without discussing this point at [2013] UKSC 35, [2013] 1 WLR 1889); *Fortress Value Recovery Fund v Blue Skye Special Opportunities Fund* [2013] EWCA Civ 367, [2013] 1 WLR 3466.

47(8)

This correlates to s 6 of the 1999 Act. Some contracts are excluded from the 1999 Act primarily because, in relation to some types of contract, legislation has already conferred third party rights in a way that would clash with the conferral of third party rights under the 1999 Act. So by section 6(1) of the 1999 Act, contracts on a bill of exchange, promissory note, or other negotiable instrument are excluded. Here third party rights are conferred under the Bills of Exchange Act 1882. By section 6(5)(a) of the 1999 Act, contracts for the carriage of goods by sea, governed by the Carriage of Goods by Sea Act 1992, are excluded; as, by section 6(5)(b), are contracts for the carriage of goods by road, rail, or air, where the relevant statutes conferring third party rights are those giving force to various international transport conventions. However, it is important to realise (hence the words 'in general' in s 47(8)(b) of the Restatement) that there is an exception to the exclusion in section 6(5) of the 1999 Act so that *exemption clauses* in contracts for the carriage of goods by sea, road, rail, or air, *do* fall within the 1999 Act. As we shall see (commentary to s 48(f) below) the enforcement of such clauses by third parties has been effected by a (difficult) common law method of evading privity. The inclusion of exemption clauses in contracts of carriage within the 1999 Act allows such clauses to be rendered straightforwardly enforceable by an expressly identified third party without the need to rely on the complex reasoning used in, for example, *The Eurymedon* [1975] AC 154, PC. Other contracts excluded from the 1999 Act for particular policy reasons include that the Act cannot be used to confer rights on third parties to enforce a contract of employment against an employee.

48   Other exceptions to, or circumventions of, the privity of contract rule

In addition to section 47, the following rules exist by way of exceptions to, or circumventions of, the privity of contract rule—

(a) an agent may make a contract on behalf of a principal, including an undisclosed principal (see section 49);

(b) a right under a contract may be assigned to a third party (see section 50);

(c) a promise to benefit a third party may be held by the promisee on trust for the third party;

(d) a covenant concerning land, whether positive or negative, may in certain circumstances benefit or burden a third party;

(e) a third party (C) may have a claim in the tort of negligence where A's breach of a contract with B also constitutes the breach of a duty of care owed by A to C, including where C's loss is the non-receipt of an economic benefit;

(f) a third party (C) may take the benefit of an exemption or exclusive jurisdiction clause in a contract between A and B where, in addition to that contract, C can establish that there is a unilateral contract by which A promises to be bound by the exemption or exclusive jurisdiction clause in exchange for a performance by C;

(g) a third party (C) may be burdened by an exemption or exclusive jurisdiction clause in a contract between A and B by which there has been a bailment or sub-bailment of C's goods provided C has consented to that bailment or sub-bailment;

(h) rules in legislation (for example, the Bills of Exchange Act 1882, section 11 of the Married Women's Property Act 1882, and the Carriage of Goods by Sea Act 1992) which, in respect of certain types of contract, allow enforcement of a contract by a third party.

48

This section primarily deals with what many commentators describe as the common law 'exceptions' to privity. However, it would appear to be more accurate to describe at least some of these as circumventions of the privity rule rather than as exceptions. Certainly, these common law techniques do not overtly recognise that a third party has the right to enforce the contract: rather, some of them treat the 'third party' as being a party to the contract or rely on the idea that the third party is not bringing an action for breach of contract (but instead for, for example, the tort of negligence). The final subsection deals with specific legislative exceptions (that is, other than the 1999 Act) to the enforcement of contracts by third parties.

48(a)

The details of the law of agency (which extends beyond the law of contract) fall outside this Restatement. However, for the purposes of this Restatement, it is important to appreciate that the making of a contract by an agent for a principal avoids the privity rule. Agency is explained further in s 49.

48(b)

The details of the law of assignment (which extends beyond the law of contract) fall outside this Restatement. However, it is plain that the law of assignment is a way of avoiding the privity rule on its benefit side. The assignment is made (often by means of a separate contract) between the promisee under the main contract, who is called the assignor, and the third party, who is called the assignee. The effect is that the third party assignee is treated as a party to the main contract and can sue the promisor (usually referred to as the debtor) under the main contract. Assignment is dealt with further in s 50.

48(c)

A trust of the promise is established where, instead of there being merely a contract for the benefit of a third party, the promise to benefit the third party is regarded as being held by the promisee on trust for the third party. That is, there is a fully constituted trust where the subject-matter is the promise itself. This draws on the well-established principle that a contractual promise is a form of personal property, namely a chose in action. It can therefore be held on trust like any other form of property. Applying normal trust rules the third party, exercising the normal rights of a beneficiary under a trust, is then able to enforce the promise. At first sight, this appears to be a very wide-ranging exception to the privity doctrine. But in order for a trust to be established, one must be satisfied that the contracting parties did intend to create a trust rather than merely to set up a contractual relationship. In some past cases the courts have been satisfied that there was that intention by implication. A famous example of this was the decision of the House of Lords in *Les Affreteurs Réunis Société Anonyme v Leopold Walford* [1919] AC 801 in which it was held that a promise in a charterparty to pay commission to the third party chartering broker created a trust of the promise enforceable by that third party. However, in the modern law that approach to intention is no longer adhered to and, in practice, it will only be where the parties have expressly stated that they are creating a trust for the third party that the necessary intention will be found. Nevertheless, the trust of the promise has remained an important method open to those drafting contracts to ensure that a third party to a contract is given enforceable rights. One should note that, if this exception applies, there can be no variation or rescission of the contract by the contracting parties without the third party's consent. One cannot unwind a trust, once constituted, without the beneficiaries' consent.

48(d)

The law allows certain covenants concerning land, whether positive or restrictive, to benefit or burden a person who is not an original contracting party. The relevant covenant may relate to freehold or leasehold land. This area of the law was developed at common law, an early famous case being *Tulk v Moxhay* (1848) 2 Ph 774, which concerned a restrictive covenant. However, the law is now largely embodied in legislation, whether s 78 of the Law of Property Act 1925, as regards freehold covenants, or the Landlord and Tenant (Covenants) Act 1995, as regards leasehold covenants.

48(e)

There are a few examples of liability being imposed for pure economic loss in the tort of negligence, which one can regard as tantamount to enforcement of a contract by a third party beneficiary. The most important example of this is *White v Jones* [1995] 2 AC 207, HL. In this case, solicitors were held to be negligent and liable to a prospective beneficiary of a will for loss of the intended legacy when they negligently failed to draw up the will before the testator died. One can argue that the prospective beneficiaries under the will were third party beneficiaries of the contract between the solicitor and the testator and that the tortious negligence action that succeeded amounted to enforcement by those third parties of the solicitor's contractual duty of care.

48(f)

One of the most discussed modern issues in relation to the privity doctrine is whether a third party can take the benefit of (that is, can enforce) an exemption clause in a contract to which it is not a party. On the face of it, the doctrine of privity prevents that: *Scruttons Ltd v Midland Silicones Ltd* [1962] AC 446, HL. However, in the context of a contract for the carriage of goods by sea, that inconvenient answer has been avoided by the courts' recognition that the exemption clause can be regarded as embodied in a separate unilateral contract—so that there is a contractual relationship—between the promisor (for example, the shipper) and the third party (for example, the stevedores): *New Zealand Shipping Co Ltd v AM Satterthwaite & Co Ltd, The Eurymedon* [1975] AC 154, PC; *Port Jackson Stevedoring Pty Ltd v Salmond & Spraggan Pty (Australia) Ltd, The New York Star* [1981] 1 WLR 138, PC; *Homburg Houtimport BV v Agrosin Private Ltd, The Starsin* [2003] UKHL 12, [2004] 1 AC 715. Note that, since the Contracts (Rights of Third Parties) Act 1999, a third party in that situation will normally be able to take the benefit of the exemption clause by reason of the Act without having to rely on this ingenious but, arguably, rather artificial common law reasoning.

The same approach was taken to an exclusive jurisdiction clause, as to an exemption clause, in *The Mahkutai* [1996] AC 650, PC.

One might think that the same approach could also be applied to an arbitration clause. However, such a development may be thought problematic as clashing with the Arbitration Act 1996, which does not deal with enforcement by a third party (hence the need for a special provision for arbitration contracts in s 8 of the Contracts (Rights of Third Parties) Act 1999: see Restatement s 47(7)).

Example 1

A, a shipper, enters into a contract with B, a carrier, for B to carry A's goods by sea. It is a term of that contract that any claim against the carrier for damage to the goods is excluded unless brought within 12 months of delivery of the goods. There is a further term whereby the benefit of that exclusion is extended to the servants, agents, or independent contractors of B. A's goods are negligently damaged while being unloaded by C, who are stevedores engaged by B. A brings a claim in the tort of negligence against C more than 12 months after delivery of the goods. Although C is a third party to the contract of carriage between A and B, there is a unilateral contract between A and C whereby, in return for C's unloading of the goods, A excludes C from liability after 12 months. C can therefore rely on the exclusion clause to defeat A's claim. (This example is based on *The Eurymedon*. Irrespective of the unilateral contract analysis, C can now rely on s 1 of the Contracts (Rights of Third Parties) Act 1999: see s 47(1) of the Restatement. Although contracts for the carriage of goods by sea are largely excluded from the Act, a third party can enforce 'an exclusion or limitation of liability in such a contract': s 6(5) of the 1999 Act and see commentary to s 47(8) of the Restatement.)

48(g)

The leading cases accepting this (which is a way round the 'burden' side of privity) are *Morris v CW Martin & Sons Ltd* [1966] 1 QB 716, CA; and *KH Enterprise v Pioneer Container, The Pioneer Container* [1994] 2 AC 324, PC.

Example 2

C sends her expensive coat to B for cleaning. B agrees with C to send the coat to A who is a specialist cleaner. In the contract between B and A, there is a clause which limits the liability of A for damage to goods during the cleaning process including damage caused by the negligence of A. The coat is damaged. C sues A in the tort of negligence. C (the third party for these purposes) is bound by the limitation clause in the contract between A and B because C consented to the sub-bailment to A (although the clause may be ineffective under, for example, the Consumer Rights Act 2015: see s 17 of the Restatement).

Some might argue that there is a further exception to the burden side of privity, namely that a restrictive covenant may run with goods so as to burden a third party. That was accepted in *Lord Strathcona Steamship Co Ltd v Dominion Coal Co Ltd* [1926] AC 108, PC, but doubted in *Port Line Ltd v Ben Line Steamers Ltd* [1958] 2 QB 146. Subsequently, any possible cause of action in that sort of situation has been viewed as being covered by the economic tort of wrongful interference with another's contract: see, for example, *Swiss Bank Corp v Lloyds Bank Ltd* [1979] Ch 548 (overturned without dealing with this point at [1982] AC 584, CA). The operation of that tort might itself be a way round the burden side of privity but it is not here included as such, primarily because, while the contract may be said to affect the third party, it falls short of requiring the third party to perform (or to pay damages for failing to perform) a contractual obligation.

48(h)

As we have seen, the Contracts (Rights of Third Parties) Act 1999 is a wide-ranging and general legislative exception to privity on its benefit side. However, over the years, a number of specific exceptions to the privity doctrine—applicable to particular types of contract—have been embodied in various legislative provisions. Three important examples are as follows. First, by s 11 of the Married Women's Property Act 1882, a life insurance policy is enforceable against the insurer by a spouse or child named in the policy. This is achieved by the statutory creation of a trust for the named beneficiaries. Secondly, by the Bills of Exchange Act 1882, a negotiable instrument (such as a bill of exchange) is enforceable by the holder even though that person is a third party to the original contract containing the payment obligation. Thirdly, by the Carriage of Goods by Sea Act 1992, replacing the Bills of

Lading Act 1855, the holder of, for example, a bill of lading is able to sue the carrier on the contract for the carriage of goods by sea evidenced or contained in the bill of lading even though the holder is not a party to that contract. Note that, under s 3 of the 1992 Act, in certain circumstances the person who has had contractual rights transferred and vested in him also becomes subject to the liabilities under the contract. In that sense, the 1992 Act may be regarded as an exception to the burden, as well as the benefit, side of the privity rule.

49 Agency

(1) An agent makes a contract with a party ('the other party') on behalf of a principal where the agent has authority from the principal to do so.

(2) The agent's authority from the principal may be—

    (a) actual (whether express or implied);

    (b) apparent (where the principal represents to the other party that the agent has actual authority to make the contract on behalf of the principal even though the agent does not have that actual authority); or

    (c) retrospectively conferred by the principal's ratification.

(3) A principal may be—

    (a) disclosed (where the other party knows that the agent is acting on behalf of a principal); or

    (b) undisclosed (where the other party does not know that the agent is acting on behalf of a principal);

but a principal can only be undisclosed if the agent has actual authority.

(4) Where the principal is disclosed and the agent has actual authority or there has been ratification, the general position is that the parties to the contract are the principal and the other party so that the contract can be enforced by, and against, the principal.

(5) Where the principal is undisclosed, the general position is that both the agent and the principal are parties to the contract with the other party so that the contract may be enforced by, and against, each of them.

(6) Where the agent has apparent authority, and there has been no ratification, the contract can be enforced by the other party against the principal but cannot be enforced by the principal.

49

An agent can act on behalf of its principal in making contracts with other parties. To do so, the agent must have the principal's authority, whether actual or apparent. Where a (bilateral) contract is concluded by an agent for its principal, the principal can both sue and be sued on the contract (although, if the agent's authority is merely apparent, rather than actual, the principal cannot sue unless it has ratified the contract). So, one *could* argue that the whole law of agency in contract is a way of avoiding the privity rule. The principal, albeit in one sense a third party to the contract concluded by her agent, is able to sue and be sued on that contract. However, in most circumstances, one can say without any fiction that the principal, not the agent, is the party to the contract concluded by the agent. Indeed in most circumstances the agent will not be named in the contract and will drop out of the picture once the contract has been concluded. But that is generally not the case where one has an undisclosed principal: that is, where the other party has not been informed, and hence does not know, that she is dealing with an agent rather than with a principal. Where the principal is undisclosed, the agent usually does not drop out of the picture: in general, the agent, as well as the principal, can sue and be sued on the contract. Therefore, it is artificial to say that the principal, not the agent, is the party to the contract. Where the principal is undisclosed, the other party has no knowledge of the principal's existence and may find that she is in a contractual relationship with someone of whom she has never heard and with whom she never intended to contract. It follows that, whatever one says about agency where there is a disclosed principal, agency where the principal is undisclosed is a way of avoiding the privity rule. Indeed, it avoids not only the benefit side of privity but also the burden side: the undisclosed principal can both sue, and be sued by, the other party.

The law on agency extends beyond the making of contracts on another's behalf. So, for example, agency has relevance in tort and unjust enrichment. Even when confined to contracts, the Restatement is not concerned with the details of the law of agency, which include, for example, the fiduciary duties owed by the agent to the principal, how one terminates an agency, and the rights of commercial agents in the event of termination under the Commercial Agents (Council Directive) Regulations 1993 (SI 1993/3053). For the details of the whole law of agency see, for example, *Bowstead and Reynolds on Agency* (20th edn, 2014).

What the provisions in the Restatement are designed to do is to explain in outline how agency in contract works with a particular focus on whether there are contractual relationships between principal, agent, and the other party, thereby making clear how agency applies despite the privity of contract rule.

49(1)–(2)

A principal consents to an agent making contracts on its behalf where it authorises the agent to do so. The key concept in the creation of agency is this giving of authority. The three types of authority are actual, apparent, and retrospectively conferred (by ratification).

Actual authority almost always arises from a contract between the principal and agent (although a contract between them is not a requirement) and may be expressly or impliedly conferred, with the scope of the authority generally turning on the ordinary interpretation of the contract: *Freeman & Lockyer v Buckhurst Park Properties (Mangal) Ltd* [1964] 2 QB 480, 482, CA.

Apparent authority arises where there is no actual authority but the principal has represented to the other party, by words or conduct, that the agent has that authority. A leading case is *Freeman & Lockyer v Buckhurst Park Properties (Mangal) Ltd* [1964] 2 QB 480, CA (director held to have apparent authority to enter into a contract on behalf of the company because the company had represented to the other contracting party that the director had that authority by permitting him to act as if he had that authority). Diplock LJ said, at 502: 'The representation, when acted on by the contractor by entering into a contract with the agent, operates as an estoppel, preventing the principal from asserting that he is not bound by the contract. It is irrelevant whether the agent had actual authority to enter into the contract.'

Ratification by the principal—which must be given within a reasonable time of the contract being made—retrospectively confers authority on the agent. The retrospectivity means that a principal can ratify an agent's acceptance of an offer even though the principal knows that the offer has subsequently been withdrawn: *Bolton Partners v Lambert* (1889) 41 Ch D 295, CA.

Example 1

On 8 December B offers to buy C's factory. Without authority this offer is accepted by A (C's agent) on 13 December. On 17 December B withdraws his offer. Over a month later, on 28 January, C ratifies A's acceptance and seeks specific performance against B. The claim will succeed. (This example is based on *Bolton Partners v Lambert*.)

49(3)–(5)

Leaving aside apparent authority (see s 49(6)), the question of whether the agent as well as the principal is a party to the contract with the other party generally depends on whether the principal is disclosed or undisclosed. A principal is undisclosed where the other party does not know that the person with whom it is contracting is an agent acting on behalf of a principal. But the concept of an undisclosed principal only applies where the agent has actual authority. It cannot logically apply to apparent authority because that is dependent on the principal making a representation to the other party (cf the controversial decision in *Watteau v Fenwick* [1893] 1 QB 346 on which see *Chitty on Contracts* (32nd edn, 2015) para 31-064; Beatson, Burrows, and Cartwright, *Anson's Law of Contract* (29th edn, 2010) 694); and it was decided in *Keighley, Maxsted & Co v Durant* [1901] AC 240, HL, that there can be no ratification unless the principal was disclosed.

Example 2

A enters into a contract with B to buy wheat on behalf of C. B does not know that A is entering into that contract on behalf of C (that is, C is the undisclosed principal). A has no actual authority to make the contract at that price on behalf of C but C later ratifies the contract. When C and A refuse to take delivery of the wheat from B, B sues C and A. The action will fail against C (but will succeed against A) because C was not a party to the contract between A and B and ratification was inapplicable where the principal was undisclosed. (This example is based on *Keighley, Maxsted & Co v Durant*.)

Where the principal is disclosed, the general position is that the contract is between the principal and the other party and the agent drops out of the picture. In other words, the parties to the contract are the other party and the principal.

However, there are exceptions to the agent dropping out. In particular, the agent may have undertaken a personal liability or given itself a personal entitlement under the contract so that the agent as well as the principal may be able to sue or be sued on the contract. Whether this is so is a matter of construing the contract. An example is *Bridges & Salmon v Owners of The Swan, The Swan* [1968] 1 Lloyd's Rep 5.

Example 3

B is a ship-repairer. A owns a ship. On his company's (C's) notepaper and signed by him as director of C, A makes a contract with B for the repair of A's ship. B carries out the repairs but C fails to pay and becomes insolvent. There is a contract between B and both A and C. A can therefore be successfully sued by B. Although A was making the contract as agent for C, A as owner of the ship was also making himself personally liable on the contract. (This example is based on *The Swan*.)

Where the principal is undisclosed, the general position is that the agent does not drop out so that both the agent and the principal are parties to the contract with the other party and can therefore sue, and be sued, on that contract: see, for example, *Siu Yin Kwan v Eastern Insurance Co Ltd* [1994] 2 AC 199, PC.

Again, that is the general position and there are exceptions to it. These can be regarded as the restrictions on the scope of the undisclosed principal concept. For example, where the contract is of a very personal nature (that is, one where the other party can justifiably argue that it is highly prejudicial to be liable to the principal as well as the agent), only the agent, not the undisclosed principal, is a party: see, for example, *Said v Butt* [1920] 3 KB 497. It may also be inconsistent with the terms of the contract for the party to be anyone other than the agent although in modern cases the courts have shown a reluctance to find that there is this inconsistency: see, for example, *Ferryways NV v Associated British Ports, The Humber Way* [2008] EWHC 225 (Comm).

49(6)

We have seen in relation to s 49(2) that apparent authority rests on a representation by the principal which estops her from denying that she is liable on the contract. That, of course, does not operate to give her rights on the contract. If the principal (who in this context must be disclosed) is to acquire rights under the contract, she must therefore ratify the contract made by the agent.

50 Assignment

(1) By an assignment, a party ('the assignor') may transfer to a third party ('the assignee'), without the consent of the other contracting party ('the debtor'), a right under a contract that the assignor has against the debtor.

(2) A right under a contract cannot be assigned if—

    (a) the contract involves a personal relationship between the assignor and the debtor such that it would be detrimental to the debtor to perform for the assignee rather than the assignor;

    (b) the contract prohibits the assignment;

    (c) the right under the contract is a right to (unliquidated) damages unless the assignee has a genuine commercial interest in taking the assignment; or

    (d) the assignment would be illegal or contrary to public policy.

(3) In a claim for breach of contract by the assignee against the debtor, the following general rules apply so as to avoid prejudice to the debtor—

    (a) the debtor can raise any defence that it could have raised against the assignor had the assignor been bringing the action against the debtor;

    (b) the assignee is not entitled to recover more from the debtor than what would have been the assignor's entitlement against the debtor had there been no assignment.

(4) If all the parties agree that a contract between two parties (A and B) is replaced by a new contract between one of the parties (A) and a third party (C) in which the same (or similar) duties are owed to, and by, C as were owed to, and by, B, this is known as a novation (which does not involve any assignment).

50

We have seen above (s 48(b)) that assignment can be regarded as a way of avoiding the privity doctrine on its benefit side. The details of the law of assignment (for example, the different methods of assignment, the distinction between statutory and equitable assignment, the relevance of notice to the other contracting party (the debtor), and the rules of priority governing successive assignments) fall outside this Restatement. Nevertheless it has been thought helpful in this section to outline some of the core principles so as to indicate how assignment works and how it avoids the privity rule. For the details of the law of assignment, see, for example, Smith and Leslie, *The Law of Assignment* (2nd edn, 2013).

50(1)

Only benefits and not burdens can be assigned (albeit that the benefit may be conditional): *Tolhurst v Associated Portland Cement Manufacturers Ltd* [1902] 2 KB 660, HL.

The assignment takes effect irrespective of the wishes of the debtor so that the debtor can find itself bound to perform for someone it did not intend to perform for. The debtor is to some extent protected by the rules laying down when a right cannot be assigned (see s 50(2)) and by the rule that the assignment takes effect 'subject to equities' (s 50(3)).

The notion of 'transfer' appears to mean that the assignor's right against the debtor is extinguished and the assignee acquires the right against the debtor (albeit that, in respect of equitable assignment, as distinct from statutory assignment under s 136 of the Law of Property Act 1925, the assignor must normally be joined to the action).

Note, however, the less orthodox view (not reflected in the Restatement but see, for example, Edelman and Elliott, 'Two Conceptions of Equitable Assignment' (2015) 131 LQR 228) that equitable assignment, as distinct from statutory assignment, does not involve any *transfer* of rights. Rather the assignee in equity is given new rights by the assignor in respect of the rights of the assignor which are still retained by the assignor: that is, the assignee's rights encumber the assignor's rights but the assignor's rights are not transferred. In effect, the assignor holds its rights on trust for the assignee. This theory runs counter to the prevailing view that an assignment in equity and a trust are different concepts (although, admittedly, it does have the merit of providing a convincing substantive reason, rather than a vague procedural explanation, for why the assignor must (at least normally) be joined to the equitable assignee's action: that is, as the assignor retains the relevant rights it follows that the assignee's action must be brought in the assignor's name).

50(2)(a)

This is a well-established restriction: see, for example, *Don King Productions Inc v Warren* [2000] Ch 291, 319 (per Lightman J); decision affirmed [2000] Ch 291, CA.

Example 1

A engages B to clean her house. If A sells the house to C, A cannot assign the benefit of that cleaning contract to C.

Note that the common law on the non-assignability of a contract of employment has been affected by the Transfer of Undertakings (Protection of Employment) Regulations 2006 (SI 2006/246).

50(2)(b)

Although this has been thought to be inconvenient in the context of 'factoring', where a company buys up multiple debts the precise terms of which cannot be realistically checked, it is clear as a matter of principle, emanating from freedom of contract, that the contracting parties are free to prohibit an assignment so that there is no valid assignment as against the debtor: *Linden Gardens Trust Ltd v Lenesta Sludge Disposals Ltd* [1994] 1 AC 85, 103, HL. On the other hand, a clause prohibiting an assignment does not necessarily prohibit a declaration of trust in favour of a third party: *Barbados Trust Co Ltd v Bank of Zambia* [2007] EWCA Civ 148, [2007] 1 Lloyd's Rep 494. Note also s 1 of the Small Business, Employment and Enterprise Act 2015, which authorises regulations invalidating some 'no assignment' clauses.

50(2)(c)

By reason of the objections to champerty and maintenance (that is, trafficking in litigation), it has been laid down that one cannot assign a 'bare right of action' (that is, a right to unliquidated damages) unless one has a legitimate commercial interest in so doing: *Trendtex Trading Corp v Credit Suisse* [1982] AC 679, HL. It follows, for example, that a right to damages for personal injury cannot normally be assigned (cf *Simpson v Norfolk and Norwich University Hospital NHS Trust* [2011] EWCA Civ 1149, [2012] QB 640).

50(2)(d)

The assignment of some types of contractual right may be illegal or contrary to public policy. For example, the assignment of the salary of a public officer is illegal: *Wells v Foster* (1841) 8 M & W 149, 151; *Roberts v Roberts* [1986] 1 WLR 437.

50(3)

The underlying principle here is often expressed by saying that the assignee takes the assignment 'subject to equities' and the underlying concern is to avoid prejudice to the debtor.

So, as regards (a), the debtor can, for example, rescind the contract as against the assignee on the ground that it was induced to enter into it by the misrepresentation of the assignor: *Graham v Johnson* (1869) LR 8 Eq 36. Similarly, if the original contract was void as against the assignor, it will be void as against the assignee. The term 'defence' includes a set-off. But this is a general rule only, principally because, after a notice of assignment has been given to the debtor, the debtor cannot normally set-off against a claim by the assignee a cross-claim that the debtor would have had against the assignor that does not arise out of the contract assigned: *Business Computers Ltd v Anglo-African Leasing Ltd* [1977] 1 WLR 578; Peel, *Treitel on the Law of Contract* (14th edn, 2015) paras 15-039–15-044. In other words, after notice, the debtor cannot 'take away' the rights of the assignee.

The rule in (b) (which again is a 'general' rule only, principally because of the law on subsequent set-offs just referred to) has given rise to the possible difficulty of damages disappearing into some 'legal black hole' where there have been assignments of building contracts and damaged or defective buildings have been sold along with the assignment of claims in contract (or tort) relating to the buildings. However, it would appear that any such problem was finally resolved by the Court of Appeal's clarification in *Offer-Hoar v Larkstore Ltd* [2006] EWCA Civ 1079, [2006] 1 WLR 2926 (applied in *Landfast (Anglia) Ltd v Cameron Taylor One Ltd* [2008] EWHC 343 (TCC)) that, in applying in this context the rule that the assignee is not entitled to recover more than the assignor, one should be asking what damages the assignor could itself have recovered but on the basis that there had been no transfer of the land to the assignee. Substantial damages were therefore recoverable by the assignee where an assignor had sold its land to an assignee along with, or prior to, the assignment of the relevant cause of action relating to the land.

Example 2

A contracts with B for the building of an office-block on A's land. After the building has been completed, A sells the land to C and assigns to C the benefit of any contractual (or tortious) claims it has against B. As a result of B's breach of contract, problems arise with the building which C pays to repair. Even though, at least on the face of it, A has not itself suffered any loss, the rule that the assignee is not entitled to recover more than the assignor requires one to ask what the position would have been had the assignor (A) neither assigned the claim nor transferred the land.

This problem will, in any event, often be circumvented because of the courts' recognition that, where the contracting parties contemplated that a third party would become the owner of the defective or damaged property or would otherwise suffer the loss, there is an exception to the general rule that a contracting party can recover damages only for its own loss and not the loss of the third party (see s 46(4) above). Where the exception applies, the contracting party (the assignor) is entitled to substantial damages for the loss suffered by the third party (the assignee): by the same token, there is no question of an award of substantial damages to the assignee infringing the rule that the assignee is not entitled to recover more than the assignor.

50(4)

At the end of this section on assignment, it has been thought helpful to distinguish novation from assignment. A novation is not best viewed as an exception to, or even as a way round, privity of contract because it involves a new contract between parties. Nor does it involve the transfer of any rights, thereby differing from assignment. Rather it involves the replacement of one contract (which is extinguished) by another contract provided all the parties agree. One might therefore think that novation belongs more naturally alongside s 12 on rescission by agreement between the parties. However, it has been thought best to consider it here because the distinctive feature of a novation, in contrast to ordinary rescission by agreement and replacement by a new contract, is that three parties are necessarily involved. The two contracting parties are agreeing that a third, who also agrees, shall become a party to the contract with one of the others.

The underlying principles of rescission by agreement apply, so that the requirements in ss 8–11 must, as usual, be satisfied. Note that the need for consideration is unlikely to present any problem given the necessary starting point for novation that all the parties must agree. So, for example, if B owes money to A, and it is agreed between them that C is to be substituted for B, and C agrees to this, A is providing consideration for C's promise by releasing B, and B is providing consideration for being released by A by providing A with the new debtor, C.

In practice, novation is very common where companies are amalgamated or there is a change in a partnership.

As novation is different from assignment, it follows that the rule that assignment is 'subject to equities' does not apply to novation. Say, for example, a contract was induced by a misrepresentation and there has then been an assignment by the person making the misrepresentation: the debtor can rely on the misrepresentation vis-à-vis the assignee. In contrast, it is irrelevant to a novation that the original contract was induced by a misrepresentation. Once there has been a novation, the original contract has been extinguished and with it the power to rescind for the original misrepresentation.

In principle, there seems no reason why there cannot be a novation of part of a contract while leaving the rest of the contract to survive although this may require some variation of the original surviving terms. Whether that is what is being achieved in any particular situation will largely turn on the intention of the parties. In principle, it further follows that there can be a novation of the whole or part of a multiparty contract with the original contract being left in place entirely as regards some parties while there is a whole or partial novation as regards other parties.

TABLE OF LEGISLATION

TABLE OF CASES

265

INDEX